Environmental Thought

Environmental Thought
A Short History

Robin Attfield

polity

Copyright © Robin Attfield 2021

The right of Robin Attfield to be identified as Author of this Work has been asserted in accordance with the UK Copyright, Designs and Patents Act 1988.

First published in 2021 by Polity Press

Polity Press
65 Bridge Street
Cambridge CB2 1UR, UK

Polity Press
101 Station Landing
Suite 300
Medford, MA 02155, USA

Cover illustration: Tanagra Darwini, plate 34 from *The Zoology of the Voyage of H.M.S. Beagle 1832–36*, by Charles Darwin (1809–92), 1840 (colour litho), English School, (19th century) / Bibliothèque de l'Institut de France, Paris / © Archives Charmet / Bridgeman Images.

All rights reserved. Except for the quotation of short passages for the purpose of criticism and review, no part of this publication may be reproduced, stored in a retrieval system or transmitted, in any form or by any means, electronic, mechanical, photocopying, recording or otherwise, without the prior permission of the publisher.

ISBN-13: 978-1-5095-3665-8
ISBN-13: 978-1-5095-3666-5(pb)

A catalogue record for this book is available from the British Library.

Library of Congress Cataloging-in-Publication Data

Names: Attfield, Robin, author.
Title: Environmental thought : a short history / Robin Attfield.
Description: Cambridge, UK ; Medford, MA : Polity Press, 2021. | Includes bibliographical references and index. | Summary: "An ambitious and wide-ranging synthesis of the history of environmental thought by a leading philosopher"-- Provided by publisher.
Identifiers: LCCN 2020030005 (print) | LCCN 2020030006 (ebook) | ISBN 9781509536658 (hardback) | ISBN 9781509536665 (paperback) | ISBN 9781509536672 (epub) | ISBN 9781509546350 (adobe pdf)
Subjects: LCSH: Environmentalism--History. | Environmentalism--Philosophy.
Classification: LCC GE195 .A88 2021 (print) | LCC GE195 (ebook) | DDC 304.209--dc23
LC record available at https://lccn.loc.gov/2020030005
LC ebook record available at https://lccn.loc.gov/2020030006

Typeset in 10 on 12.5 Sabon LT Pro by
Servis Filmsetting Ltd, Stockport, Cheshire
Printed and bound in Great Britain by TJ Books Limited

The publisher has used its best endeavours to ensure that the URLs for external websites referred to in this book are correct and active at the time of going to press. However, the publisher has no responsibility for the websites and can make no guarantee that a site will remain live or that the content is or will remain appropriate.

Every effort has been made to trace all copyright holders, but if any have been overlooked the publisher will be pleased to include any necessary credits in any subsequent reprint or edition.

For further information on Polity, visit our website: politybooks.com

Contents

	Introduction	1
1	Pre-modern Attitudes and Influences	8
2	Early Modern Reflections	33
3	Darwin and His Successors	60
4	The American Debate	82
5	Foundations of the Science of Ecology	103
6	Further Origins of Conservation	122
7	Early Environmentalism	143
8	Environmental Philosophy and Kindred Studies	164
9	Green Issues and Movements	183
10	The Environmental Crisis	203
	Conclusion	216
References		220
Index		243

Introduction

Environmental thought concerns reflections on nature, and related attitudes and intuitions. The vulnerability of natural systems to human destructiveness came to full awareness only in the nineteenth century, with the publication of George Perkins Marsh's *Man and Nature* (1965 [1864]), and in the wake of the publication (in 1859) of Charles Darwin's theory of evolution by natural selection, although some limited grasp of the impact of human interventions dates back to Theophrastus (371–287 BCE), one of Aristotle's followers, in the ancient world (Glacken 1967: 129–30; see also Chapter 1), and to John Evelyn in the early modern period (Glacken 1967: 485–91; see also Chapter 2). Yet it took until the disclosures of Rachel Carson (1962) about emissions of DDT in Europe reaching the flesh of Antarctic penguins (see Chapter 6) for the urgency of redressing the impacts of human interventions to be taken seriously.

There have been many different conceptions of nature across the centuries. For some, nature is everything that is not supernatural, and in this sense humanity is generally regarded as part of nature. For others, the natural is everything that is not (or largely not) the result of human artifice or intervention, and in this sense humanity is often regarded as distinct from nature, since most people are formed by human nurturing and education. The parenthetic 'or largely not' is important, for the regions of Earth unaffected by humanity are diminishingly slight, and in some views nonexistent. Yet whole tracts are *largely* unaffected, and it is these tracts and their living inhabitants that are most often meant when people speak of 'nature'.

There is, of course, another sense of nature, where a thing's nature is its character or composition, as in the expression 'the nature of the beast'. This is why it even makes sense to talk about 'the nature of nature'. But that is not the sense of nature intended in this book, except where the context indicates otherwise. However, some people have regarded nature as an autonomous force, with laws (and in some views even purposes) of its own, and this sense survives into the present, as when Barry Commoner (1972) presented as one of his laws of ecology the suggested law that 'Nature knows best' (see Chapter 7). Aspects of this conception will be used here to the extent that there are laws of nature to which human beings – as well as everything else in creation – are subject, but the suggestion that nature is an autonomous force should not in my view be credited, let alone the view that it has knowledge or a will of its own. The related Gaia theory of James Lovelock (1979), according to which the Earth is a self-regulating system or superorganism, will also be discussed and sifted (see Chapter 8).

The recentness of the discovery that human action is affecting and sometimes undermining ecosystems worldwide may suggest that there is little to learn from pre-modern or early modern environmental thought. But here we should heed the warning of George Santayana (1863–1952): 'Those who do not remember the past are condemned to repeat it.' More positively, John Passmore has brought to light some environmentally promising stances which he finds in ancient literature, for one of which humanity is nature's steward, answerable (whether to God or to posterity) for its care, and another for which the role of humanity is to complete, adorn or perfect nature, regarded as an incomplete creation (1974: 28–40). While Passmore claimed that these were minority stances that disappeared from view until the modern period, there is evidence that there was a continuity among their adherents across the Christian centuries, and that these approaches were in due course adopted by Jews and Muslims as well. Passmore considered these stances important as being seeds within the Western tradition on which contemporary environmentalism could be built; if he was right to this extent, then these ancient stances have great contemporary importance.

This suggestion, however, gives rise to a debate concerning whether ideas and thought are capable of exercising influence on the course of history as opposed to economic and related social factors. Many Marxists and others have regarded economic forces as the motors of history, and ideas as mere epiphenomena or by-products, with little or no influence of their own. It is not necessary to be a determinist to hold this, for economic factors could predispose people both to beliefs and forms of behaviour which they could have resisted but have lacked the determination to reject. Others, however, have held opposed positions, maintaining either that ideas are what shape the future more than anything else, or, more moderately, that beliefs, ideas and cultural factors exercise some degree of influence alongside economic forces and social and technological trends.

My own inclination coheres with this more moderate stance, evidence for which may be found in whichever passages in this book concerning thinking of the past ring bells with readers and stimulate environmental concern. (In particular, one cogent example, discussed in Chapter 1, is the influence of Plato's *Timaeus* on centuries of subsequent thought, while an even clearer case may be found in the passage of Chapter 4 concerning the influence of the ideas of Henry David Thoreau and George Perkins Marsh on the inauguration of the Yellowstone National Park by President Ulysses Grant in 1872.) And if this more moderate stance is credible, then (for example) the ancient traditions of Passmore's account remain worth considering, even if his account is open to qualification in detail. There again, other ancient and environmentally sensitive traditional schools of thought, such as Daoism, should not be forgotten, but taken into account when the prospects for contemporary environmentalism are being considered. If the West needs to build on its own ancient traditions, so does China, and so too does (for example) the world of Islam. Accordingly, some longstanding Daoist traditions will receive mention in Chapter 1, and, likewise, consideration will be given to some longstanding Islamic themes. Yet in the modern 'global village', historical attitudes of past centuries are the history of humanity as a whole, and none of these traditions can be regarded as irrelevant to any of us, however emancipated we may claim to be from the social constraints and narrow nationalisms of the past.

This granted, the scope of this book is perforce broader than that of ecological science and its origins, important as this science has been to environmental awareness. So, for example, I have not followed Frank N. Egerton in omitting the Bible and early Christianity as neglectful of science (2012: 17), in view of their profound environmental teachings, presuppositions and influence. Nor have I omitted the divergent stances of Reformers such as Luther and Calvin, together with their long-term impacts. At the same time, I have attempted to bring onto the stage significant literary and artistic works, from Hesiod and Virgil to Traherne, Wordsworth, Turner and Gerard Manley Hopkins.

But the major drawback of this inclusiveness of scope has perforce been the omission of much of the detail covered by authors with more specialist concerns (and with more space to deploy). Thus I have had to omit mention of many medieval Muslim scholars (while acknowledging the contribution of this period of Islam), and the many Renaissance scholars who revived the study of ancient botanists and zoologists, including their fascinating dispute of around 1500 about the vulnerability of Pliny and other ancient authorities to error (Egerton 2012: 33). My brief was in any case to focus largely on Darwin and the subsequent period, and that has required selectivity with respect to much of the detail of the preceding ages, including even the detail of the biological science of the modern world prior to Darwin. Readers intent on accessing this phase of the history of the science of biology are advised to read Egerton.

Similarly, this book does not seek to cover the scientific revolution of the early modern period, or its technocratic late modern counterpart, despite its discussion of the central advocates of mechanism in Chapter 2, and of Darwin and his successors in Chapter 3. A penetrating investigation into these aspects of the history of science can be found in Pepper (1984). There again, this book does not seek to depict in any detail the history of either landscape gardening in England or the related enclosure movement (except for the related protests of the poet John Clare: see Chapter 2). Readers wishing to study these movements are recommended to consult Coates (1998). Likewise, more detail is to be found about American environmentalists of the nineteenth century in the books of Nash (2014 [1967]; 1989) than in this one, although Chapter 4 presents the developing ideas both of the American Transcendentalists (including Marsh) and of the controversy about preservation between John Muir and Gifford Pinchot. There again, there is ampler detail to be found in Worster (1985 [1977]) about the origins and rise of ecological science, topics which the fifth chapter of this book re-examines with the aid of more contemporary sources.

Darwin and Darwinism are discussed in Chapter 3, with emphasis on Darwin's own understanding of the ecological implications of his theory. Chapter 4 considers 'The American Debate', focusing on the writings and influence of Marsh and of John Muir, and the controversies about National Parks. Chapter 5 concerns the origins and development of the science of ecology on both sides of the Atlantic.

In Chapter 6, further sources of conservation are studied, including the poet Gerard Manley Hopkins, the forester and ecologist Aldo Leopold and the biologist Rachel Carson, whose *Silent Spring* (published 1962) ignited the ecological movement. Chapter 7 introduces a range of contributions to early environmentalism movements, from *Blueprint for Survival* (1972) to *Our Common Future* (1987). In Chapter 8, we encounter the pioneers and main schools of environmental philosophy; this discussion is continued in Chapter 9, where further schools are introduced, together with ecological issues and movements, including the

Green movement. Chapter 10 presents the global environmental crisis of the twenty-first century, and the Conclusion brings together historical strands that have contributed to contemporary environmental thought and allow the crisis to be addressed.

The above-mentioned debate about the influence of beliefs and ideas can be illustrated by the discourse surrounding the thesis put forward by Lynn White Jr. in an article in *Science* in 1967. White maintained that the roots of our ecological (his word was 'ecologic') crisis lie in Judaeo-Christian theology, which makes Christianity, particularly in its Western version, 'the most anthropocentric religion the world has seen'. White's specialism was medieval technology, and he regarded the distinctive technological advances of Western Christendom during the Middle Ages as manifesting an aggressive form of belief in the human domination of nature. His thesis will be discussed more than once (in Chapters 1, 8 and 9), because of its interpretation of Christianity, as well as of the Middle Ages, and detailed discussion can be left for the relevant sections. However, it is worth remarking that among the many criticisms to which his stance has been subjected, no fewer than two forms of misguided determinism have been ascribed to him.

For example, in a review in *Past and Present*, R. H. Hilton and P. H. Sawyer (1963: 97) accused him of 'technological determinism', the suggestion that the shape of history and the structure of society were determined by technological innovations such as the new form of heavy ploughing of the early Middle Ages (on which White made human attitudes and behaviour towards nature turn), or later innovations such as clockwork and gunpowder. This approach clearly has its limits, since technology is itself heavily influenced both by economic factors and trends and sometimes by cultural factors (and even possibly ideas). There is a case for ascribing the intensity of some modern ecological problems to contemporary technology (carbon-based energy generation and the manufacture of plastics being leading examples), but once again the forces that drive this technology must also be taken into account.

However, this criticism of White is not consistent with another form of determinism often ascribed to him, the view that the roots of our problems lie in religious beliefs, and that their solution correspondingly lies in a change of religious beliefs, such as either the adoption of Zen Buddhism or reversion to the kind of Christianity advanced by St Francis of Assisi. Certainly, the suggestion that religious beliefs drive history to such a profound extent is implausible, particularly if the claim is that the conversion of the West (of Northern Europe) to Christianity in the centuries around 700 CE is what drove the industrial revolution of over a millennium later, or the subsequent industrial revolutions of the twentieth and twenty-first centuries. Critics have rightly commented that religious beliefs have often formed a rationalization of trends that were taking place already, themselves to be otherwise explained. Thus, even if White's theory is held in a nondeterministic form, it can be criticized for exaggerating the formative influence of religious beliefs.

Yet the possibility remains that such beliefs are capable of making a difference, alongside many other factors. And this makes it important to consider whether, as many others have claimed, White mischaracterizes both Christianity and also characteristic medieval attitudes to nature. It also makes it important to consider religious stances like the stewardship approach, as identified by Passmore, since approaches of this kind may also make a difference, this time in the direction of motivating environmental concern. While there are undoubtedly other sources of environmental concern, such as recognition of the full implications of Darwinism, and of the ordered but vulnerable character of global ecological systems, attitudes such as these remain significant sources of potential motivation.

But so does simple love of nature and natural beauty. This can be acquired from direct experience (for example, through hiking, boating and field-trips), from films and television programmes, through appreciation of art, and by retrieving the love of nature and landscape found in ancient thinkers such as Virgil and the author of the *Song of Solomon*, in patristic writers such as Basil the Great, in early modern poets such as Thomas Traherne and in modern thinkers such as Rachel Carson. Historical environmental thought, then, can influence contemporary agents not only through its teachings about ethical responsibilities, but also through renewing the jaded vision of the dwellers of modern cities, and opening or reopening our eyes and ears to the colours, sounds and variety of the world around us.

I would like to express thanks to my Cardiff colleague, Dr Hefin Jones, for checking an early draft of part of Chapter 5, to two anonymous referees for looking over Chapters 3 and 5 respectively, and to two others for reviewing a draft of all ten chapters. I am grateful to my colleagues at the Cardiff University Institute for Sustainable Places for inviting me to give a presentation there on 'Myths about Darwin and Marsh' (based on relevant sections of Chapters 3 and 4) and for their participation in that seminar, and to Steven Goundrey for much-needed technical assistance. Thanks are also due to Pascal Porcheron and Ellen MacDonald-Kramer of Polity Press for their longsuffering and constant helpfulness. Above all, I am particularly grateful to my wife, Leela Dutt Attfield, for encouragement, love and support throughout, and also for daily companionship as we shared together the COVID-19 lockdown during which the later stages of this book were completed. Without her, this book would not even be a dead letter; it would not exist.

Recommended reading

Carson, Rachel (1962). *Silent Spring*. London: Hamish Hamilton.

Coates, Peter (1998). *Nature: Western Attitudes since Ancient Times*. Berkeley: University of California Press.

Egerton, Frank N. (2012). *Roots of Ecology: Antiquity to Haeckel*. Berkeley: University of California Press.

Marsh, George Perkins (2003 [1864]). *Man and Nature: Or, Physical Geography as Modified by Human Action*, ed. David Lowenthal. Seattle: University of Washington Press.

Nash, Roderick Frazier (2014 [1967]). *Wilderness and the American Mind*, 5th edn. New Haven, CT: Yale University Press.

Nash, Roderick Frazier (1989). *The Rights of Nature: A History of Environmental Ethics*. Madison, WI: University of Wisconsin Press.

Pepper, David (1984). *The Roots of Modern Environmentalism*. London: Routledge.

Worster, Donald (1985 [1977]). *Nature's Economy: A History of Ecological Ideas*. Cambridge: Cambridge University Press.

1

Pre-modern Attitudes and Influences

This chapter concerns attitudes to nature in the period before 1500 CE. With the exception of one allusion to ancient China and one to ancient India, it is concerned with Western cultures, broadly enough interpreted to include the rise of Islam and its spread into much of the Middle East, and beyond that to the lands once conquered by Alexander, such as Iran and Afghanistan. Yet it primarily focuses on the Greeks and the Romans, on the Old and New Testaments, on early Christianity and on Europe in the Middle Ages. For these were the periods and the cultures from which many more recent attitudes have derived, as becomes clear in Chapter 2, which depicts the early modern period of Europe.

While the predominant ancient stance was that humanity can and should be in control of nature, it was from the Greeks, in particular, that we have received, on the one hand, belief in human stewardship of the natural world (a belief to which Christianity later contributed: see Chapter 2), and, on the other, belief in the world as a living being, an ancient theme echoed many centuries later in James Lovelock's theory of Gaia (see Chapter 8). Greeks such as Empedocles and Romans such as Lucretius were among early adherents of speculative versions of the theory of evolution by natural selection, more recently supported with empirical evidence and a different conceptual scheme by Charles Darwin (see Chapter 3); this theory has in turn fostered a new ecological awareness (see Chapter 4 and onwards).

Thus, while some readers may prefer to turn to the chapters about Darwin and environmental thought in the subsequent period, it may be rewarding to review first the beliefs and theories of the ancient and medieval worlds. These are the focus of the current chapter.

Greeks and Romans

This section concerns the ancient worlds of the Greeks and the Romans – the period from 700 BCE to the Emperor Constantine in the early fourth century CE. (The Homeric poems, which may have attained their current form around 700 BCE, bear many traces of earlier thought and practice, but are not considered here.) The thousand years under consideration nourished beliefs, attitudes and practices of immense diversity, and embodied a large variety of attitudes to nature, the land and the natural environment. No claim is made to anything like comprehensive coverage here. Instead, I have selected certain prominent, significant and contrasting claims and statements, whether in prose or verse, in song, drama or philosophy. (As we shall see, some of these were overlapping categories, with much drama and much philosophy expressed in poetic form.) Some have been selected because of their later influence, whether ultimately misleading, like Empedocles' belief in four basic elements, or far-sighted, like his belief in a kind of natural selection (albeit without any recognizable belief in adaptation). Predominantly, however, ancient writers must be allowed to speak for themselves, and ancient practices, however questionable, to receive attention, if only because they supply the context of related thinking and protests, both contemporary and subsequent.

Hesiod and Virgil

All ancient civilizations were agrarian, observes J. Donald Hughes (1994: 131), and dependent on agriculture and the soil. (Some, however, could remember a nomadic past.) So it is not surprising that the fifth-century BCE tragedian Sophocles wrote of Earth as the greatest of the gods, from whom the other gods were descended (*Antigone*, 338–41; Hughes 1994: 130). There are many other passages of the fifth-century tragedians celebrating the Earth as universal Mother, despite recognition of Zeus as the supreme deity.

Nor is it surprising that one of the earliest surviving poems in the Greek language is the poetic guide to farmers (of several centuries earlier than Sophocles) on how to scratch a living from the soil of Boeotia (central Greece), Hesiod's *Works and Days* (around 700 BCE). Hesiod encourages farmers to plough diligently and thus garner enough of a harvest to survive the winter without needing to beg from neighbours. His world is one of small-scale farming and peasant proprietors, albeit also one where much of the hard work is done by slaves.

Hesiod thus became the father of didactic verse, poetry intended to teach a message. This was accomplished in hexameters, the same rhythm as that of the Homeric poems, the *Iliad* and the *Odyssey*, with their heroic themes. But there is nothing heroic about *Works and Days*; Hesiod is aware of living in an Age of Iron, in which the Earth has greatly degenerated from the golden age when 'the fruitful field bare fruit abundantly and without stint' (*Works and Days*, 117–18, 176–7; Hughes 1994: 130). Such belief in decline, both in nature and in human nature, was widespread in the ancient world, although, as we shall see, there were some significant exceptions.

Nearly seven hundred years later, the Roman poet Virgil (70–19 BCE) wrote another didactic poem to foster farming, again in hexameters, but this time in Latin, the *Georgics*. Virgil lived in an age of farms both large and small, and of large armies. He was an influential supporter of (and propagandist for) the first Emperor, Augustus, who ruled the Roman world, which extended to almost all the shores of the Mediterranean and half of Europe (but not yet Britain). Virgil's poem is elegantly written and reflects patriotic pride in the beauty of the Italian landscape; it was written as much for poets as for farmers, although some in our own day have attempted to implement his precepts (presented in his final book) for bee-keeping.

As Peter Coates (a historian of attitudes to nature since ancient times) has written, Virgil's poem extols 'the husbandman's self-reliance, celebrating honest, open-air toil as man's ... pursuit' (1998: 35), though not, as Coates declares, humanity's original pursuit, as there had been a previous age of plenty, when all needs had been met without effort (an echo of Hesiod's golden age). Virgil explains that Jupiter, the Roman equivalent of Zeus and father of farming, did not want the human path to be easy, but sought to stimulate human skill and effort through introducing a hostile environment, inhabited with dangerous creatures like snakes and wolves, in which humans had to earn their livelihoods (*Georgics* I: 122–46).

Despite exceptions, most ancient writers accepted the rightness of human control of nature. For Virgil, though, human control was limited, and the human relation to the land served as a means of building human character. Yet others adopted a sunnier view of nature than Virgil; thus, in his *Natural History* (77 CE), Pliny the Elder, who wrote about agriculture voluminously (in prose), 'celebrated nature as a storehouse' (Coates 1998: 28), fit for humans to mine, till and domesticate. Sadly (and perhaps ironically), he was killed by the eruption of the volcano Vesuvius in 79 CE.

Hesiod and Virgil represent different ages, the first an age of small-scale agriculture and small Greek states, albeit ones spread around much of the Eastern Mediterranean, and the second an age of large-scale farming and large empires, and with much greater literacy and a much larger city-based reading public. Their shared role of briefing farmers showed that the problems of deriving a living from the land persisted. Yet while with Hesiod the struggle was pursued in bitter earnest, Virgil wrote with greater consciousness of the beauty of landscape, but with little or no sense that preserving it might become a problem. Many centuries later, Virgil became a source of inspiration for the eighteenth-century naturalist Gilbert White of Selborne (see Chapter 2) (Worster 1985 [1977]: 27–8).

Empedocles

It is time for philosophy to enter the story. During the sixth and fifth centuries BCE, philosophy arose among the Greeks of Miletus in Asia Minor, and spread to the Greek colonists of Italy and Sicily. Several wrote tracts on the true or underlying nature of nature. For present purposes, our focus will be on the Sicilian Greek, Empedocles of Acragas (c. 490–430 BCE), not because he was the most profound of the Greek philosophers, but because of his unique contributions, centrally relevant to how we should understand nature.

Empedocles was probably a Pythagorean (or follower of Pythagoras), believing in reincarnation, and in the possibility of returning as an animal. This may be why he advocated vegetarianism (Coates 1998: 33), a minority stance in the ancient world, but one followed much later by some of the Neoplatonists. The possibility of humans being transformed into animals was later to be explored by the Roman poet Ovid (43 BCE–17 CE) in his *Metamorphoses* (a work of great influence in the Renaissance period). In faraway China it was also developed in the late fourth century BCE by Zhuangzi, who imagines a fish being transformed into a giant bird, to the amazement of smaller creatures. Zhuangzi's aim was to show us how different from our own the perspective of the large bird would be, and thus how we can be liberated from our habitual, narrow human perspectives (Hourdequin 2015: 82–3). I am not suggesting any influence from the Pythagoreans of the West to the Daoists of China (or vice versa), or from or to either school to or from the Jains of sixth-century India who also taught respect for all creatures, but rather that all three of these schools of thought can open up the possibility of transcending perspectives focused on human beings alone.

We would, however, be mistaken if (with Hughes) we trace environmentalism back to the ancient Pythagoreans, whose stance was an ascetic, dualistic and ritualistic one, and for whom there is no evidence of belief in the vulnerability of species, conservation or concern for sustainability. Nor (come to that) should we credit the ancient legend that Empedocles died by casting himself into the crater of Mount Etna, despite Matthew Arnold's poem depicting his death in this manner.

Perhaps Empedocles' most original contribution was his theory of the evolution of living creatures by a kind of natural selection. At one stage, he held, all kinds of monstrosities came into being, alongside the ancestors of surviving creatures, but the monsters did not prove viable, and thus the range of species was winnowed down to those that survive today. Aristotle later poured scorn on this theory, although Epicurus (fourth to third centuries BCE) adopted a revised form of it. Much later still, Charles Darwin acknowledged Empedocles as a predecessor for his different but related theory; indeed, Darwin wrote of Empedocles: 'We see here the principle of natural selection shadowed forth' (Burrow 1985: 53). Empedocles combined this theory with belief in the kinship of human beings and (other) animals, a belief seldom recaptured until the time of Darwin.

Empedocles also devised the theory that everything is made of the four elements, earth, air, fire and water, his solution to the problem of finding something permanent that underlies change. This theory was enthusiastically adopted by Aristotle, and in consequence was held in high favour until the atomic theory was gradually adopted instead by seventeenth-century scientists. Atomism itself was put forward by Democritus of Abdera (fifth century BCE), and adopted in the later ancient world by Epicurus and his followers; but the authority of Aristotle overshadowed it for two thousand years. The four-element theory could be seen as a false start; but it remained an important contribution to people's understanding of nature for centuries to come. Understanding historical attitudes to nature cannot be limited to successful theories, as if ancient people were trying to anticipate modern findings; that approach is prone instead to mischaracterize the past, and to underestimate its distinctiveness. Nevertheless, Empedocles' speculative theory of evolution by natural selection was eventually found to be partially (and almost accidentally) on target by nineteenth- and twentieth-century scientists (see Chapter 3).

Greek medicine: Hippocrates and 'Airs, Waters, Places'

Hippocrates of Cos (*c.* 460–*c.* 375 BCE) was one of the founders of ancient medicine, and travelled around the islands of the Aegean sea, teaching medical students. For present purposes, his most relevant tract was 'Airs, Waters, Places', which seeks to trace the influence of seasons, winds, waters and climates on both human health and human temperaments and cultures. This tract can be seen as prefiguring the late twentieth-century subject of bio-climatology, and has recently been hailed by Anthony Capon (in an address at Cardiff University) as an ancient anticipation of modern ecological studies.

I am not suggesting that 'Airs, Waters, Places' exercised any direct influence on modern bio-climatology. Yet many classically educated writers, such as Alexander von Humboldt (1767–1859), took up the theme of the influence of climate on culture, and could well have derived inspiration from the would-be empirical approach of this tract, while newly introducing data from his own study of the new world; and von Humboldt has almost certainly influenced the development of modern climate science (Rajan 2017: 21–50). Hippocrates' detailed claims are often less than impressive, such as his assertion that cities exposed to hot winds and with plentiful waters have inhabitants with excessive phlegm, leading to dysentery, fevers, eczema and haemorrhoids ('Airs, Waters, Places', III). But his approach was later to open up valuable realms of investigation, such as the study of occupational health, and also that of tropical medicine. And that makes it worth a mention here.

Plato and later Platonism

Most of the philosopher Plato's writings are in the form of dialogues, and so it is not always easy to discover which participants of a given dialogue Plato (428/427–348/347 BCE) himself supported (not even his central character Socrates). It is clear, however, that his characters appreciated natural beauty (*Phaedrus*, 30b), and that they were aware of some (what we call) environmental problems such as soil erosion and deforestation. Thus at *Critias* 111b–d, he writes about Attica (the region around Athens): 'There are remaining only the bones of the wasted body, as they may be called ... all the richer and softer parts of the soil having fallen away, and the mere skeleton of the land being left' (Passmore 1974: 175; John Passmore was a leading philosopher and historian of ideas, based in Australia). But it is less clear that he felt any need to take steps to preserve or restore the landscape, since for Plato reality consisted in universal forms (such as justice itself or goodness itself) and not in particular objects or places (Hargrove 1989: 16–26), which are mere shadows of what is real. Besides, none of the Greeks (with the possible exception of Theophrastus, discussed in the next section) were aware of humanly caused environmental problems as such.

However, in Plato's *Phaedrus* the claim is made that 'it is everywhere the responsibility of the animate to look after the inanimate', one of the foundation texts for belief in the human stewardship of nature (*Phaedrus*, 246b; Passmore 1974: 28). Some of the subsequent Platonists, such as Iamblichus, interpreted passages like this to mean that humans were sent to live on Earth by God 'to administer earthly things' and to care for them in God's name (Passmore 1974: 28). Passmore took the view that this approach did not appear in Christian teaching until the seventeenth century (1974: 29–30); some evidence for a different interpretation will be advanced in the section on biblical and Christian attitudes.

But the Platonic dialogue that has proved most influential has been *Timaeus*, with its claim that the world is a living creature (*Timaeus*, 30c), and with Plato's account of its ordering by the Demiurge, or cosmic architect (*Timaeus*, 29a). These themes were later taken up by Renaissance Platonists such as Paracelsus (1493/4–1541) and others, who maintained that the universe was to be viewed 'as a vast organism, everywhere quick and vital, its body, soul and spirit . . . held tightly together' (Merchant 1990 [1980]: 104; Whitney 2006: 40). They also contributed to the later (widely influential) belief in the balance of nature (Egerton 2012: 3).

These perspectives can also be understood as contributory factors in the eventual development during the twentieth century of holistic environmental theories of the Earth (see Chapter 8), such as the Gaia theory of James Lovelock (1979), the holistic ethic of Aldo Leopold (1966 [1949]), the holistic views of Deep Ecologists (Naess 1973) and those of eco-holists such as J. Baird Callicott. Callicott also sought at one stage to appeal to and reinterpret Plato's ethical holism, in which the good of the whole is what matters, rather than the good or the suffering of the individual, in support of Leopold's 'land ethic' (*Republic*, 462a–d; Callicott 1980), but he later retracted these claims. The goddess Gaia is actually mentioned passingly in Plato's *Timaeus* (Goldin 1997: 198); maybe this was known to the novelist William Golding, who suggested this name to Lovelock to epitomize his theory of the Earth as a self-regulating superorganism.

According to Alfred North Whitehead, 'The safest general characterization of the European philosophical tradition is that it consists of a series of footnotes to Plato' (1979 [1929]: 39). This claim has proved more than controversial, even construed strictly about European philosophy. Yet if someone were to apply it to environmental thought, while their claim could be seen as even more controversial, it would not be obvious that they would be wrong. However, another view is possible: the critical insights and the curiosity of the early Greek philosophers (including Empedocles), of historians such as Herodotus (who discusses the distinctive reproductive capacities of hares), of Hippocrates and of Plato himself, derive much of their importance from their supplying the foundations for the original studies of Aristotle and Theophrastus, the founders of several disciplines including biology (Egerton 2012: 4).

Aristotle and Theophrastus

Aristotle (384–322 BCE) studied at Athens in Plato's Academy, but set off in new directions, founding biology and spending long periods studying, together with his follower Theophrastus, the creatures of a lagoon on the island of Lesbos. He also founded the study of logic. Eventually he founded his own school, the Lyceum. In place of Plato's theory of forms, for which the highest reality consisted in goodness itself and other such abstractions, Aristotle located reality in observable particulars (an approach much more congenial to most modern environmentalists).

For Aristotle, it is not only human beings who have souls, but other creatures as well; their 'psyche' is what makes them the living creatures that they are. One problem passage (in the *Politics*) claims that all other living creatures exist for the sake of humanity; but Aristotle's usual view is that all living creatures have a good of their own, which should be respected where possible. Aristotle paid detailed attention to the study of animals in his books *Generation of Animals*, *History of Animals* and *Parts of Animals*, and found some animals to display virtues such as wisdom. (Some of his biological works were translated and studied by medieval Arabic scholars: see Egerton 2012: 20–1.) As he says in *Parts of Animals* in response to students reluctant to participate in such study, '[i]f there is anyone who thinks it is base to study animals, he should have the same thought about himself' (Nussbaum 2006: 348).

Aristotle's tenets that all kinds of living creatures shade into one another, and that all creatures can be ordered in a scale of comparative greatness, have been regarded by Arthur O. Lovejoy as contributions (in conjunction with others from Plato) to belief in 'the great chain of being', adhered to subsequently by the Neoplatonists and widely held across Europe until its rejection by the German Romantic writer von Schelling (Lovejoy 1936). But Aristotle actually rejected key components of this (later prevalent) 'chain', such as the principle that all possibilities are fulfilled. Nor probably did he adhere to the view that the implicit goal of everything is human benefit; animals aside, it is implausible that the sun and the stars have such a goal. Some of the Stoics may later have adhered to such an anthropocentric view; but their ideas should not be read back into Aristotle. Aristotle's own views enjoyed a revival in Europe in the late Middle Ages, having earlier been cherished in such Islamic centres as

Baghdad and Córdoba. But by that time, being an Aristotelian usually meant deferring to his authority, and not, as in his own day, basing theories on empirical fieldwork. (For a more detailed account of Aristotle's zoology, see Egerton 2012: 4–7.)

As for Theophrastus, who took over the leadership of the Lyceum after Aristotle's death, he recognized that humanmade change (such as deforestation) can have impacts on the local climate. Theophrastus here departs from Aristotle's view (expressed in the *Meteorologica*) that the world is permanent and ultimately unchanging. We find here the first glimmering of awareness of the systemic vulnerability of the natural world to human influence. But Theophrastus (despite his impact on Pliny the Elder) did not exercise sufficient influence for such awareness to prevail for over two thousand years; after the first century CE, his ideas seem to have been largely forgotten, despite translations during the sixteenth century (Egerton 2012: 33), at least until the time of von Humboldt (eighteenth century: see the above section on Hippocrates, and also Chapter 2).

Lucretius

One other Roman poet is too important to omit. Lucretius (*c.* 99–*c.* 55 BCE) was the first Roman poet to write philosophy in Latin, and was thus a predecessor of Virgil in composing didactic Latin verse. He was an adherent of Epicureanism, a philosophical stance which adopted (and adapted) the atomism of Democritus, and which advocated the pursuit of pleasure and avoidance of pain. Besides writing on physics, Lucretius also wrote on the development of life on Earth as well as on the rise of human culture. His account of the development of living creatures embodied an adjusted version of the relatively crude account of natural selection pioneered by Empedocles, a poet on whom he also modelled his verse.

Lucretius includes a passage (towards the end of his *De Rerum Natura*, Book II) about the Earth being past its prime and in a state of decline (rather as had Hesiod). But he also extols, in Book V, the development of human culture (agriculture and navigation included), and supplies one of few ancient examples of belief in progress. Coates (1998: 27) aligns this passage with the widespread ancient belief in a cosmic purpose to be found in all creatures, and even with belief in a purposive great chain of being, with each creature serving a higher stage in the chain, and with humanity as its apex. However, these were not remotely the views of the Epicureans, but rather those of their rival philosophical school, the Stoics. Lucretius, by contrast, rejected belief in cosmic purpose, holding that the gods were exemplars of tranquil indifference, which human beings should imitate. It is important to avoid stereotyping ancient attitudes, which were as varied as those of the modern world.

Yet Lucretius also had an eye for natural beauty, whether in landscape, streams or clouds, and presents many similes drawn from nature to illustrate his message about atoms and molecules. This part of his message (his atomism, that is) remained influential when, after his works were rediscovered during the Renaissance, many seventeenth-century scientists adopted his atomism, albeit adjusted to fit their belief in divine creation. Later still, the poet Thomas Gray (1716–71) composed a poem in Latin hexameters extolling the empirical philosophy of John Locke (1632–1704), imitating the verse and the similes of Lucretius, and echoing his love of landscape, estuaries and seas. Indeed, Lucretius' influence lives on as much in pastoral poetry and its appreciation of nature as in modern science.

Roman circuses and related protests

Greek hunting was inhibited by the expectation that hunters would respect the sanctity of sanctuaries such as groves sacred to deities (Coates 1998: 37). But leading Roman public figures introduced so-called 'hunts' (*venationes*) to public arenas as popular entertainment, with contests between, for example, bulls and rhinoceroses, or between spearsmen and elephants. These spectacles attained such proportions that the procurement of larger wild animals, both from Roman territories and from dependent states, may have been responsible for the complete disappearance of these species from North Africa and the Near East (Coates 1998: 38). The Romans were so unconcerned about biodiversity that they did not even notice that they were curtailing it.

The best-known protest against these displays was expressed by Marcus Tullius Cicero, in one of his letters to his friends (*Epistulae ad familiares* VII, 1, 3). Cicero relates, in Torill Christine Lindstrøm's paraphrase: 'When the elephants tried to escape by starting to break down the iron bars that held them in place, people were terrified and, finally, when the elephants simultaneously started to trumpet in desperation, the spectators rose to their feet and, weeping, cursed Pompey for his cruelty' (2010: 319). Although this was an untypical reaction, Cicero found in it '*misericordia*' or compassion, and a sense that there was after all some common bond between people and beasts. Later, a more general protest about the maltreatment of animals in the arena was expressed by Plutarch, the celebrated Platonist writer (46–120 CE) (Hughes 1994: 111).

Yet such responses were rare, and Coates rightly remarks that the characteristic Roman (and Greek) attitude to natural creatures was 'manipulative' (1998: 39). Modern bull-fighting is a relic of such ancient entertainments. But it is worth adding that Christians of the Roman Empire were forbidden to attend gladiatorial contests, or contests between beasts or between humans and beasts, on pain of excommunication (Singer 1975: 210), and that the reason given by the Christian Minucius Felix (early third century CE) for this ban was that the games were both impious and cruel (Migne 1844–63: 3:354). Eventually, contests between men and beasts were condemned by the Council of Trullo (691–2) and had ceased in the Eastern Empire by the end of the seventh century (Lecky 1913 [1869]: 2:37); they ceased in the Western Empire with the fall of Rome (fifth century CE). The cessation of these contests should not have taken so long; but the more recent lengthy struggle to end slavery shows for how long vested interests can defend the indefensible. It is at least to the credit of Christians that these contests were finally abolished.

Ancient Greek and Roman perspectives on nature thus prove to have been extremely diverse, while many have had lasting impacts on later history (Schliephake 2016). But understanding later history also involves grasping the largely distinct history of Judaism and Christianity at that time. To this history we now turn.

The Old and New Testaments and Early Christianity

The Old Testament (also known as the Hebrew Bible) enshrines the history, poetry, prophecy and laws of the Jewish people, and was composed over at least a thousand-year period. The New Testament, by contrast, was written during the century following the death of Jesus. Christianity, however, became the religion of the Roman Empire, which may be held to have lasted until 1453 (with the fall of Constantinople to the Ottoman Turks). This section outlines aspects of Christian thought only up to Augustine, who wrote around the fall of the Western Empire (early fifth century CE), and selects significant attitudes to the land and to nature among Jews and Christians. While attitudes are again diverse, their diversity has a focus in the common belief of Jews and Christians in God, God's creative purposes, and his message for humanity transmitted through both Judaism and Christianity. Many of the attitudes of Europe and its worldwide diaspora were strongly influenced by Judaism, Christianity and the Bible, of which some of the more significant strands are highlighted here.

The Old Testament

In the course of the thousand years over which the Old Testament was written, beliefs about God, humanity and nature underwent change and development. Different documents from different periods have often been spliced together, such as the two creation narratives in the early chapters of Genesis. Hence, total consistency cannot be expected. Yet central overall themes can be elicited, and were among those widely taught when first Judaism and then Christianity spread across the Roman world and beyond.

One of these themes is the creation by God both of humanity and of the rest of the universe. Everything in creation is continually dependent on God, and nothing but God is to be worshipped. The world of nature consists of his or her creatures, and has its own value as such; yet to worship creatures rather than the creator is idolatrous. These themes are prominent both in Genesis and also in part of the book of Isaiah (chapters 40–55) composed in the sixth century BCE, after the exile in Babylon.

They also appear in the book of Job, which challenges Job to describe and explain the creatures of land, sea and air, and makes it clear that they all have their appointed places, and that God cares for them as well as for humanity (see Job 38–41.) A similar message about God's care for wild creatures is expressed in the book of Psalms (particularly Psalm 104); psalms were regularly sung in at least the period of the last five centuries BCE.

Relatedly, the Psalms recognize God's presence in the world; thus Psalm 139 conveys the impossibility of escaping God's presence. This theme re-emerges in the New Testament, in Paul's speech in Athens, where he speaks of God 'in whom we live and move and have our being' (Acts 17:28).

Another theme is that, despite human sinfulness, God has given dominion over the creatures of the Earth to humanity (Genesis 1; see also Psalm 8. The precise meaning of 'radah', the Hebrew term for 'have dominion', is debated.). This theme may be a retrospective validation of the domestication of farm animals, but it also authorizes humanity to kill animals for food. In Genesis, humans are represented as originally vegetarian, but as receiving a covenant after the flood, allowing them to eat meat (Genesis 8–9). However, dominion does not involve treating other living creatures as having no value of their own, and can reasonably be interpreted as involving the kind of stewardship foreshadowed in the story of God placing Adam in the garden of Eden to 'dress it and to keep it' (Genesis 2:15). Stewardship is certainly the interpretation of dominion in the Bible as a whole adopted by Clarence J. Glacken (1967: 152, 155, 168). (Glacken (1909–89) was the author of a magisterial history of the relations of nature and culture from earliest times to the end of the eighteenth century; in Chapter 3, some of his subsequent writings about the nineteenth century will also be introduced.) Coates (1998: 50) suggests that the stewardship tradition may be 'enlightened despotism' (on the part of humanity), but this hardly tallies with the passages that he cites, such as the instruction in Deuteronomy 22 to spare the mother bird when taking eggs from her nest, or ones that he omits, such as the teaching of Proverbs 12 that 'the righteous man regardeth the life of his beast', and the opening of Psalm 24: 'The Earth is the Lord's, and the fulness thereof' (consciously echoed in I Corinthians 10:26 in the New Testament), which implies that humanity does not own the Earth, but is answerable to its creator.

The Old Testament also re-emphasizes the goodness of creation, not only in Genesis 1:31, but also in Song of Solomon 2, with its celebration of spring, and in Proverbs 8:22–31, where the wisdom of God is represented as God's agent in creation, 'rejoicing before him always, rejoicing in his inhabited world and in the sons of men'. This theme is developed in the intertestamental book, Wisdom of Solomon, which stresses that God is well satisfied with his creation (1:13–16). Elsewhere in the Old Testament, and not least in the writings of the prophets (see Isaiah 55), the fertility of the land is standardly treated as a token of divine favour, while the rivers 'clap their hands' and 'the hills sing together for joy' in praise of God (Psalm 98). (This theme of nature praising God was taken up later by St Francis; see the later part of this chapter.)

Glacken often writes of God in Judaeo-Christian theology as not being immanent in the world. In the Bible, God is certainly the world's transcendent creator, but, despite Glacken's comment, God is often represented as also omnipresent. Psalm 139, for example, expresses the impossibility of escaping from God's presence, while, in the New Testament, Paul, speaking at Athens, proclaims that, in God, 'we live and move and have our being' (Acts 17:28). Thus, in the Bible as a whole, God is both the world's transcendent creator and immanent in the world as well. This combination of beliefs has proved important for subsequent attitudes to the Earth and its multiple inhabitants.

The New Testament and the Christian message

The New Testament was written over roughly a century, mostly in the eastern Mediterranean, but partly in Rome. Despite their differences of emphasis, its writers largely assumed the overall message of the Old Testament; but as they were concerned to express the Christian message to non-Jews, including their belief in God as creator, they conveyed this message in distinctive ways, seeking to explain and summarize for Gentiles what the Jews had learned gradually over a long period.

Thus Paul suggests that many of these people had failed to see God's works in nature, clear as they were: 'Ever since the creation of the world his invisible nature, namely his eternal power and deity, have been clearly perceived in the things that have been made' (Romans 1:20). Likewise in Acts, Paul and Barnabas affirm that, even in past generations, 'he did not leave himself without witnesses, for he did good and gave you from heaven rains and fruitful seasons, satisfying your hearts with food and gladness' (Acts 14:17; Glacken 1967: 161). These passages were later used to supply arguments for God's existence based on nature and its order.

Jesus too assumed God's existence and care, but used common experience to express this. 'Consider the lilies of the field, how they grow ... And yet I say unto you that even Solomon in all his glory was not arrayed like one of these' (Matthew 6:28–29). The 'fowls of the air' are treated similarly in the same passage, with the rider that people are more valuable than they are (Matthew 6:26). But even this rider presupposes that the birds and the flowers have an independent value of their own, a stance nowadays known as 'biocentrism', which is compatible with the belief that people, with their ampler capacities, are of greater value. (Biocentrism need not imply that all creatures are of like value. For an elucidation of biocentrism, see Chapter 2.)

Problem passages from the gospels, about Jesus sending the Gadarene swine to their deaths (Mark 5:11–14) and cursing a barren fig-tree (Mark 11:12–14), were taken by Augustine to indicate that refraining from killing animals and destroying trees is 'the height of superstition' (Passmore 1974: 111–12). But this passage tells us far more about Augustine and his polemical powers (directed against contemporary opponents) than about Jesus. Stephen Clark suggests that the narrative about the Gadarene swine may have originated in a parable, rather than as a historical event (1977: 196), while Luke 13:6–9 records a parable that could easily have been transformed into the story about the cursing of the fig-trees in Mark. (For other examples of New Testament narratives probably originating in parables, see Attfield 1991 [1983]: 30.) These problem passages, then, need not constitute obstacles to Jesus holding the biocentric attitudes shown in the passage about the birds of the air and the lilies of the field (Matthew 6:26–29), and suggested also by his consorting with the wild beasts in the wilderness (Mark 1:13), which is an echo of the behaviour associated in the Old Testament with the Messiah. (Biocentrism is discussed in greater detail in the next chapter.)

Paul, for his part, was clear that the whole of creation was involved in God's plan of salvation, 'groaning in travail' and yearning for its fulfilment (Romans 8:19–22). And the author of Revelation foresees that in the last days there will be a tree of life, the leaves of which 'are for the healing of the nations' (Revelation 22:2). Glacken (1967: 163) regards the passage of Romans just mentioned as far more representative of Paul's thinking than passages later interpreted as concerning sin being inherited from Adam, the first human. The Bible, then, regards nature as both God's creation and as being involved in his plan for redemption.

Lynn White (1967) has claimed that Christianity is 'the most anthropocentric religion the world has seen'. 'Anthropocentrism' is variously used to mean either the view that everything exists for the sake of human interests (teleological anthropocentrism), or the view that the criterion of moral rightness is fostering human interests alone (normative anthropocentrism). White may intend both of these, but qualifies his claim with 'in its Western form', thus referring in the first instance to two millennia of Christianity in the West. However, it is appropriate to remark at this stage that, despite occasional anthropocentric biblical passages (e.g., Paul's stance on oxen at 1 Corinthians 9:9), the Old Testament is clearly incompatible with anthropocentrism in both of these senses (see Psalm 104, Proverbs 12:10 and Job 38–41), and that the overall message of the New Testament is, in this regard, no different. I will, however, return to White's claims in the section below on the Middle Ages, to which they most directly refer.

Early Christianity

Some of the Church Fathers have been cited as sources of inspiration by modern environmentalists. The theologian Paul Santmire, for example, finds a neglected but ecologically promising motif in the second-century Christian theologian Irenaeus, who wrote of the whole cosmos being renewed in the end times: 'The whole creation shall, according to God's will, obtain a vast increase, that it may bring forth fruits such as Isaiah declares (30:25–26)'; indeed, it 'is full of goodness, harmony, beauty, and life at all times' (Santmire 1985: 43). And then there is Chrysostom's teaching (in the fourth century) about the beasts – 'Surely we ought to show them great kindness and gentleness for many reasons, but above all because they are of the same origin as ourselves' – which has been cited with approbation by C. W. Hume (1957: 26) and Andrew Linzey (1976: 103). Basil the Great (*c.* 331–79 CE) prayed for 'the humble beasts who bear with us the heat and burden of the day' (Passmore 1974: 198), suggesting that the attitudes of the book of *Proverbs* persisted into the patristic period. However, others, such as Origen (third century CE), seem to have adhered to a more anthropocentric stance, holding that the creator has made everything to serve rational beings (Glacken 1967: 185–6).

Nevertheless, Glacken attests the widespread presence of the belief among the Church Fathers, including Ambrose (fourth century CE) and Theodoret (fifth century CE), that humanity has the role of adorning and perfecting God's creation (1967: 192, 299, 300). There again, implicit belief in the human role as stewards of nature was also found among Christians such as Cosmas Indicopleustes (early sixth century), who writes of humanity completing and adorning the house of creation which God has prepared (Glacken 1967: 300–1). Yet these are precisely the two ancient traditions which Passmore (an admirer of Glacken) detects in pagan antiquity, and then (amazingly) as absent across the entire period of early Christianity and the Middle Ages (Passmore 1974: 28–34).

A frequent literary form among early Christians was that of commentaries on the six days of creation, each bearing the name of 'Hexaemeron'. This tradition was pioneered by the first-century CE Jewish writer Philo (Glacken 1967: 187–9); its most celebrated exponent was Basil the Great, whose work became known in the West through the Latin hexaemeron of Ambrose, which was based on it. Basil's work was praised many centuries later by von Humboldt in *Cosmos*, his major work of the early nineteenth century(Glacken 1967: 177: for von Humboldt, see Chapter 2).

One passage of Basil's work illustrates well the theme of an unfinished Earth which God has yet to complete with the aid of human farming and arboriculture: 'For the proper and natural adornment of the earth is its completion: corn waving in the valleys – meadows green with grass and rich with many-coloured flowers – fertile glades and hill-tops shaded by forests' (Glacken 1967: 192). Phrases from this sentence about the completion of God's creation were echoed to convey much the same message more than a thousand years later by the English naturalist John Ray (1627–1705). Such passages give the lie to the once-popular claim that early and medieval Christians lacked an awareness of natural beauty.

Augustine (354–430) too wrote a hexaemeron. Although, as we have seen, he adhered to a kind of anthropocentrist theology (everything being made, in his view, either for human benefit or for the glorification of God), he importantly countered aspects of Origen's degraded view of creation (see Santmire 1985), holding that life on Earth and the beauties of nature are not to be despised because they are low in the scale of being (Glacken 1967: 196). (For the great chain of being, see the subsection above on Aristotle and Theophrastus.) For Augustine, indeed, God is immanent in the world, and also transcends it (Santmire 1985: 208; Peacocke 2007: 22; Attfield 2016: 96). Rather surprisingly, in view of his usual reputation, Augustine also praises the achievements of human art and invention (agriculture and navigation included), and was one of many to argue to God from the beauties of the world.

> Ask the loveliness of the earth, ask the loveliness of the wide airy spaces, ask the loveliness of the sky, ask the order of the stars . . . ask all these things, and they will all answer thee, Lo, see we are lovely. Their loveliness is their confession. And these lovely but mutable things, who has made them, save Beauty immutable? (Glacken 1967: 200; Vivès 1872–8, vol. 18: 237–45)

Despite the fallen nature of humanity, human beings participate fully in the order of creation (Glacken 1967: 200), an order that retains its created goodness, and can, as in the passage cited, serve as a profound source of wonder.

Augustine also continued the tradition, present already in Chrysostom, of comparing nature to a great book, and one which, as he wrote, even the unlettered can read (Glacken 1967: 204). Reflection on nature as one of God's two books (the other being the revelation as conveyed in the Bible) has echoed down the centuries, being taken up (for example) in the seventeenth century by Francis Bacon (1561–1626) and Galileo (1564–1642), and in the nineteenth by the American naturalist John Muir (1838–1914). Those who could understand this book could at least begin to experience wonder, and to feel awe before its creator. This sense of awe and wonder has proved to be (as in Muir's case) one of the central springs of modern environmentalism.

The Middle Ages

This is the period from the fall of the Roman Empire in the West to 1500 and the dawn of the modern period. It includes the centuries which were at one time known as the 'Dark Ages', but which turn out to have been a period of considerable agricultural and technological development. It is also the period in which Christianity reached lands outside the Roman Empire, and returned to lands overrun by non-Christian invaders after the Romans withdrew. Many of those commemorated as saints, such as Patrick, Brendon, Columba and Cuthbert, played leading roles in this latter process. Several of these saints also enjoyed friendly and cooperative relations with wild animals, in the tradition of St Antony, the third-century founder of living as a hermit, in his case in the Egyptian 'inner desert' (Bratton 1988; Coates 1998: 55).

This section traces the attitudes to nature, land and animals of people in the Middle Ages, from St Cuthbert of Northumbria to St Thomas Aquinas. It also encompasses the rise and spread of Islam, and the life's work of Hildegard of Bingen and of Francis of Assisi. The narratives to be related are divergent and diverse. The one common factor was belief in God and the divine purposes, together with attempts to comprehend them. Lynn White has claimed to detect further common factors, and these claims are also discussed.

Saints and beasts, monks and farming

The successors of St Antony spread his ideas and practices, and tales of gentleness towards animals became associated with Celtic saints such as Brendon (sixth century) and Northumbrian saints such as Cuthbert (seventh century) (Waddell 1995). The detailed veracity of these stories matters less than the widespread veneration of these saints among Christians throughout the Middle Ages (and beyond). This veneration fostered a gentle attitude to animals, both wild (such as seals and ravens) and domestic (such as sheep and dogs), albeit one contrasting with traditions of hunting (in which, for example, Basil the Great joined) (Coates 1998: 56), and also with anthropocentric teachings spread by followers of church fathers such as Augustine. While this was an age when many wild animals were hunted to extinction, the lives of the saints also exercised an important influence on attitudes to nature, particularly among the poor and the unlearned. Meanwhile, some small contributions were made by Byzantine scholars to both zoology and botany (Egerton 2012: 17).

We now turn to monasticism, and the emergence of monasteries and nunneries. Following the Rule of Benedict (*c.* 480–*c.* 544), itself based on the teachings of Basil the Great in the East, the Benedictines founded the first of many monasteries at Monte Cassino in Italy in the early sixth century. The monks' main activities, besides prayer and worship, consisted in gardening and farming. 'St Benedict', writes René Dubos, 'believed that it was the duty of the monks to work as partners of God in improving his creation . . . implicit in his writings is the thought that labour is like a prayer which helps in recreating paradise out of chaotic wilderness' (1974: 126, 131–2; see also Coates 1998: 56–7). Dubos finds here a continuation of the ancient tradition (as depicted by Passmore) of completing and perfecting an unfinished creation, adding that such a creative stewardship of the earth is compatible with reverence for nature. While not all monasteries always lived up to these ideals, Western monasteries contributed to establishing a pattern of fertile farmland, and also of islands of order, in turbulent and unpredictable times.

Before we turn to White's discussion of medieval technology, it is appropriate to pause to remark other changes to the landscape taking place in this period, with special reference to England and Wales.

Pre-Roman deforestation seems to have emptied these lands of bears, and largely of beavers, and by 1400 wolves were extinct here too, but not yet in Scotland. The Saxon invaders found a land rich in fields, villages and farmsteads, adding places with names ending in 'ley' (a forest clearing), such as King's Langley and Abbot's Langley in Hertfordshire, and 'hurst' (a settlement in a clearing) such as Chislehurst in Kent, albeit not in great abundance (Coates 1998: 43–4). Much later, in the early twelfth century, Cistercian monks arrived and by 1300 had established 230 abbeys and priories, from the Moray Firth in Scotland to Tintern in Wales (and across Europe as far as Hungary). They adhered to the Rule of Benedict, and cleared land for cultivation at the same time, but sometimes displaced local people as they did so (Coates 1998: 44). Much forest clearance was also conducted at their behest (Glacken 1967: 214).

Lynn White and medieval technology

White's understanding of the attitude of Christianity to nature (as anthropocentric and despotic) has already been encountered (see above, 'The New Testament and the Christian message'). But his main specialism concerned medieval technology, and he wrote illuminatingly about wind-power and late medieval clocks and organs (White 1962). In this work he also discussed the introduction of heavy ploughing in Christian seventh-century Europe (use of ploughs equipped with a vertical knife to cut the soil, a ploughshare to slice it and a mouldboard to turn it over). But he always did so with qualifications and nuances, recognizing that such ploughing had occasionally been used much earlier (in Roman times) and was introduced to Britain and Normandy much later by the pagan Vikings (White 1962: 51; Attfield 2009b). But in his famous 1967 essay in *Science*, the nuances are omitted, and heavy ploughing, together with its implications for land tenure, is claimed as epitomizing the supposed new despotic Christian attitude of mastery over nature. 'Formerly man had been part of nature; now he was the exploiter of nature.' These claims appear to be upheld by White's (controversial) despotic account of Christian theology.

While this form of ploughing was much more effective than the scratch-ploughing that preceded it, its introduction was not confined to Christian cultures; nor was it universal among them. Besides, the suggestion that humanity had, until that century, been 'part of nature' conflicts with the vigorous forms of agriculture promulgated long before by Hesiod, Virgil and Roman prose writers such as Columella (first century CE), and the suggestion that fear of nature and belief in spirits animating it had disappeared conflicts with the attitudes assumed in, for example,

Beowulf (probably composed in the eighth century) (Coates 1998: 58). Nor does White's ascription of a despotic view fit the attitudes of Basil, Benedict or their followers. In any case, his basing of this change of West European attitudes on a single technological development ascribed to the seventh century strikes many (including Coates) as disproportionate and 'idiosyncratic' (Coates 1998: 62).

White seems correct in ascribing growing technological superiority to Western Europe across the Middle Ages, and finding some of the roots of current ecological problems in its subsequent impacts. But since those roots more cogently turn on the industrial revolution of over a millennium later than the period to which he traces their origins, his case, even if it were better supported by early medieval technology, would require many additional explanatory factors to bridge this thousand-year chasm. Others have indeed detected an industrial revolution in the thirteenth century, citing the fulling-mill and the windmill (Carus-Wilson 1954; Coates 1998: 63), but without associating these developments with such wide-ranging changes of human self-understanding as those alleged by White. Besides, as Coates proceeds to show, this period also saw the beginnings of an increasing appreciation of nature and 'the greenwood' (Hutchinson 1974; Coates 1998: 64), rather than a monolithic posture of human mastery. White's depiction of medieval attitudes as dependent ultimately on his account of theological beliefs in any case gives undue prominence to a single kind of underlying cause (ideas and beliefs), disregarding many other factors, among which are social, economic and cultural trends.

The Rise of Islam

Islam originated in seventh-century Arabia, but before long took over Egypt and the rest of North Africa and also the former Roman province of Syria, soon expanding into most of Spain, Sicily, Mesopotamia, Persia and the lands north and east of it once conquered by Alexander the Great. It proclaimed a purer and less diluted version of monotheism than Christianity, and embodied the belief that the Qu'ran conveys God's literal message to humanity. In the late Middle Ages, Mohammedans lost Sicily and Spain but captured Asia Minor, the Balkans and (in 1453) Constantinople.

Islam has always maintained that human beings are God's vicegerents (*khalifa*) on Earth, and the custodians of the entire natural world, charged not to violate the 'due measure' and 'balance' that God has created. Thus, although the entire bounty of nature has been created for the sake of human beings, this anthropocentric stance does not imply that humanity is granted unbridled exploitative powers, for nature has been made for all generations, and not just for one, and human beings remain answerable to God. Within Islamic tradition (*Hadith*), there is provision for recognizing *hima* (protected pasturage, with special protection for indigenous flora and fauna), and also for *harun*, sanctuaries where killing animals of game species is forbidden, and where springs and watercourses are respected (Nomanul Haq 2001).

The Islamic philosopher Averroes, or Ibn Rochd (1126–98) flourished in the relatively tolerant Muslim kingdom of southern Spain in the twelfth century (where by the end of the tenth century the royal library at Córdoba was said to have had more than 400,000 volumes: Whitney 2004: 11). He was influenced by Aristotle, and his work is a Muslim counterpart to Christian theology, conveying belief in divine purpose and concern for humanity. Like many Christian thinkers, he was impressed by the natural world as a work of art, and argued that it discloses the work of a craftsman-like creator (Glacken 1967: 220–1). He also defended science, replying to *The Incoherence of the Philosophers*, an anti-scientific treatise of al-Ghazali (1058–1111), with his formidable counter-sceptical work *The Incoherence of the Incoherence* (Whitney 2004: 13).

Thus Islam during the Middle Ages fostered the scientific quest for laws of nature, particularly at centres of learning such as Córdoba and Baghdad. These studies made a large difference when, in the late Middle Ages and the Renaissance period, West Europeans, influenced by Islamic science, resumed the study of mathematics, physics and astronomy.

St Francis of Assisi (1182–1226)

Francis of Assisi has been suggested by White as the patron saint of ecologists; White (1967) considered him an isolated exception to what he considered the Christian postures of anthropocentrism and mastery of nature. But this was a case of what Coates calls 'making figures from the past over in our own image', adding that 'nineteenth-century Romanticism . . . launched the modern process of reinvention by casting Francis as a nature mystic' like 'a medieval Wordsworth' (1998: 53).

The historical Francis, however, as Susan Bratton has concluded, fits into a long line of saints who respected and befriended animals as fellow-creatures: 'St. Francis was not . . . an aberration, but the product of a thousand-year tradition beginning with Antony in the inner desert, and kept alive by the great monastic libraries of Europe' (1988: 52). He is said to have talked and preached to bees, doves and even a wolf, chiding those that harmed human beings, reminding them of their indebtedness to their creator, and urging them to praise God (rather as the Psalms had done). Brother Thomas of Celano relates that he called all creatures by the name of 'brother', and Francis himself, during his final years, composed *The Canticle of Brother Sun* in which he addressed the sun and moon, fire and the wind as 'brothers' and water as 'sister'. Stories of his preaching to swallows and at Gubbio to a ravenous wolf are recounted by Ugolino de Monte Santa Maria in *The Little Flowers of St. Francis*, composed a century after his death (Glacken 1967: 214–16), while the Franciscan order continued his teaching, albeit in diluted form.

Even if these stories display the embroidery developed during an oral tradition, their telling in the early fourteenth century is itself significant, belying Passmore's claim that 'In any case, Francis had little or no influence' (1974: 112). Many of Francis's ideas were in fact transmitted by his follower, the theologian Bonaventure (1221–74), who qualified Francis's teaching by adding that the relation to God of different creatures differs according to their capacities (Santmire 1985: 98). Certainly, Francis's attempts to humanize or make responsible citizens of wolves would not commend him to modern ecologists. In his beliefs, he was a man of this own time, with an unusually intense rapport with nonhuman creatures, alongside a related concern for economic and social justice among human beings. The main reason he appeared so exceptional to White was White's controversial characterization of Christianity as uniformly committed to a despotic attitude to nature.

In 2015, Pope Francis paid tribute to St Francis of Assisi in his Encyclical *Laudato Si'* for his joyful communion with fellow-creatures ranging from the stars to the animals and flowers. After quoting Romans 1:20, he also noted that Francis asked that part of the friary garden should be left untouched so that wild flowers could grow there, and so that those who saw them could raise their minds to the creator of such beauty (Pope Francis 2015: 10–12). While the assumptions of our day are not those of St Francis, retrieval of the awe and wonder that he showed towards the natural world could, as Pope Francis suggests, rescue us from attitudes of mastery and lifestyles of exploitation (see Attfield 2016: 99–100.)

Hildegard, Albert and Thomas Aquinas

Shortly before the birth of Francis of Assisi, Hildegard of Bingen (1098–1179) became abbess of two Benedictine nunneries in north central Germany, composed music and, between 1150 and 1160, wrote several books, including visionary works and also *Causae et Curae* (Causes and Cures) and *Physica* (Natural History). *Causae et Curae* begins with an account of the creation and the impacts of the sun, moons, planets and winds on the earth and human bodies. She goes on to discuss the four elements (see the sections above on Empedocles and on Aristotle), the four humours (blood, phlegm, yellow bile and black bile), reproduction, the effects of the fall of humanity on human health and the physiological basis of personality, finishing with herbal and other remedies for ailments.

Physica covers the elements, animals, stones, fish, birds, metals and, especially, plants, with regard to their relation to the four humours and to remedies. Thus, Hildegard added environmental factors to the ancient medical teachings of Galen (129–199/200 CE), supplied original views about the male and female roles in conception, and devised (among other metaphors drawn from the natural world) the metaphor of greenness (*viriditas*) for the force of life generated by God.

Hildegard was one of the last of a series of learned abbesses known to us from the middle ages (Whitney 2004: 162–5). Neither Glacken nor Coates mentions her, and her books have largely been overlooked, but her musical compositions have become well known, and her understanding of human physiology and its relation to religious ideas are beginning to receive scholarly attention. She can in any case be credited with anticipating, to some extent, the modern green movement by introducing the term 'greenness' for the force of life to be found in nature.

Soon after the death of Hildegard, Albert the Great (1193–1280) wrote about geography, climate, the seasons and their influence in his book *De Natura Locorum*, probably based on his travel on foot between the Dominican monasteries of France, Italy and Germany (Glacken 1967: 227–9). Like Theophrastus, he was aware that human interventions can change the impact of geography, as when trees are felled. His writings were influenced by bestiaries (which used animals to teach moral messages) and also by astrology (regarded then as a legitimate science; Lindberg 1992: 274–7).

Yet Glacken regards Albert's work as 'the most important and the most elaborate discussion of geographical theory with relation to human culture since the Hippocratic *Airs, Waters, Places*' (1967: 270). He was interested in the details of soil preparation and of grafting, and, building on Aristotle's works, wrote *On Animals*, the foremost medieval work of zoology (Lindberg 1992: 353; Whitney 2004: 189–93); but at the same time, he was just as prone as ancient (and many modern) writers to overgeneralization about human characteristics and to racial stereotyping (Glacken 1967: 270). Nevertheless, Albert played a key part in the transmission of ancient ideas to the thinkers of the early modern and modern periods.

Thomas Aquinas (*c.* 1225–74) was a pupil of Albert, and an early advocate of biodiversity (albeit using different terms), holding that 'it is better to have a multiplicity of species than a multiplicity of members of one species' (Glacken 1967: 230). This multiplicity makes the universe more perfect, as the great chain of being had long maintained (see the subsection above on Aristotle and Theophrastus). In the fifth of the 'Five ways' of his *Summa Theologiae*, Thomas reasons from the order and apparent directedness of natural beings that lack intelligence to the direction supplied by their creator, 'and this being we call God' (Glacken 1967: 229). And like Averroes, Thomas in his *Summa Contra Gentiles* regards the heavens and the earth as the handicraft of a craftsman. He supports this view with passages such as Psalm 104, and also Paul's letter to the Romans (see the subsection above on the New Testament). At the same time, he derives further support for his natural theology from Aristotle's claim that nature does nothing in vain (Glacken 1967: 231–2).

Thomas frequently seeks to demonstrate the goodness of nature, replying both to the Manicheans of the ancient world and to the Albigensians of his own time. Evils are due not to the primary cause (the creator), but to the exercise of their powers by lower agents or secondary causes, exercising delegated powers which they hold because of the ends for which they were created. Foremost among lower agents is humanity, which Thomas believes to be master over the animals, and authorized to domesticate selected animal and plant species. But this is a derivative dominion, and its derivativeness calls for human beings to show humility (Glacken 1967: 236).

Even so, there is a marked difference of tone between Thomas Aquinas' despotic view of humanity and the tone that we have met in Chrysostom, Basil, Cuthbert and Francis. The diversity of Christian medieval assumptions helps explain the diversity of modern readings of the period, which range from interpreting everyone except Francis as anthropocentric and despotic (including Thomas's late medieval successors) (White 1967) to locating a patron saint of ecology in St Benedict, and celebrating the Benedictines and Cistercians accordingly (Dubos 1974). Borrowing Passmore's approach to the ancient world, we could reasonably find the seeds of enlightened approaches and compassionate perspectives in the medieval world, alongside widespread exploitative attitudes, all of them prone to influence that period's modern successors.

This chapter has selectively surveyed environmental thought in the ancient world, the Bible, early Christianity and the medieval period (including the rise of Islam in the early part of that period). In the next chapter we turn to the successors of that period who lived in the part of the modern period prior to the working life of Charles Darwin. While ancient and medieval influences underlay their thought, many were determined to make a new start. They sought to match the discovery of the new world of America with new beginnings in science, in art, in literature and in poetry, and to reform religion by returning to Christian origins. Their attitudes to the natural world reflect these changed perspectives. So it is to the early modern period that we now turn.

Recommended reading

Attfield, Robin (1991 [1983]). *The Ethics of Environmental Concern*, 2nd edn. Athens: University of Georgia Press.
Bratton, Susan Power (1988). 'The Original Desert Solitaire: Early Christian Monasticism and Wilderness', *Environmental Ethics*, 10(1): 31–53.
Coates, Peter (1998). *Nature: Western Attitudes since Ancient Times*. Berkeley: University of California Press.
Dubos, René (1974). 'Franciscan Conservation and Benedictine Stewardship', in David and Eileen Spring (eds), *Ecology and Religion in History*. New York: Harper & Row, pp. 114–136.
Egerton, Frank N. (2012). *Roots of Ecology: Antiquity to Haeckel*. Berkeley: University of California Press.
Glacken, Clarence J. (1967). *Traces on the Rhodian Shore: Nature and Culture in Western Thought from Ancient Times to the End of the Eighteenth Century*. Berkeley: University of California Press.
Lovejoy, Arthur O. (1936). *The Great Chain of Being: A Study of the History of an Idea*. Cambridge, MA: Harvard University Press.
Passmore, John (1974). *Man's Responsibility for Nature*. London: Duckworth.
Santmire, Paul (1985). *The Travail of Nature: The Ambiguous Ecological Promise of Christian Theology*. Philadelphia, PA: Fortress Press.
White, Lynn, Jr. (1962). *Medieval Technology and Social Change*. Oxford: Clarendon Press.
White, Lynn, Jr. (1967). 'The Roots of Our Ecologic Crisis', *Science*, 155(37): 1203–1207.
Whitney, Elspeth (2004). *Medieval Science and Technology*. Westport, CT: Greenwood Press.

2

Early Modern Reflections

The Sixteenth, Seventeenth and Eighteenth Centuries

This chapter is concerned with the whole of the modern period from the Reformation up to the decades prior to the publication of Darwin's *Origin of Species*. This first section considers theologians, poets, scientists and philosophers from 1500 onwards; the next section looks at the Romantic movement in Germany, Britain and America.

It may help readers if some of the concepts employed below are clarified. Some of the figures mentioned below (including Jean Calvin and John Evelyn) were (what we would now call) anthropocentrists, holding that what matters is limited to the interests or welfare of human beings. Some environmentalists continue to ground their beliefs and campaigns on this idea, but many find it too impoverished, and prefer to hold either a sentientist position (as Jeremy Bentham did), for which the interests or welfare of all sentient beings also matter, or a biocentrist stance (as was held by John Ray), for which the good of all living creatures matters, whether equally or unequally, or an ecocentrist stance, for which what matters further includes the good of species and/or ecosystems. All these classifications derive from the late twentieth century, but serve to convey significant distinctions of attitude and conviction characteristic of earlier centuries.

The concept of theocentrism is also used below. This does not exclude any of the above stances, but recognizes the value of anything held to be loved and cherished by God as creator. Thus Calvin combined anthropocentrism with theocentrism (though he was, of course, a stranger to both of these concepts), and could oppose on this basis the maltreatment of any of God's creatures not for their own sakes, but because of the will and the good purposes of God. Yet others, such as Alexander Pope (1688–1744), were able to combine theocentrism with sentientism (and others with biocentrism). Another theological concept deployed below is panentheism, the belief that, as well as being the universal creator, God is present in all creatures; as will be seen, this was the stance of Martin Luther and some of his followers (see the passages of Luther quoted in the next section). It should be emphasized that there is no contradiction between belief in God as transcendent creator and belief in God's indwelling in the created world. (For a review of different shades of meaning of panentheism currently in use, see Attfield 2019.) Pan*en*theism contrasts with pantheism, the belief that God and the universe are one and the same, a stance upheld in the seventeenth century by Baruch Spinoza (1632–77), and revived in the nineteenth by Schelling (see the section later in this chapter, 'The Romantic Movement').

It may also help to explain the concept of mechanism, introduced by René Descartes (1596–1650), for bodies (human and nonhuman) as opposed to minds. For mechanists, living bodies are basically machines, operating on principles similar to clockwork. The material universe can also be regarded as a machine, movements in which are produced by contiguous forces. This belief was held by Descartes, but not strictly by Isaac Newton, who believed in action at a distance, as in the case of gravity. Mechanists were opposed by vitalists, such as the Cambridge Platonists, who held that living creatures behave as they do because of the presence of animating spirits, and also by Aristotelians, who held (and continue to hold) that the behaviour of animate organisms is to be understood by their inbuilt purposes. The philosopher Gottfried Wilhelm Leibniz (1646–1716), for example, revived belief in such 'final causes' or inbuilt purposes. (These classifications too, with the exception of 'Aristotelians', come from a later period, when there was an explicit debate in the decades prior to the First World War between mechanists and vitalists.)

However, one of the distinguishing features of the modern period was a widespread desire to break with the Aristotelianism of the late Middle Ages, and to resort to new explanations. These included atomism (belief that the fundamental components of physical objects were indivisible particles or atoms), a belief adopted by Pierre Gassendi (1592–1655), Robert Boyle (1627–91) and John Locke, and belief in laws of nature, observable regularities uniform across space and time (a stance championed by most of the members of the Royal Society, which was given a royal charter by Charles II in 1662).

There were also artists of the Renaissance period who broke new ground, such as Albrecht Durer (1471–1528), with his drawings of landscape and of clumps of turf (see Egerton 2012: 33), which challenged people to look at the world around them anew, and such as the Italian masters who reintroduced perspective into their painting, similarly challenging their clientele. Limits of space prevent any detailed treatment of these particular innovations here.

While these concepts and distinctions will shortly be brought into play, this chapter inevitably opens with the attitudes to nature and the environment of the two principal founders of the Reformation, Martin Luther and Jean Calvin. Although their followers and successors were often (but not always) politically aligned, their own stances (theological and otherwise) were both influential and mutually distinctive. Since they each changed the way large numbers of people came to understand their own relation both to God and to nature, it is important to consider them briefly in turn.

Luther, Calvin and Hale

Martin Luther (1483–1546), the pioneer of the Reformation, stressed in his writings the sovereignty of God over nature, together with his distinctive stance on human salvation. But he also believed in God's hiddenness and in his immanence in nature. He wrote: 'God is substantially present everywhere, in and through all creatures, in all their parts and places, so that the world is full of God and he fills all, but without his being encompassed and surrounded by it' (Santmire 1985: 129). Here we find a remarkable affirmation of the world, including its living creatures, to a degree which harmonizes with what modern theologians call 'panentheism', the belief that God is present in the world as well as being its creator. (As we have seen in Chapter 1, beliefs of this kind are expressed in the Bible in Psalm 139 and in Acts 17:28.)

Luther also wrote: 'You cannot in one glance survey this most vast and beautiful system of the universe in all its wide expanse without being completely overwhelmed by the boundless force of its brightness.' Thus he held that if we truly understood the growth of a grain of wheat, we would die of wonder (Santmire 1985: 129–30). These remarks echo the tradition of German mysticism, founded by the Dominican monk Meister Eckhart (*c.* 1260–*c.* 1328).

Santmire comments that Luther's sense of the presence and power of God in nature are far removed from the stress invoked by Thomas Aquinas on the distance between the infinite creator and finite creatures (1985: 129). While Luther's emphasis was on doctrines such as justification by faith, he also left his followers a legacy of immersion in the wonders of the natural world, which many were to disregard, while others gladly embraced them, as will be seen as this chapter unfolds. Luther's belief in God's immanence in nature was to be most strongly echoed in the writings of the Lutheran mystic Jakob Boehme (1575–1624), who was widely influential on other mystics in later generations. Among later Lutherans, it was, perhaps, the Romantic movement that most fully recaptured this immanentist stance. However, some twentieth-century theologians, conscious of evolution and of ecological processes, have turned more explicitly to panentheism. A good example is Jürgen Moltmann, in particular in his book *God in Creation* (see Chapter 9).

As for the more activist stance of the other principal leader of the Reformation, Jean Calvin (1509–64), his emphasis on people's callings (as well as on their justification and divine election) made him understand the human dominion of nature as 'vocational dominion'. Even more than in the theology of the Benedictines (see Chapter 1), people were to transform the world (Santmire 1985: 126). In this connection, Calvin expressly resuscitated the New Testament metaphor of stewardship, both with regard to a person's own resources and to caring for the Earth as a whole; indeed, he decried the 'plundering of the earth of what God hath given it for the nourishment of man' (Derr 1973: 20).

In Calvin's view, everything in creation has been made for humanity, but people are to use the world around them responsibly, so that no one is deprived of its resources. This, indeed, is the historical point at which the tradition of stewardship becomes explicitly avowed: 'Let everyone regard himself as the steward of God in all things which he possesses,' he taught (Welbourn 1975: 563). This remark, in fact, begins to cast doubt on the influential thesis of Max Weber (1864–1920) that the Protestant Reformation initiated the process that he called 'the disenchantment of the world' (2002 [1905]), which barely fits the teachings of Calvin, and appears to ignore altogether the very different teachings of Luther. In the next century, some of the adherents of the stewardship tradition were to interpret this tradition in a less anthropocentric manner than that of Calvin. Calvin, however, would have disowned the label of 'anthropocentric' (if he had encountered it), and might well have preferred, if offered it, that of 'theocentric'. Besides, another of Calvin's persistent emphases was God's presence in nature, a theme which was to prove influential among his followers (Stoll 2015: 21).

If we now move to the next century, we can find a development of the Reformers' theology in the statement of the Protestant Chief Justice of England and Wales, Sir Matthew Hale (1677), who wrote: 'The end of man's creation was, that he should be the viceroy of the great God of heaven and earth in this inferior world; his steward, villicus [farm-manager], bailiff or farmer of this goodly farm of the lower world.' Only for this reason, to follow Passmore's paraphrase, was man

> invested with power, authority, right, dominion, trust and care, to correct and abridge the excesses and cruelties of the fiercer animals, to give protection and defence of the mansuete [tame] and useful, to preserve the species of diverse vegetables [growing things], to improve them and others, to correct the redundance of unprofitable vegetables, to preserve the face of the earth in beauty, usefulness and fruitfulness. (1974: 30: the phrases in square brackets are Passmore's modern translations)

Passmore comments that this passage would have the sympathy of modern conservationists, though not preservationists, even if they did not agree about humanity being God's deputy. He also considers that it is an expression of seventeenth-century humanism, and has a (heretical) Pelagian emphasis on what the human will can achieve (1974: 30). I suspect that many modern conservationists would have reservations, alongside preservationists, not only about curbing the fiercer animals, but also about correcting the excesses of 'unprofitable vegetables'. Nevertheless, the passage is a fine expression of the stewardship position. As for seventeenth-century humanism, Hale's words fit well into Francis Bacon's aspirations, expressed in his utopian novel *New Atlantis*, to rescue humanity from the fall, as he interpreted it, and to improve fruit-bearing plants, thus 'effecting all things possible'; rather than being Pelagian or otherwise heretical, Hale's remark is also a continuation of Calvin's message about humanity's vocation to stewardship (as just described), with rather more of an emphasis on landscapes and the environment, and less of an anthropocentric outlook. We shall see how similar ideas were soon to be expressed by the naturalist John Ray. Generally, this passage should not be regarded as an isolated one, as Passmore regards it, but as a valuable development of the ancient stewardship tradition (see Chapter 1 on Plato, Ambrose, Theodoret and others), now explicitly revived by Calvin.

The metaphysical poets

This cluster of seventeenth-century English and Welsh poets often wrote about the relations of humanity, nature and God, to an extent that exceeds their predecessors of the Elizabethan age, profound as Shakespeare and his contemporaries undoubtedly were (Martin 2015), and also their successors of what is often called 'the Age of Reason'. For example, George

Herbert (1593–1633), who has become known as 'laureate of the Church of England' (Passmore 1974: 31), composed some anthropocentric lines, as cited by Passmore: 'For us the winds do blow; / The earth doth rest, heaven move, and fountains flow'; he goes on to speak of the world being our servant, and to pray that both the world and humanity may be God's servants (Passmore 1974: 31). Yet elsewhere, in a well-known (and still much-loved) hymn, Herbert develops the language of the Psalms, praying for nature's participation in praising God – 'Let all the world in every corner sing / "My God and King"' – in language reminiscent of that of St Francis and his *Canticle*. Thus to represent George Herbert as unqualifiedly anthropocentric seems a distortion; for he captures not only the language of human dominion (Psalms 8) but also that of nature's adoration of God (as in Psalms 148 and 150).

Thomas Traherne (1637–74) was a clergyman, poet and mystic, who wrote poems such as 'Wonder' and also poetic prose, including 'Centuries of Meditation', the influence of which has been comparatively recent, after this long-lost work was rediscovered. Traherne presents both an original twist to belief in humanity's dominion and an identification with the natural world:

> You never enjoy the world aright, till the Sea itself floweth in your veins, till you are clothed with the heavens, and crowned with the stars: and perceive yourself to be the sole heir of the whole world, and more than so, because men are in it who are every one sole heirs as well as you. ('Centuries of Meditation'; see Ridler 1966)

The world, including the sea and the stars, are to be enjoyed and appreciated as the unique inheritance of each of us. This is a figurative uniqueness, but Traherne's language nevertheless evokes the distinct delight to be found in identification with the world and in a shared awareness of createdness and of creation, comparable with that of the Psalms and of Luther.

Around the same time, Andrew Marvell (1621–78) pretends in 'The Garden' that he holds that trees far exceed the beauty of a human mistress, and that life in the 'happy garden-state' of Eden was better for Adam when his enjoyment of the garden was unshared. This is a many-layered and nuanced poem, which at one point appears to envisage that gardens (and the world in general) are generated by human minds (as in philosophical idealism), but it pulls back from this view to accept the objective beauty of the original garden, a view at odds with the philosophy of Descartes, which we will shortly encounter. In another poem, 'Bermudas', Marvell recounts a hymn of praise to God for the beauty and fruitfulness of those islands, as sung by the original English colonists (Wilcher 1986), and echoing the tone of the biblical Psalms.

There again, at much the same time, the Welsh poet, Henry Vaughan (1976), wrote of the restoration of all things at the end of the world:

> O knowing, glorious spirit! when
> Thou shalt restore beasts, trees and men,
> When thou shalt make all new again,
> Destroying only death and pain,
> Give him amongst thy works a place,
> Who in them loved and sought thy face!

Here the poet, besides including all living beings in God's new creation (Revelation 21), shows how in his own understanding God was present in them all already, as Luther had likewise taught. The metaphysical poets, then, adopted a mixture of (what would later be called) anthropocentric, theocentric and panentheistic stances, which modern environmentalists who share their theistic beliefs are free to follow, and from which those who do not are free to select, not least these poets' characteristic sense of the wonder of the world (best expressed in Traherne's 'Wonder', as long before in Psalm 139).

The scientific revolution: Bacon, Descartes and the Royal Society

In *New Atlantis* (posthumously published in 1627), Francis Bacon portrayed a research community of scientists (Salomon's House), on the mythical island of Bensalem, whose research was to cover the accessible parts of the entire natural world, to provide for human needs and improve the fruits of nature for the sake of the kingdom of humanity. In *New Organon* (1620), Bacon depicted a new methodology for the conduct of such scientific research. Later, the Royal Society (1662) was founded in London for the sake of collaborative research employing this same methodology. Bacon's anthropocentrism was combined with advocacy of humility, but has been widely accused – particularly by Carolyn Merchant (1990 [1980]) – of being arrogant, of transforming nature from an organism to a machine and of having an aggressive attitude to both nature and women.

It is doubtful whether we can ascribe the mechanistic view of nature to Bacon, as much as to his contemporaries René Descartes and the reviver of atomism, Pierre Gassendi; indeed, Bacon's metaphor of putting nature to the test probably reflects enthusiasm for experimentation rather than support for torture or sexual violence. His essay on gardens (1625) even advocates the inclusion of an area set aside for wild flowers (Coates 1998: 116). Nor did his thought spell the end of the model of nature as an organism, which remained the view of the Cambridge Platonists of later in the seventeenth century. Yet Bacon certainly initiated a major shift in attitudes to nature, away from Aristotelianism and from varying forms of belief in the intrinsic value of natural beings, and towards an experimental and inductive approach, which the Royal Society was later to carry forward, decades after his death.

In the philosophy of Descartes, qualities such as scent, colour and taste are understood as secondary, and as generated by ourselves, and the primary qualities of nature are limited to mass, motion and position. This would mean, as Santmire says, that the beauty and wonder of nature belong to the realm of human subjectivity (Santmire 1985: 133), rather than having the objectivity ascribed to them in Andrew Marvell's 'The Garden' (see above). More fundamentally, Descartes proposed an analytic and reductive method of investigation, which he employed fruitfully in devising coordinate geometry. Descartes held that human beings are essentially minds ('*sum res cogitans*', or 'I am a thinking thing', was one of his conclusions), albeit closely connected to material bodies, whereas animals and other living creatures are essentially machines, incapable of reflection and self-consciousness. Many have also ascribed to him a denial of feelings in animals, but John Cottingham (1978) has supplied convincing evidence that Descartes (somewhat inconsistently) did not deny animal sensations, but recognized that animals feel emotions, pleasure and pain. Some of his followers, sadly, were more consistent.

Descartes's dualism of mind and matter was widely influential for the following three centuries, although it was contested in his own century, both by the materialist Thomas Hobbes (1588–1679), and by the Cambridge Platonists, for whom nature was suffused with spirit. Meanwhile, Leibniz maintained that the physical universe consisted of units of perception or monads, each perceiving the others from its own perspective. Leibniz also revived Aristotle's belief in final causes (purposive explanations), which Bacon had regarded as unknowable and Descartes as no part of science.

Bacon and Descartes, together with Isaac Newton (1642–1727), have been widely pilloried 'as supreme bogeymen in many environmentalist accounts' (Coates 1998: 71), not least by Merchant, having been made spokesmen of the scientific revolution. They certainly either advocated this revolution (Bacon and Descartes) or developed it (Descartes and Newton), with far-reaching consequences. Yet Bacon was hardly a mechanist; nor strictly speaking was Newton, who believed in action at a distance. And while they presented new methods for the conduct of 'natural philosophy' (science, that is), they can hardly be held responsible for its later more extreme developments or applications. Nor can their predecessors be regarded as having formed a golden age of sustainability or of belief in nature as a nurturing mother (think of the Spanish *conquistadors* and their extraction of the mineral wealth of the Americas.) Besides, as Coates maintains, the new belief in mechanism presupposed belief in God as the creator of the mechanism of creation (1998: 81); historically, for many decades to come, most scientists shared in the theism of Bacon, Descartes and Newton. So even those whose attitudes were anthropocentric held standardly (as had Calvin) that natural organisms were creatures of God, and should be treated accordingly in a stewardly manner, although some of the members of the Royal Society nevertheless resorted to vivisection, as will shortly be seen.

The Royal Society received its charter from Charles II in 1662, and began a process of collaborative research along Baconian lines, in an attempt to discover the creator's laws from his workmanship in the observable world. The Fellows held varied views, from the sceptical empiricism of Joseph Glanvill (1636–80) to the confident atomism of Robert Boyle, and later of Isaac Newton. It was indeed at this stage that the atomism of the ancients, after its revival by Descartes's contemporary Pierre Gassendi, returned to the mainstream of science, and was adopted by Boyle and by John Locke. Yet Boyle, it must be acknowledged, took part in the vivisection of live animals, a practice at which Alexander Pope was to protest on the basis of his (far from anthropocentric) belief in human stewardship of 'the inferior creation' (Turner 1964: 48).

One of the members of the Royal Society, its secretary John Evelyn (1620–1706), composed two works that mark him out as a proto-environmentalist, aware of some of the adverse side-effects of human activities. In *Fumifugium* (1661), he exposed and complained about the air pollution of London; while in *Silva, or, A Discourse of Forest Trees* (1664), he drew attention to deforestation, as another unintended side-effect of the human modification of nature. Certainly, one of his motives was concern for the availability of timber for the construction of ships for the English navy, but he was also concerned for the conservation of forests: he quoted freely from Theophrastus, Virgil, Pliny and Columella, and advocated a large scheme of tree-planting to make good the damage that had already taken place (Glacken 1967: 485–91). Here was a further example of an anthropocentric approach being allied to belief in stewardship, and to a dawning (and virtually unprecedented) realization of the vulnerability of the natural world.

Evelyn also wrote a tract defending vegetarianism on grounds of human health. In this, he was following the ideas of Thomas Tryon

(1634–1703), who in 1657 gave up meat and fish and refused to wear leather, partly on grounds of animal welfare (Thomas 1983: 291–2). Others adopted both Tryon's theory and his practice, not least through the influence of translations of Ovid's *Metamorphoses* (see Chapter 1); in 1700, John Dryden (1634–1700) interpolated into his own translation the striking couplet: 'Take not away the life you cannot give: / For all things have an equal right to live' (Dryden 1958; Thomas 1983: 292). Thus were the ancient seeds of vegetarianism (sown by Empedocles, Plutarch and Porphyry) revived by a significant minority in early modern England.

Another writer influenced by Evelyn was Hans Carl von Carlowitz of Saxony (1645–1714). In 1713, Carlowitz wrote *Sylvicultura oeconomica*, appealing to Genesis 1 about dressing and keeping the original garden (see Chapter 1), warning of excessive deforestation, and using the term 'nachhaltend' about timber-usage, thus employing 'sustained' in its modern sense for the first time (Grober 2007: 19). (Two centuries after Evelyn, George Perkins Marsh was given the accolade of 'Our American Evelyn: see Chapter 4.)

Another member of the Royal Society was John Ray, a plant biologist, who rejected the view that everything had been made for the sake of humanity, as opposed to human beings and animals alike (Thomas 1983: 167). Ray was mentioned above in Chapter 1 as having been influenced by Basil the Great. In his book *The Wisdom of God Manifested in the Works of the Creation* (1691) he echoes some of Basil's words in writing:

> I persuade myself that the bounteous and gracious Author of Man's Being and Faculties, and of all Things else, delights in the Beauty of his Creation, and is well-pleased with the Industry of Man, in adorning the Earth with beautiful Cities and Castles ... with regular Gardens and Orchards, and Plantations of all Sorts of Shrubs and Herbs ... with Shady Woods and Groves, and walks set with Rows of elegant Trees, with Pastures cloathed with Flocks, and Valleys cover'd with Corn, and Meadows burthened with Grass, and whatever differenceth a civil and well-cultivated Region, from a barren and desolate Wilderness. (Glacken 1967: 484)

Here we find a striking expression of cooperation with nature from a nonanthropocentric perspective. Roderick Nash (the pioneering historian of American and related attitudes to nature) cites a further, even more memorable, passage: 'It is a generally received opinion that all this visible world was created for Man; that Man is the end of the Creation, as if there were no other end of any creature but some way or other to be serviceable to man ...yet wise men nowadays think otherwise.' Animals and plants in fact exist to glorify God (Ray 1691: 127–8; Nash 1989: 21). Ray was no lover of wilderness, but preserved into the age of modern biology the ancient tradition of the human role of enhancing the creator's workmanship in pursuance of his original intentions, and also of plants and animals having an independent place in the design of the creator. Glacken hails this work as 'probably the best natural theology ever written' (1967: 379). (For the botanical achievements of Ray and his Dutch collaborator Antoni Van Leeuwenhoek – the discoverer of bacteria – see Egerton 2012: 60–6. For the renewal of zoology on the part of the sixteenth-century anatomist Vesalius, see Egerton 2012: 36, 39. For the influence of the seventeenth-century Oxford microscopist Robert Hooke's *Micrographia* on Leeuwenhoek and others, see Attfield 2016: 142–3.)

The new world

Despite the rapacity of the *conquistadors*, many of the environmental problems of the new world seem to have been due to the practices of the indigenous people of those lands. At Head-Smashed-In Buffalo Jump in Alberta, for example, local people used to stampede buffaloes to jump off cliffs, not only in the pre-Columbian era but right through the seventeenth century, while in Nevada only 1 per cent of the bodies of buffaloes that similarly jumped to their deaths were put to human use; the rest were left to rot. Several species of large mammals were driven to extinction long before European settlers arrived (Coates 1998: 90). And while the irrigation systems of northern Mexico made possible both double-cropping and an elaborate social organization, the network of canals of the Hokokam people of modern New Mexico proved unsustainable, and collapsed (Coates 1998: 94).

Hence the portrayal of American Indians as ecologically benign appears misguided, despite the works of writers such as J. Baird Callicott (1989a: 207–10; 1989b: 201), J. Donald Hughes (1983) and Kirkpatrick Sale (1990). Yet a whole chain of writers, beginning with Bartholomé de Las Casas (1474–1566), have creditably argued for the virtues of these indigenous people and against their forcible conversion and slaughter (Las Casas 1992 [1552]; see Attfield 2015 [1999]). And although the most famous apparent environmentalist statement attributed to an American Indian (Chief Seattle) turns out to be a forgery (Coates 1998: 92; Attfield 2018a: 104), other evidence, such as the panentheistic words of Black Elk, of the Oglala Lakota (Sioux) (1863–1950), suggests that some of them cherished traditions of a preservationist character:

> We should know that He (sc. the Great Spirit) is within all things: the trees, the grasses, the rivers, the mountains, and all the four-legged animals and the winged peoples ... When we do understand all this deeply in our hearts ... then we will be and act and live as he intends. (Attfield 2018a: 105)

More tangible benefits for the rest of the world are to be found in the maize and tomatoes of Mesoamerica and the potatoes of Peru. Maize and tomatoes enhanced European and Asian diets, while potatoes became the staple foodstuffs of Ireland and parts of the Balkans. Compared with these exports to the old world, the main import to the new world from the old (sugar cane) was a more dubious benefit, requiring intensive labour either from slaves or, after slavery was abolished, from indentured labour (Ponting 1991: 112–14).

It should be added that, as Ponting relates, the exposure of indigenous people to European and African diseases caused a population decline following the arrival of the first settlers from sixty million to six million within a century (Ponting 1991: 130–4, 230–1). This calamity led to the return of previously cultivated land to wilderness, and hence absorption of more atmospheric carbon dioxide by vegetation, and could well have contributed to the worldwide 'Little Ice Age' of the seventeenth century.

Further contributions from Americans to environmentalism (in addition to that of Black Elk) are discussed in the section of this chapter below, 'The Romantic movement' (such as William Bartram's discovery of the sublimity of mountains there), and also in Chapter 4, 'The American debate'.

The humanitarian movement

In *Man and the Natural World* (1983), Keith Thomas expounds factors which gradually eroded the widespread attitude that the world was made for humanity and that other species were to be regarded as subordinate. One such factor was the rise of natural history, and we have already remarked the stance of one of its proponents, John Ray. A further key moment in the development of natural history was the introduction by the Swedish botanist Linnaeus of the binomial classification of plants (in Latin) by genus and species, in his *Species Plantarum* of 1753, and its spread to England and other countries in the following decades. Thomas adds the hypothesis that the new nomenclature helped 'shatter the assumptions of the past' in which the very names of plants, birds and beasts, with their 'human analogy and symbolic meaning' made them seem 'responsive to human affairs'. Instead, wild creatures began to be regarded as a 'detached natural scene', studied for their own sake by impartial observers from a different world (1983: 89–91). If so, we may comment, this change will only have affected the attitudes of the learned who understood Latin.

Nevertheless, explicit condemnation of vivisection is found with Alexander Pope writing in 1713: 'The more entirely the inferior creation is submitted to our power the more answerable we should seem for our mismanagement of it' (Turner 1964: 48). Pope's use of the phrase 'the inferior creation' shows that he remained committed to belief in the great chain of being (see the section on Aristotle in Chapter 1); yet at the same time he was explicitly rejecting both anthropocentrism and cruelty to animals. Like many others, Pope was here influenced by the humanitarianism of Anthony Ashley Cooper, third Earl of Shaftesbury (1671–1713), widely celebrated for his *Characteristicks* (1711). Pope could also have been influenced by the yet more famous John Locke, who in *Some Thoughts Concerning Education* (1693) advocated teaching children kindness to animals.

Many other writers made their own contributions to the humanitarian tradition, including the philosopher Gottfried Wilhelm Leibniz, the Christian moralists William Wollaston, John Balguy and Francis Hutcheson, the hymn-writer William Cowper, the celebrated sceptic French *philosophe* François-Marie Arouet (Voltaire), and other religious sceptics such as David Hume and Jeremy Bentham. In *Introduction to the Principles of Morals and of Legislation* (1781), Bentham wrote: 'The question is not, Can they reason? nor, Can they talk? but, Can they suffer? Why should the law refuse its protection to any sensitive being?'

Many participants in this tradition campaigned for the abolition of slavery as well as of cruelty to animals, William Wilberforce among them (Nash 1989: 25). In their view, if it was permissible to sell human beings into slavery and the savage treatment that often accompanied it, or to profit from these practices, then there could be few objections to cruel treatment of animals. Conversely, better treatment of nonhuman creatures required those advocating it to abolish slavery and the slave trade and to ameliorate working conditions that effectively treated many agricultural and industrial workers as slaves.

Some of the moralists even held that compassion towards suffering creatures is irresistible (Fiering 1976). Yet in this same period, the trade in fur, based on trapping, was expanding in America, Russia and elsewhere, and continued to do so until the twentieth century, except where the species concerned were driven to extinction (Ponting, 1991). Nevertheless, there was clearly an increase in concern about animal suffering across these centuries, fostered by Evangelicals, Quakers, Methodists and (later) utilitarians, at least in Britain, France and USA, which resulted in a succession of acts of legislation to ban one or another cruel practice (from legislation in Massachusetts in 1641 onwards), and also later in the foundation in the UK of the Society for the Prevention of Cruelty to Animals (in 1824; its subsequent royal status was granted in 1840).

Classical economics and belief in progress

The conviction that the passage of time would bring continual advances and benefits not only in science but also in the well-being of society was advanced towards the end of his long life by Bernard de Fontenelle (1657–1757), and adopted by a succession of Enlightenment *philosophes*, Voltaire included. Subsequently a number of philosophers propounded would-be laws of society or of history, beginning with Johann Gottfried Herder (1744–1803) and continuing with Saint-Simon, Auguste Comte, Karl Marx and Herbert Spencer.

Belief in progress is discussed in greater detail in the fifth chapter of my book *The Ethics of Environmental Concern* (1991 [1983]), to which interested readers are referred. The main bearing of this belief on environmental thought is to be found in the relative disregard for nonhuman nature on the part of most of the advocates of progress just mentioned (Voltaire being an exception), and in the influential blend of attitudes to nature on the parts of Marx (1818–83) and his follower Friedrich Engels (1820–95).

The relative disregard for nature is well illustrated by the characteristic stance of classical economists such as Adam Smith (1723–90) and David Ricardo (1772–1823). These economists believed in a self-regulating market that works through a balance between supply and demand, and, despite some differences of theory, bequeathed to their successors, Marxian and Keynesian economists included, the 'fundamental flaw' (as Ponting puts it) of ignoring resource depletion. The characteristic assumption is that resources (plants, micro-organisms and other wildlife included) are infinite and inexhaustible, that economic growth can continue indefinitely, and that there is no limit to the substitution of resources derived from nature with humanmade substitutes (Ponting 1991: 155–6). This assumption went largely unchallenged until the publication of *Limits to Growth* (Meadows et al. 1974 [1972]), by which time the pursuit of progress through economic growth had led to global problems of pollution, deforestation, desertification, species-loss and (we were soon to discover) climate change. Economic theory is prone to encourage the gratification of short-term self-interest, not least through discounting the value of future costs and benefits, and thus the neglect of all future human generations (let alone the continued existence and thus the future of nonhuman species).

While Marx and his followers adhered to belief in progress along the lines of the 'humanization of nature', which supposedly gave nature a 'meaning' that it was deemed to lack otherwise, it is only fair to note that he, and to a greater extent his collaborator Engels, rejected the predatory exploitation of nature characteristic of capitalism and of science-based technology, and advocated the recycling of the waste products of industry, nonpolluting technology, and the need to take account of side-effects and long-term consequences. Engels stressed the unintended side-effects of apparent progress, and in particular the loss of the soil of the Cuban uplands when Spanish planters burned down the forests for the sake of one generation of quick profits from coffee plantations. Yet he also adhered to the belief that through growth and new technology the tensions between humanity and nature would eventually be overcome (Attfield 1991 [1983]: 78–81).

However, belief in progress, whether of a capitalist, free-market kind or of a Marxist kind, prevailed widely into the twentieth century, partly through confidence that one or other of the theorists of progress – such as Spencer (1820–1903) or Marx – had grasped the laws of history, despite an increasing recognition of the vulnerability of nature and natural systems. The key challenge to belief in such laws was presented by Karl Popper, when he argued conclusively that there are no laws of history (Popper 1960), and that human culture and society are in principle largely unpredictable. This work was intended to commemorate the victims of totalitarian ideologies of both the left and the right, usually grounded in belief that the laws of history guaranteed the triumph of one or another favoured form of society.

Since Popper's intervention, belief in the inevitability of progress has waned, but not belief in its possibility (Passmore 1970). Kinds of belief in progress that recognize the vulnerability both of nature and of humanity, and seek forms of existence in which human society lives in harmony with natural systems, remain open possibilities. Yet to achieve this, they need the kind of better understanding of nature that only became possible with changing attitudes to the natural world and in particular with the rise of Darwinism. Grasping how these changes came about requires us to return to new forms of understanding that arose in the eighteenth century.

New forms of understanding

Gilbert White (1720–93), for much of his life curate of Selborne in Hampshire, gave close attention to the wildlife of his area, particularly in his book *Natural History and Antiquities of Selborne* (1789). In more than one of his remarks, he showed an awareness of the interdependence of living creatures and the landscape. For example, he wrote: 'Earthworms, though in appearance a small and despicable link in the chain of nature, yet, if lost, would make a lamentable chasm ... worms seem to be the great promoters of vegetation which would proceed but lamely without them.' He also recognized that the trees of woods and copses are vital for the continuing existence of rivers.

Another eighteenth-century writer who contributed to a new approach to nature was Erasmus Darwin (1731–1802), grandfather of the more illustrious Charles, who advocated belief in the evolution of species, and encapsulated it in his poem *The Temple of Nature* (published in 1803). Natural selection was no part of his thought, but the struggle for survival was, as it had been for Empedocles and the ancient Epicureans. This poem was admired by William Wordsworth (1770–1850), whose work was beginning to flourish just as it was published.

Erasmus Darwin's younger contemporary, Jean-Baptiste Lamarck (1744–1829) held that there is evolution from one species to another in accordance with natural laws. He is widely known for his belief in the inheritability of acquired characteristics (which, if true, might have accounted for the emergence of new species); this stance is widely known as Lamarckism. But it played only a small part in his theories and writings. Indeed, his stance was rejected by Charles Darwin on other grounds, and not on this one. When the French National Assembly founded the *Musée nationale d'Histoire naturelle* in 1793, Lamarck became a professor of zoology there, and remains honoured in France as one of the greatest French contributors to biology.

Another pioneer in biology was Erasmus Darwin's older contemporary, the aristocratic Comte de Buffon (1707–88). Buffon pioneered palaeontology with his study of lost species. Also, in his massive work *Histoire naturelle*, he spoke of the common ancestry of humans and apes. This work extended to thirty-four volumes; it was begun in 1749, and was completed by others some years after his death. He was well known and well regarded during his lifetime (which shows how, at least in France, evolutionary ideas were already becoming mainstream) – much more so than Lamarck.

With Immanuel Kant (1724–1804), we find reflection in his (early) pre-critical period on astronomical phenomena, expressed in flamboyant language, but little that is new in his understanding of terrestrial nature. In his critical period, his characterization of nature in the *Groundwork of the Metaphysic of Morals* makes it a mere backdrop to a human good will, which shines like a jewel 'even if, by a special disfavour of fortune or by the niggardly provision of a step-motherly nature, this will should wholly lack the capacity to carry out its purpose' (Kant 2005 [1785]). One of the serious problems for Kant's ethics is that his Categorical Imperative requires agents to treat human beings (*qua* rational beings) as ends and not means, but makes no such provision for less rational creatures. Yet in *The Metaphysics of Morals* (1797), he condemned cruelty to animals on grounds of duty to humanity (Denis 2000).

Isaiah Berlin (1909–97) used to claim, in lectures at Oxford in the early 1960s, that Kant's thought introduced 'the Romantic movement in political thought', because his emphasis on autonomy supposedly implied that no single solution to political issues is ultimately preferable to any other. But this interpretation hardly coheres either with Kant's own realist view of the mandatory nature of the Categorical Imperative or with the form of internationalism (Kant called it 'cosmopolitanism') to be found in Kant's *Perpetual Peace* (1795). Others, including Gilles Deleuze (1925–95), have traced the origin of the Romantic movement to Kant's *Critique of Judgement* (1790; see Lloyd 2018: 71), but this work plays down nature's irresistible forces, and was written long after the pivotal works of Jean-Jacques Rousseau (see the section below, 'The Romantic movement'). Indeed, some find here 'intimations of what will later become the Romantic mood of endless longing for the unattainable' (Lloyd 2018: 195).

Kant's greatest contribution to the aesthetics of nature is to be found in his distinction, in 1764, between the beautiful (which arouses joy and happiness) and the sublime (scenes where enjoyment is blended with awe or horror) (Coates 1998: 132). The concept of the sublime dates from the ancient text *On the Sublime* of Longinus (first century CE), and was revived in a 1757 work of the Irish philosopher Edmund Burke (1729–97). But while Kant's focus on the sublime contributed to the growing appreciation of mountains, the Romantic movement, to which we will shortly turn, effectively began in Germany not with Kant, but with the traveller and polymath Alexander von Humboldt, who will shortly be discussed.

Meanwhile, the nineteenth-century philosopher Arthur Schopenhauer (1788–1860) sought to retain elements of Kant's thought, but gave greater stress to compassion, and at the same time made nonhuman animals objects of direct moral concern (Schopenhauer, 2010 [1818–19]; Shapshay 2017). This appears a commendable attempt to make Kant's austere ethics more humane, but it is doubtful whether a consistent ethical system emerges, particularly since Schopenhauer also held that nonexistence is preferable to any life with the slightest amount of suffering, and on this basis that the value of most life is negative. On the other hand, his contribution signifies that it may be possible to combine humanitarianism with systematic ethics, and thus that ethicists need not erect a barrier between humanity and the rest of nature on pain of falling short as ethicists, and that followers of Kant need not carry forward into the contemporary period Kant's own moral (as opposed to aesthetic) disregard for whatever is overtly nonrational.

No treatment of eighteenth-century attitudes to nature would be complete without mention of von Humboldt, who travelled in South America (the Humboldt Current is named after him), and who sought to unify human knowledge in his large work *Kosmos* (1845–62; the later parts were published posthumously). As previously mentioned (see the section in Chapter 1, 'Greek medicine: Hippocrates and "Airs, Waters, Places"'), he was interested in the influence of climate on civilizations, a study that now bears the name 'biogeography'. As early as 1800, he even wrote of human-induced climate change (Hawken 2017), but this phenomenon was not widely understood until the United Nations Conference on Environment and Development (Rio de Janeiro Earth Summit) in 1992 established the Framework Convention on Climate Change. While von Humboldt's attempt to unify knowledge in a single work was characteristic of the Enlightenment, his awareness of the dynamic change that results from the interaction of human society and its natural environment makes him a pioneer of the Romantic movement. So too does his belief in communion with nature, expressed in *Kosmos* 1:25: 'Everywhere, the mind is penetrated by the same sense of the grandeur and vast expanse of nature, revealing to the soul, by a mysterious inspiration, the existence of laws that regulate the forces of the universe' (Rajan 2017: 25).

The Romantic Movement

Whether or not the Reformation led to the disenchantment of nature, the Romantic movement sought in different ways to re-enchant it. While some of its themes can be traced to the early eighteenth-century philosopher and aesthetician Shaftesbury, a more significant influence was Jean-Jacques Rousseau (1712–78), whose works – such as *Émile* (1762) – were often set in the Swiss Alps, and whose *Discourse on the Origin of Inequality* (1756) disseminated the concepts both of a pristine state of nature and of the noble savage. Rousseau was also a prominent champion of the nonformal 'jardin anglais', but his influence had more lasting effect on thinkers like William Godwin, who chose to set his novel *St. Leon* (1799) in the Swiss Alps (to which his aristocratic hero retires to live the simple life), and then on the poets of the English Lakeland, Wordsworth and Coleridge.

Rousseau was not the first primitivist. As Roderick Nash relates, primitivism made its appearance more than two hundred years earlier in Hans Sachs's *Lament of the Wild Men about the Unfaithful World* (1530), in which protestors against the vices of urban life left and led lives of tranquillity in wilderness caves. This was followed fifty years later by Montaigne's essay *Of Cannibals* (Nash 2014 [1967]: 48). These writings led to an increasing enthusiasm (among the leisured classes) for noble savages. Meanwhile, the general attitude of disdain for civilization and appreciation of the charm of the deserted island was enhanced by Daniel Defoe's *The Life and Surprising Adventures of Robinson Crusoe* (1719; see Nash 2014 [1967]: 48–9). Yet Rousseau's praise of the sublimity of wilderness scenes and the charms of the simple life did more than these predecessors to initiate what amounted to a new movement.

Rousseau's contemporary, the American Quaker and botanist William Bartram (1739–1823) was struck not only by individual plants, but also by the sublimity of the wildernesses of the American Southeast, which he explored extensively from 1773. Nash quotes him as being 'seduced by these sublime enchanting scenes of primitive nature' (Bartram 1958: 212–13; Nash 2014 [1967]: 54). Bartram was thus writing about sublimity soon after Burke and Kant had done so, but applied this concept to overpowering mountain scenery in a spirit resembling the romanticism of Rousseau. He also related the sublime in nature to the grandeur of God, whose 'wisdom and power' were manifested in wilderness (1958: 69, 229; Nash 2014 [1967]: 54; for more on Bartram, see Attfield 1994: 73). Meanwhile, in 1793, the Reverend Nicholas Collin asked the American Philosophical Society to support the protection of species of birds that were on the verge of extinction, until naturalists could discover 'what part is assigned to them in the oeconomy of nature', the grand biological system created by God (Collin 1793: xxiv; Nash 1989: 36). The phrase 'the oeconomy of nature' had been coined by Linnaeus, and was here used, perhaps for the first time, as a ground for ecological protection; not to heed the God-given system of nature was 'both imprudent and irreverent' (Nash 1989: 6).

William Wordsworth (1770–1850) more memorably related his experience of nature and his sense of oneness with it in a manner that came close to pantheism. This is expressed in his 'The Prelude' (1805):

> I held unconscious intercourse with beauty
> Old as creation, drinking in a pure
> Organic pleasure from the silver wreaths
> Of curling mist ...

and yet here the feelings found in nature are ones with which the poet expressly endows it. It is also present in his 'Lines Composed a Few Miles above Tintern Abbey' (1798)

>   And I have felt
> A presence that disturbs me with the joy
> Of elevated thoughts; a sense sublime
> Of something far more deeply interfused,
> Whose dwelling is the light of setting suns,
> And the round ocean and the living air,
> And the blue sky, and in the mind of man.

where the poet's pantheist tendencies are more clearly in evidence, for while the joy is his own, its source dwells in sunsets, Homer's all-encompassing ocean, and the blue sky, as well as in human consciousness.

Wordsworth also wrote poems in praise of Lakeland shepherds (such as 'Michael: A Pastoral Poem') about the resilient but tragic life of a shepherd of Grasmere Vale, published in the first edition of *Lyrical Ballads*, 1800), which express more clearly the influence of Rousseau. Such poems implicitly praise rural life and independence, by contrast with the drabness and conformity of life in cities.

A few months earlier, Wordsworth's friend Samuel Taylor Coleridge (1772–1834) composed his two most famous poems. One was 'Kubla Khan' (1797), reflecting his own sense of the sublime in lines such as:

> Where Alph, the sacred river ran
> In caverns measureless to man,
> Down to a sunless sea.

The other was 'The Rime of the Ancient Mariner' (1797), where the heinous sin of the mariner was to shoot an albatross needlessly, and where his path to forgiveness and restoration began when, as an isolated shipwreck survivor, he was able to bless the slimy sea-creatures of the surrounding ocean. Here the underlying theme is one of the whole creation being loved by the forgiving God of Christianity; Coleridge was at this stage returning to Christianity from the Unitarianism of his earlier years (Guite 2017). Despite the burgeoning slaughter of wild creatures going on all over the Earth at this time, Coleridge recognized how, in the Psalms and the Wisdom literature, God loves and provides for creatures of every kind. Coleridge's epic poem was included by Wordsworth in *Lyrical Ballads* (1800).

As Coates relates, Coleridge went on to refer to torrents and cataracts in the Savoy Alps as 'glorious as the gates of heaven'. This was in his poem 'Hymn before Sunrise in the Vale of Chamouni' (1802).

The Romantic celebration of mountains and of pastoral scenes can also be found in the opening of William Blake's (1757–1827) poem widely known as 'Jerusalem' (1804)

> And did those feet in ancient times
> Walk upon England's mountains green?
> And was the holy lamb of God
> On England's pleasant pastures seen!

These lines, sung to Hubert Parry's music, may sound trite to contemporary ears, but, in combination with their denunciation of 'those dark Satanic mills' (the factories of the early industrial revolution) will have conveyed a strand of radical freshness at their first appearance. It should be added that Blake was writing the preface to his *Milton, a Poem*, in which he urged Milton to recognize the heroism of the depraved, rather than the elect, and requested Milton to return to rectify the errors of his (relative) orthodoxy. Blake also believed that nature was holy, but rejected all religious authorities. Similarly, most of the Romantic poets were far removed from being religiously orthodox.

Considerations of space prevent a detailed review of the perspectives of other Romantic poets, such as Percy Bysshe Shelley, Lord Byron, John Keats, Robert Burns and John Clare on the natural world. Shelley addressed the west wind and the skylark, but in the latter case (1820) was addressing the poetic spirit, ('Bird thou never wert'); generally, nature was for him a source both of inspiration and of symbolism. In Byron's *Childe Harold's Pilgrimage* (published in 1812), 'the book of nature' is more meaningful to the hero than books of men, and communing with nature is preferred to immersion in human culture (Coates 1998: 127). John Keats's *Ode to Autumn* and *to a Nightingale* (both from 1819) are as evocative and as autobiographical as his *On First Looking into Chapman's Homer* (1816), which compares the discovery of Chapman's verse to that of the Pacific by Cortez's men 'with a wild surmise, Silent, upon a peak in Darien'. Robert Burns had earlier expressed compassion for a wild creature in *To a Mouse, on Turning Her up in her Nest with a Plough* (1785), and in Germany Friedrich Hölderlin (1770–1843) had written between 1797 and 1800 'The Death of Empedocles' (for whom, see Chapter 1). And later John Clare (1793–1864) inveighs against enclosures in 'The Village Minstrel' (1821), writing how:

... desolation struck her deadly blows
As curst improvement 'gan his fields enclose:
O greens, and fields, and trees, farewell, farewell. (Coates 1998: 114)

This and other works, as Coates remarks, explain how Clare is often regarded as a forefather of present-day radical environmentalism. (We will encounter another such forefather in Gerard Manley Hopkins, of just a few decades later, in Chapter 6.)

Meanwhile in Germany, Johann Wolfgang von Goethe (1749–1832) became a leader of the *Sturm und Drang* proto-romantic literary movement. He also contributed to botany in his *Metamorphosis of Plants* (1790), presenting his discovery of the homologous nature of leaf organs in plants ranging from cotyledons to leaves to the petals of flowers. This discovery has widely been regarded as a significant contribution to our understanding of plant evolution. Another participant was Friedrich Schiller (1759-1805), who also wrote the 'Ode to Joy' celebrated in Ludwig von Beethoven's Ninth Symphony (first performed 1824).

This brings us to the emergence of the Romantic movement in place of the classicism of Joseph Haydn and Wolfgang Amadeus Mozart in music. The first Romantic symphony is widely regarded as Beethoven's Symphony No. 3, the 'Eroica' (first performed in 1805). In this work, Beethoven was initially celebrating the heroic leadership of Napoleon, but on learning that the latter had declared himself Emperor, he tore up the dedication. However, Beethoven's celebration of nature and rural life really came with his Symphony No. 6, the 'Pastoral' (first performed in 1808), which offers representations of birdsong, and has movements with names like 'Scene by the brook' and 'Shepherd's song. Cheerful and thankful feelings after the storm'. In contrast with such music, these were turbulent times, with the Napoleonic wars still raging, but this symphony conveyed the kind of rural idyll loved in an increasingly urban society. Admiration for this symphony has remained strong, and it regularly appears in the highest ranks of the UK radio station Classic FM's annual 'Hall of Fame', alongside Beethoven's Fifth Piano Concerto (first performed in 1811), which still bears the title 'The Emperor'.

To return to the romantic celebration of mountains and wild cataracts, the painter of landscapes and seascapes, J. M. W. Turner (1775–1851), after focusing on British and particularly Welsh mountain scenery, was able to visit Switzerland in an interlude during the Napoleonic Wars in 1802, and returned in more peaceful times during the 1840s. This enabled him to travel on a steamer on Lake Lucerne, and to make a cluster of paintings of Mount Rigi in different lights and different weathers, which added to his already considerable reputation. Their popularity must have contributed to the decision to build a railway from the lake to the summit of the Rigi in 1871, which remains to this day a magnet for tourists. In this way, Turner's work fostered and broadened the appeal of wild scenery among many in Northern and Western Europe.

After considering the Romantic poets, Coates proceeds to discuss the limitations of the Romantic movement, expressing reservations about both its profundity and its social influence. He quotes Wordsworth as saying: 'Cataracts and mountains are good occasional society, but they will not do for constant companions' (Coates 1998: 135). Yet the mere fact that Wordsworth was blessed with a sense of proportion does not detract from his influence and is compatible with his having introduced and popularized a profoundly changed attitude to nature. And although not everyone was affected (hardly likely at a time of such deep inequality and dire poverty), a significant proportion of European and later American society became open from this time to new possibilities of recuperation and a renewed sense of self-understanding.

New philosophies of nature

Reacting to the idealist view of Johann Gottlieb Fichte (1762–1814) that everything in reality results from the self-consciousness of the mind, Friedrich Wilhelm Joseph Schelling (1775–1854) responded that nature is independently real, and is the sum of whatever is objective. But its reality may not comply with human conceptions (here Kant's influence is apparent); it results from dynamic transformations of matter, light and organism (or life). His belief in nature's independent reality and its conformity to natural laws comprise the stance that has become known as *Naturphilosophie* (nature-philosophy), which was regarded in Germany as an aspect of the Romantic movement.

Schelling in his later works saw himself as an heir of the seventeenth-century pantheist philosopher Spinoza, and also as a critic of 'the great chain of being' (see Chapter 1), which, in his eyes, had long since been wrongly represented as complete, immutable, and as a system of being rather than of becoming. Georg Wilhelm Friedrich Hegel (1770–1831) initially supported Schelling against Fichte, but later, in *Phenomenology of Spirit* (1807) criticized his view of reality as implying that reality embodies no real distinctions, like 'the night in which all cows are black'. Others were later to criticise Schelling (more fairly) for the absence of any empirical basis for his philosophical system.

A little later, Ralph Waldo Emerson (1803-1882) presented a distinctive approach in his essay *Nature* (1836), and at the same time launched the American variety of Romanticism, which came to be known as 'transcendentalism'. Emerson was trained at Harvard Divinity School, but later, on returning to Concord, Massachusetts, he abandoned Christian orthodoxy and became something of a pantheist, believing in mystical relations between humanity and the world of plants. (Later he was influenced by the ancient Indian *Vedanta*.) For Emerson, nature both facilitates a sense of a person's solitariness and supplies a soothing balm to those oppressed by work or society. Thus it forms in effect a route towards human spiritual fulfilment; there is no apparent awareness in Emerson of nature's bearing an independent value of its own. But at the same time, a person's relation with nature makes that person a small part of God. These ideas later became widely popular in America.

At the same time, Emerson remained a follower of Francis Bacon (see the section above on the scientific revolution) and a believer in progress (see the section above on classical economics and belief in progress). He urged his readers to 'Build, therefore, your own world' (Coates 1998: 136–7), and he believed that the railroad would help America to fulfil its destiny.

More critical of industrialism was Emerson's fellow-transcendentalist, Henry David Thoreau. Thoreau withdrew for around two years from Concord to live in a rustic hut beside Walden Pond, and later wrote *Walden* (1854), an autobiographical work that has become one of the key texts of American environmentalism. Besides growing his own food, Thoreau became immersed in the life of the woods and the swamps around him, and came to recognize nature's otherness and independent value, such as that of the soaring falcon (Thoreau 1968 [1854]: 279). He certainly considered it worth taking time away from productive activity to spend it on contemplating natural processes, appointing himself to the calling of 'inspector of snowstorms'. Indeed, Thoreau is often considered the father of modern American nature writing, and a proto-environmentalist. (For more about Emerson and Thoreau, see the opening section of Chapter 4.)

Overview

We have come a long way from Luther and Calvin to the Romantics and to Emerson and Thoreau. The ideas of this period must be understood against a background of a vast expansion of European power and capitalist enterprise, but towards the end of the period some of the thinkers mentioned were preparing the way for a challenge to such a posture of dominance over colonial peoples and over nature. From the eighteenth century onwards, there are also clearly emerging strands of belief in the evolution of natural species, and yet not even in the early nineteenth century were these ideas systematized in a suitable manner for most earlier thinking to be challenged. The systematizing of evolutionary thought had to wait for Charles Darwin and his successors, the theme of the next chapter.

As we have seen, the Reformation brought new attitudes to nature, ranging from the implicitly panentheistic insights of Luther (seldom surfacing again until the late twentieth century), to the stewardship tradition, a biblical approach newly articulated by Calvin and explicitly brought to bear on nature during the seventeenth century by Sir Matthew Hale. The ensuing period of religious wars brought widespread destruction to much of European society and its environment. Yet during this period new insights and attitudes to nature emerged through the works of the metaphysical poets, which expressed, often in beguiling verse, a blend of anthropocentric, biocentric and theocentric themes.

The scientific revolution also issued in a blend of mechanical theories and dominion-oriented attitudes, together with (what we could call) a more biocentric stance on the part of John Ray and others. These were carried forward into the Enlightenment by the humanitarian movement and writers such as Alexander Pope, even though at the same time there was a spread of colonial exploitation of virgin lands, of which a striking example is the worldwide spread of the trapping of animals for fur. The rise of classical economics and simultaneously of belief in the inevitability of progress involved (in most versions) a failure to grasp the value of natural resources and of nonhuman creatures; yet the same period saw a new awareness of the natural world from people like Linnaeus and Gilbert White, and the dawning of (what could in our day be called) ecological and related insights on the part of Alexander von Humboldt.

The Romantic movement, in which von Humboldt can fairly be regarded as an early participant, turned attention back to the sublimity of nature (a theme revived from the ancient world by Burke and Kant), and led to changed attitudes to wild and mountainous regions, expressed in the works of Wordsworth and others. One of their themes was a protest at economic and industrial expansion, expressed by poets like Wordsworth and later John Clare. In America, Emerson, despite his mysticism, supported the growth of industry and railroads, whereas his associate Thoreau saw fit to turn his back on urban life and celebrate rural life and nature's cycles. (We shall return to these 'transcendentalist' thinkers in Chapter 4.) Meanwhile in Germany, Schelling and Hegel cast doubt on traditional concepts such as that of the great chain of being, and Schelling in his later work sought to revive the pantheism of the seventeenth-century philosopher Spinoza.

As has just been mentioned, evolutionary thought made its appearance during the eighteenth and early nineteenth centuries, through the work of Erasmus Darwin, Buffon, Lamarck and von Humboldt. But their theories of evolution (revived from ancient thinkers such as Empedocles, Epicurus and Lucretius: see Chapter 1) proved unconvincing, even when new discoveries in geology (see Chapter 3) suggested that life on Earth had a much longer history than had widely been credited. Also, the bearing of their theories remained ambivalent, since they could be used either to extol humanity as the pinnacle of the evolutionary process, or to draw attention to the common origins and kinship of humanity and other creatures. During this period, the first of these attitudes was predominant. Not even Charles Darwin was to overcome the ambivalence of evolutionary theories, but, as will be seen, his work led to new debates and new insights among his contemporaries and successors.

This chapter has concerned selected thinkers from Luther and Calvin in the sixteenth century to the Romantics and to scientists such as Lamarck in the late eighteenth and early nineteenth centuries. While the Romantics made the greatest impact on attitudes to nature, earlier poets, theologians and naturalists were also influential in this respect. This chapter paves the way for a study, in the next chapter, of Darwin, his immediate predecessors and his immediate and longer-term influence, not least on ecology.

Recommended reading

Attfield, Robin (1991 [1983]). *The Ethics of Environmental Concern*, 2nd edn. Athens: University of Georgia Press.

Attfield, Robin (2018). *Environmental Ethics: A Very Short Introduction*. Oxford: Oxford University Press.

Attfield, Robin (2019). 'Panentheism, Creation and Evil', *Open Theology*, 5: 166–171.

Coates, Peter (1998). *Nature: Western Attitudes Since Ancient Times*. Berkeley: University of California Press.

Glacken, Clarence J. (1967). *Traces on the Rhodian Shore: Nature and Culture in Western Thought from Ancient Times to the End of the Eighteenth Century*. Berkeley: University of California Press.

Merchant, Carolyn (1990 [1980]). *The Death of Nature: Women, Ecology and the Scientific Revolution*. San Francisco, CA: HarperCollins.

Nash, Roderick Frazier (2014 [1967]). *Wilderness and the American Mind*, 5th edn. New Haven, CT: Yale University Press

Nash, Roderick Frazier (1989). *The Rights of Nature*. Madison: University of Wisconsin Press.

Ponting, Clive (1991). *A Green History of the World*. London: Sinclair Stevenson.

Rajan, S. Ravi (ed.) (2017). *Genealogies of Environmentalism: The Lost Works of Clarence Glacken*. Charlottesville: University of Virginia Press.

Santmire, Paul (1985). *The Travail of Nature: The Ambiguous Ecological Promise of Christian Theology*. Philadelphia, PA: Fortress Press.

Thomas, Keith (1983). *Man and the Natural World: A History of the Modern Sensibility*. New York: Pantheon Books.

Thoreau, Henry David (1968 [1854]). *Walden*. London: Dent.

Wordsworth, William and Coleridge, Samuel Taylor (1800). *Lyrical Ballads*. London.

3

Darwin and His Successors

Influences on Darwin

This chapter mainly concerns Charles Darwin, his associates (such as Alfred Russel Wallace, Thomas Henry Huxley and Herbert Spencer), his influence (including the bearing of his work on ecology) and his successors, including the authors of the Darwinian synthesis of the twentieth century. But it is first necessary to set the scene by reviewing the beliefs and theories held before Darwin published *The Origin of Species* (1859), including those which impressed him but he later rejected, those which prepared the intellectual climate for his work, and those which showed the strength of feeling against theories of the transmutation of species, and which served to discourage the publication of his theories for some twenty years after they were formed.

When Charles Darwin was an undergraduate at Cambridge, one of the texts that he was required to study was William Paley's *Natural Theology* (1810 [1802]; see also Gillispie 1969: 35–40). At the time, Darwin found Paley's arguments for design based on anatomy (such as the intricate structures of the human eye, apparently devised to serve the purpose of sight) highly impressive. But later in life he replied well to such arguments, supplying natural explanations of such phenomena, and cases of dysfunctionality in nature (see below on upland web-footed birds). However, it is worth noting how Paley (1743–1805), in common with many others of the two centuries that his life spanned, argued for divine design from such structured regularities; and further how such arguments are always prone to be undermined when a law is discovered, applying to all times, which provides a natural explanation of the regularity in question. There are much better forms of design argument (like arguments from laws themselves, not vulnerable to this objection), but in the early nineteenth century Paley's variety appeared conclusive (Attfield 2006). In any case Paley aroused Darwin's interest in anatomical detail and in apparent design.

Yet, as we have already seen in Chapter 2, several figures of the late eighteenth century had abandoned belief in the fixity of species – biologists such as Erasmus Darwin, Lamarck, Buffon and von Humboldt. Such ideas of the transmutation of species opened up new possibilities for Darwin during his voyage on *The Beagle*, despite his dissatisfaction with these earlier theories. He was also influenced by Goethe's discovery of homologies between species, mentioned earlier in Chapter 2.

A further influence on Charles Darwin was Thomas Robert Malthus (1766–1834), whose theory that the human population continually expands until it reaches the limits of its food supply was intended to apply also to the populations of other species, which were held to compete with each other, and expand as and when food supplies permitted. Glacken reports that Darwin came across Malthus's *Essay on Population* in 1838, and at once recognized that in these circumstances 'favourable variations' would arise and be preserved, leading to 'the formation of new species' (Rajan 2017: 63–4; in this book, Rajan valuably publishes some important lost writings of Clarence J. Glacken). For Darwin, this was a confirmation of a theory formed on a separate basis a few years earlier.

Malthus's theory did not go unopposed. It was fiercely and tenaciously contested by William Godwin (1756–1836), a prominent believer in social progress, to which Malthusianism appeared to comprise a major objection. In *Of Population* (1820), Godwin pointedly protested at Malthus's selective use of the population increase of the New England settlers, where special factors applied, presented China and India as counter-evidence, and concluded that Malthus's principle of population is not the law of nature 'but the law of very artificial life' (Rajan 2017: 13–14). In other words, Malthus was reading the competitiveness of current English society and economic theory into the processes of nature. Darwin, by contrast, was centrally a natural historian, and was influenced not so much by economics or politics, but by the struggle of natural species to survive, a struggle that his studies gave little room to doubt (Rajan 2017: 64–5). His reading of Malthus served as a confirmation of natural selection, and he certainly credited him with 'the principle of geometrical increase' (Darwin 1859: 63; Ruse 2001: 22), but he need not be taken as a card-carrying Malthusian. Indeed, Malthus's view that population rises geometrically whereas food supply rises (at best) arithmetically is highly contestable in both these regards, and is rejected by many contemporary Darwinians.

Another more profound influence on Darwin was the work of the geologist Charles Lyell (1797–1875), whose *Principles of Geology* (1830–3) maintained that the forces of nature currently operative had been so all along (uniformitarianism, a theory devised earlier, in a qualified form, by James Hutton, 1726–97), and that the history of the earth must therefore have been far more extensive in time than had usually been supposed. Darwin took a copy of this book with him on his voyage on the *Beagle*, discussed it with Robert FitzRoy, and was thus encouraged to seek explanations of fossils and species distribution involving the same extensive past as Lyell claimed for geological strata.

While Lyell advanced the classificatory study of past geological eras, he also adhered (for most of his life) to a belief in the fixity of species, and to their creation at various different past stages. He introduced his readers (Darwin included) to Lamarck's belief in the development of some species from others, but firmly rejected it, until, many decades later, he came round to Darwinism (Gillispie 1969: 130–5). However, his book effectively undermined the hitherto widespread belief that the flood described in Genesis was a universal and uniquely potent geological agency. And despite his denial of any 'transmutation' of species, his theory, as Gillispie remarks, seemed almost to cry out for an evolutionary theory of organic life (1969: 138). Darwin was not slow to draw the appropriate conclusion, when confronted with fossils of maritime creatures in elevated ancient strata, and a little later with the modifications of the finches on particular islands of the Galapagos archipelago.

Followers of Lyell proceeded to show how uniformitarianism could readily be allied to the appearance of new species as new geological and climatic conditions arose. One was Gideon Mantell (1790–1852), whose *Wonders of Geology* (1838) added to popular understanding of the geological past, but presupposed acts of special creation to explain the origination of new forms of life (Gillispie 1969: 137–9). Darwin, however, already had in mind a different theory. While Mantell made more of the public take on uniformitarianism, his works had little or no influence on Darwin.

Much the same applied to the work *Vestiges of the Natural History of Creation*, published anonymously by Robert Chambers (1802–71) in several editions across the 1840s. This work combined uniformitarianism with belief in the transmutation of species, together with some ill-fated theories about how the latter took place. It resulted in a deluge of protest against its acceptance of 'development' from geologists and theologians of a wide range of stances, but sold widely: the first ten editions sold twenty-five thousand copies (Gillispie 1969: 172). Darwin himself considered it inaccurate and incautious, but 'regarded the work as a valuable lightning rod in channelling off the initial thunders of orthodoxy' (Gillispie 1969: 217). One of the more influential critics of *Vestiges* was the Christian geologist Hugh Miller (1802–56), who argued that belief in 'development' conflicted with the Christian belief in immortality. His *Testimony of the Rocks* (1857) sold forty-two thousand copies, while his *Old Red Sandstone* (1841) ran to twenty editions (Gillispie 1969: 172). Miller's following helps explain Darwin's reluctance to publish his theories until he had amassed enough counter-evidence.

However, another influence on Darwin from his Cambridge days helps explain both his laborious and cumulative method and his own approach to science. For he was taught there by the historian and philosopher of science William Whewell (1794–1866), whose works (1837, 1840) illustrate his belief that the best form of scientific work involves a 'consilience of inductions'. These are cases where strands of evidence from different areas are explained by the same hypothesis, and the diverse inductions drawn from these fields thus leap together, or exhibit 'consilience' (Ruse 2001: 13). Whewell's own scientific and religious views were orthodox ones. Yet his approach to scientific method helps explain Darwin's reasoning, as we shall now see.

Darwin's Argument

Between devising his theory of evolution by natural selection and his belated decision to publish, Darwin worked on several studies of barnacles, which increasingly convinced him that his overall theory was correct. However, he remained unwilling to rock the scientific boat until he heard from Alfred Russel Wallace (1823–1913) that Wallace had hit on the same theory through his studies of birds (including birds of paradise) in New Guinea. So it was agreed that they would present a joint paper to the Linnaean Society (in London in 1858), and Darwin was also emboldened to publish his main findings the next year.

Darwin described the theme of his *On the Origin of Species* as 'one long argument'. He argued that evolution by natural selection is the best explanation of the findings of several different fields. One was palaeontology, and the progressive fossil sequence from extinct forms to organisms similar to those currently extant. Another was biogeography, the subject revived by von Humboldt (see Chapter 2) from the ancient tract 'Airs, Waters, Places' (see Chapter 1). Here Darwin drew attention to the nonrandom distribution of plants and animals in places such as the Galapagos Islands, and the small differences between the birds and the reptiles of different islands and those of the mainland; this suggested that these organisms had migrated from the mainland and diversified to suit the conditions of the different islands.

Another relevant field was that of anatomy. Thus the bone structures of very different animals display remarkable similarities (or 'homologies'), as had been stressed by the *Naturphilosophen*. For example, the forelimbs of humans, horses, seals, bats and moles have different functions, but highly similar structures, and this is best explained by common ancestry and diversification in the process of evolution so as to equip the different creatures for grasping, running, swimming, flying and digging (respectively).

Yet a further field is known as systematics. Organisms turn out to be arrangeable in groups, suggestive of development from more basic to more specialized kinds. Again, common ancestry seems much the best explanation. A further field again is embryology; organisms of very different species turn out to have embryos that are indistinguishable. This again suggests a shared origin, followed by evolutionary differentiation (Ruse 2001: 12–18).

Darwin also argued from the facts of human selective breeding. Breeders select and breed from variations. But if artificial selection can produce such strikingly successful strains as can be seen on farms and race-courses, how much more, he argued, can be achieved by nature, making its own selection from random variations? He had no theory of the source of the variations, nor of how they came to be transmitted, and here inclined to Lamarck's theory of the inheritability of acquired characteristics (mistakenly, as it later emerged). But for natural selection to operate, all that was required was the fact of variation, and of that there was no room for doubt.

Besides, there was a long tradition that appealed to natural selection, originating with Empedocles, and adopted in adjusted form by the Epicureans (see Chapter 1). Darwin was aware of Empedocles as a predecessor, but did not accept that variations included monstrous forms such as centaurs (half-equine and half-human), as Empedocles had (Burrow 1985: 53). He did, however, follow the Epicurean line that viable variations usually had to be small, and took place gradually (Ruse 2001: 23). But unlike the ancient theorists of natural selection, Darwin was able to claim a scientific basis for his inductions, based on observation and on the fields already mentioned (biogeography, palaeontology, anatomy etc).

However, Darwin also produced empirical arguments against special creation and the adaptedness of organisms to their environment from creation onwards. He wrote:

> He who believes that each being has been created as we now see it, must occasionally have felt surprise when he has met with an animal having structure and habits not in agreement. What can be plainer than that the webbed feet of ducks and geese are formed for swimming? Yet there are upland geese with webbed feet which rarely go near the water; and no-one except Audubon has seen the frigate-bird, which has all its four toes webbed, alight on the ocean. (1859: 132; Rajan 2017: 55)

As Rajan comments, 'this illustration could have been the perfect example for the natural theologian who assumed that God first made the environment and then created the webbed feet to deal with the problem of the water' (2017: 55). Darwin continues:

> [With regard to him] who believes in the struggle for existence and in the principle of natural selection . . . it will cause him no surprise that there should be geese and frigate-birds with webbed feet, living on dry land and rarely alighting on the water.

This is because each species constantly tries to increase in numbers. So if any variation, however small, gives it an advantage over other species, it will seize on their habitat, however different it may be from its own. Thus Darwin rejected the view that environment and climate determine the distribution of animals and plants. In its place he substituted the theory of natural selection (Rajan 2017: 55–6). Yet, as we shall see in the next section, this does not mean that he had little to say about ecology.

It is worth noting here that Darwin's friend, the Harvard biologist Asa Gray (1810–88), argued in 1860 that natural selection was compatible with divine creation; God could have chosen natural selection as part of the process of creation, and made provision for a range of suitable possibilities (what we nowadays call 'mutations'), and thus variation, to arise and be selected from. Gray's response shows that Darwin's ideas were known in some circles in America from the outset. They also indicate that there was no need for Darwinians to reject theistic belief. The possibility of combining natural selection with belief in creation was also voiced by Charles Kingsley (1819–75), who, in *The Water Babies*, has his creative mother-figure 'making creatures make themselves' (1930 [1863]: 248).

It is also noteworthy that John Stuart Mill (1806–73), possibly the greatest philosopher alive at this time, rejected Darwinism on grounds of methodology. For no consilience argument could deliver the kind of proof that Mill, as an empiricist, was looking for (Ruse 2006: 1036). In some ways, Mill was right, since the hypothesis presented by Darwin had an unstable basis; the range of variations on which he relied was unexplained, and the persistence across the generations of selected variations appeared inexplicable. But Mill seems to have overlooked the scientific progress that Darwinism epitomized.

However, the implications of Darwin's conclusions for humanity were not drawn within *Origin*, except for the tantalizing remark 'Light will be thrown on the origin of man and his history' (Ruse 2001: 24). To this topic, however, he returned in *The Descent of Man* (1871), which is discussed below, although related controversies arose as soon as *Origin* was published.

Darwin on Ecology

Darwin enjoyed rambling and geological study, but Coates holds that he lacked interest in issues of ecology, despite his discovery of the kinship of humans and nonhuman animals (1998: 139), and (it might be added) his book on animal emotions (Darwin 2009 [1872]). Nevertheless, Coates recognizes that one of Darwin's passages anticipated ecological science and foreshadowed the concept of food chains (although he is mistaken in taking this to be an isolated passage). In the course of illustrating what he called the 'web of life', or 'how plants and animals, remote in the scale of nature, are bound together by a web of complex relations', Darwin gives the example of the relations of red clover to bees, mice and cats. The humble-bee is indispensable for the fertilization of clover, but the humble-bee population size is regulated by the size of the population of field mice, which is itself in turn regulated by the number of cats in the area. Since there are more cats in or around towns and villages, this is where there will be more humble-bees and more clover (1859: 82–3; Coates 1998: 139–40).

Coates represents this passage as having 'nothing to do with the principle of natural selection or the struggle for existence' (1998: 139). Yet the regulation of the populations of clover, humble-bees and field mice by cat populations seems in fact to have a good deal to do with this principle; for this passage recognizes the ecological interplay of otherwise unrelated species. This is borne out by the title of Chapter 3 of *Origin of Species*, 'Complex relations of all animals and plants to each other in the struggle for existence'.

David Pepper cites a further relevant passage on linkages 'in what we might now call a Paraguayan "ecosystem"'. Describing parasitic flies that lay eggs in the navels of newborn cattle, horses and dogs, Darwin wrote:

> The increase of these flies, numerous as they are, must be habitually checked by some other means, probably by other parasitic insects. Hence, if certain insectivorous birds were to decrease in Paraguay, the parasitic insects would probably increase, and this would lessen the number of the navel-frequenting flies – then cattle and horses would become feral [wild] and this would certainly greatly alter the vegetation: this again would largely affect the insects: and thus ... the insectivorous birds, and so onwards in increasing circles of complexity. (Pepper 1984: 102)

Glacken finds several further passages where Darwin showed awareness of such a mutual interplay of species, and thus what would later be called an ecological awareness. Here is one such:

> The tail of the giraffe looks like an artificially constructed fly-flapper; and it seems at first incredible that it could have been adapted for the present purpose by successive slight modifications, each better and better fitted, for so trifling an object as to drive away flies ... It is not that the larger quadrupeds are actually destroyed (except in some rare cases) by flies, but they are incessantly harassed and their strength reduced, so that they are more subject to disease, or not so well enabled in a coming dearth to search for food or to escape from beasts of prey. (Darwin 1859: 144; Rajan 2017: 71)

And there are more such passages, explaining the relations between flowering plants and insects, the role of sexual selection in the genesis of the beauty of male birds, fishes, reptiles, mammals and butterflies, and how the hooks of some trailing plants arose as a defence against browsing quadrupeds, but later acquired the different function of assisting their attachment to tall trees (a change of function that would nowadays be termed an 'exaptation'). Glacken also remarks that Darwin's talk of natural webs expresses the concept of ecosystems, and that where humans are involved in such webs, this has spurred the study of the relations of nature and culture (Rajan 2017: 70–1).

Indeed, as J. Arthur Thomson concluded, 'it seems fair to say that no naturalist, before or since, has come near Darwin in his realization of the web of life, in his clear vision and picture of the vast system of linkages that penetrates throughout the animate world' (1910: 45; Rajan 2017: 71). Yet Thomson's appraisal could be challenged in the light of the discovery by Louis Pasteur in 1861 of anaerobic bacteria, and later of their role in fermentation and putrefaction, and of the germ theory of disease (Egerton 2012: 195), thus considerably augmenting the understanding of the web of life bequeathed to us by Darwin.

In later chapters of *Origin of Species*, Darwin makes it clear that environmental conditions alone could not, in his view at that time, account for the origin of species, and that natural selection was more significant. This was the basis of his rejection of Lamarck's ideas. Yet later (in 1876) he wrote to Moritz Wagner: 'In my opinion the greatest error which I have committed, has been not allowing sufficient weight to the direct action of the environment, i.e. food, climate &c., independently of natural selection' (Rajan 2017: 74). Wagner had written of Darwin's neglect of factors such as migration and isolation, and so this was a partial concession on Darwin's part. Thus Darwinists are not obliged to attribute all biological phenomena to natural selection in order to be true to Darwin.

The First Darwinians, Humanity and Nature

In 1871, Darwin published *The Descent of Man*. His view was that the same processes that operated in the evolution of other forms of life had operated in human evolution as well, and that variations arose through the same factors in both cases. Further, the laws of population growth applied to humanity as to other species, and humanity was part of the same struggle for survival.

In this struggle, Darwin claimed that from the days of early man onwards, humanity established dominance over other forms of life.

> Man in the rudest state in which he now exists is the most dominant animal that has ever appeared on this earth. He has spread more widely than any other highly organised form: and all others have yielded before him. He manifestly owes this immense superiority to his intellectual faculties, to his social habits, which lead him to aid and defend his fellows, and to his corporeal structure. (1871: 431; Rajan 2017: 76)

Darwin described early humans as skilled technologists with the ability to interfere in the natural world through weapons and through fire. The discovery of fire was 'probably the greatest ever made by man, excepting language', and took place in prehistoric times (1871: 432; Rajan 2017: 76–7).

Accordingly, Darwin's account of the relations of humanity and nature concerned an inevitable dominance on the part of humanity. Coates comments that there was no suggestion of how human powers were subject to ethical constraints, or of the need for the preservation of biodiversity (1998: 140–1), but Nash provides evidence of an ethical sensitivity; humans would eventually put aside 'baneful customs and superstitions' and might attain 'disinterested love for all living creatures' (1989: 44). Darwin's findings generated plenty of religious controversy, but no direct debate about environmental ethics. He did, however, undeniably endorse the view that humanity is distinctive in having ethical capacities. 'I fully subscribe to the judgment of those writers who maintain that of all the differences between man and the lower animals, the moral sense or conscience is by far the most important' (1871: 471; Rajan 2017: 77). Indeed, for Darwin this was the main if not the sole basis of human superiority.

Yet in Darwin's day, his recognition of the skills of primitive peoples (such as knowledge of useful plants and of watering holes in the desert) was unusual, and importantly different from that of Wallace.

> These several inventions, by which man in his rudest state has become so pre-eminent, are the direct results of the development of his powers of observation, memory, curiosity, imagination and reason. I cannot, therefore, understand how it is that Mr. Wallace maintains that 'natural selection could only have endowed the savage with a brain a little superior to that of an ape. (1871: 432; Rajan 2017: 77)

Indeed, for Darwin the impacts of natural selection on civilization were not profound: 'With civilized nations, as far as an advanced standard of morality, and an increased number of fairly good men are concerned, natural selection apparently effects but little; though the fundamental social instincts were originally thus gained' (1871: 504; Rajan 2017: 78).

As Glacken cogently adds, 'it was not Darwin but his enthusiastic supporters that were responsible for reimporting the struggle for existence (Malthusianism applied to nature as a whole) into the social world' (Rajan 2017: 78). He may have been worried by the tendency of the weaker members of society to propagate faster than the rest, and (unlike Wallace) lacked compassion for their condition (Rajan 2017: 78), but he did not favour social policies promoting the survival of the fittest.

Lenn E. Goodman has, however, recently explained that Darwin had to devise a way of speeding up the course of evolution, because the scientist Lord Kelvin (b. William Thomson, 1824–1907) had argued, on the basis of contemporary physics, that neither the sun nor the earth was old enough to afford the time needed for natural selection to do its work.

(This was only realized to be an illusory problem with the later discovery of nuclear fusion as the source of the sun's energy and of radioactivity in the earth's core as the source of much of the earth's heat.) Darwin's solution was to appeal to Lamarckism, and to represent numerous forms of behaviour as hereditable, from social attitudes to the atrophy of muscles, within just a single generation, and thus including many transitory phenomena among the sources of new species. This solution chiefly skewed his treatment of humanity, involving the introduction of much racism and sexism, but it also affected his treatment of animal species, and is thus of greater current relevance than might at first sight be apparent (Goodman 2019: 47). It was only with the later synthesis of Darwinism and Mendelian genetics that these distortions of Darwinism (albeit ones devised by Darwin himself) could be discarded, in favour of a Darwinism purged of Lamarckism and more largely focused on natural selection.

To turn now to Darwin's champion in the famous encounter with Bishop Wilberforce at Oxford in 1860, Thomas Henry Huxley (1825–95) published in 1863 *Evidence as to Man's Place in Nature*. As in his debate with Wilberforce, Huxley thus diverted to himself much of the opprobrium that might otherwise have been directed at Darwin. He had no doubt that the gulf between humanity and the highest forms of animal life could be accounted for by evolutionary theory. But he was also convinced of the greatness of that gulf: 'At the same time no one is more strongly convinced than I am of the vastness of the gulf between [the] civilized and the brutes; or is more certain that whether from them or not, he is assuredly not of them' (1863: 102; Rajan 2017: 79).

For Huxley, the great dividing line between humanity and the higher primates was language and the power of speech. He further objected to the widespread use of the abstract term 'man', not on feminist grounds, but because of the huge differences between ancient, primitive and civilized man (Rajan 2017: 80).

Huxley was a humanitarian, who wanted to distinguish between prehistoric humans, among whom 'there was an authentic struggle no different from the struggles among the animals' (Rajan 2017: 82) and 'the history of civilization', which was 'the record of the attempts which the human race has made to escape from this position' and where 'the ethical man tries to escape from his place in the animal kingdom ... and to establish a kingdom of Man, governed upon the principle of moral evolution' (Huxley 1894 [1888]: 203–5; Rajan 2017: 82). He continued to struggle with these themes, not least in view of the response of Petr Kropotkin (1842–1921), the Russian biologist and anarchist, who in essays, published later as *Mutual Aid: A Factor of Evolution* (1902), stressed the naturalness of human cooperation, and its continuity with the intraspecific sociality of many nonhuman species. (Kropotkin believed in group selection, a belief that Mary Midgley (2014: 26-28) has ascribed to Darwin himself, and that was also held by the Darwinian Konrad Lorenz (1903–89), the founder of ethology, the study of animal behaviour.) Huxley also sought to oppose the view of Herbert Spencer that fitness can be identified with (moral) goodness; in his 1888 essay 'Evolution and Ethics', he wrote that 'the ethical progress of society depends not on imitating the cosmic process ... but in combating it' (1894 [1888]; Passmore 1970: 245).

But his critics rapidly pointed out that this suggestion is barely consistent with Darwinism, for Darwinists hold that man is part of nature and subject to its forces, rather than able to resist them. Hence Huxley added a note to the printed version of his lectures that largely conceded the point. 'Strictly speaking', he admitted, 'social life, and the ethical process in virtue of which it advances toward perfection, are part and parcel of the general process of evolution', adding that even in primitive forms of society 'the general cosmic process begins to be checked by a rudimentary ethical process, which is, strictly speaking, part of the former' (1894 [1888]: 101). Thus, as Darwin had already maintained, evolution by natural selection is capable of generating ethical progress, possibly among primates and other mammals, and certainly among humans (Passmore 1970: 245). And if so, the kind of sociality within animal species depicted by Kropotkin, and further evidenced more recently by Frans de Waal (1996), must form part of this process. (On Kropotkin, see also Midgley 2014 [2010]: 46–8.)

A very different view was taken by Wallace. Wallace had a much greater respect for primitive peoples than Darwin or Huxley. His admiration for their intellectual and moral powers led him to the conclusion that these powers were not generated by natural selection. He agreed with Lyell, who, in the tenth edition of his *Principles of Geology* had accepted 'the derivation of man from the lower animals' (Wallace 1869), but added that accepting this does not prevent one rejecting the possibility of either natural selection or evolution in general explaining humanity's intellectual and moral nature. Neither the emergence of conscious life on earth nor human intellect and human morality could originate on the basis of any law of evolution (Wallace 1869: 391). Effectively, Wallace was invoking divine supervision of natural laws to explain these unique phenomena. He was also, of course, refusing to recognize any seeds of morality or social collaboration within nonhuman species.

Wallace's travels and experiences in Southeast Asia led him to the view that the primitive peoples of that region were endowed with qualities 'that were unnecessary for their survival in the struggle for existence'

(Glacken, in Rajan 2017: 85). He found, for example, that they had knowledge of their environments far superior to that of missionaries, and based on prolonged association (Wallace 1872). This did not lead him to a Rousseauesque advocacy of returning to nature, nor to an idealized primitive way of life. Nevertheless, he held that primitive peoples were endowed with skills that they did not need, and which, accordingly, could not be ascribed to natural selection. He was thus initiating a debate about the extent to which human culture can be held to evolve through natural selection, or, because it depends in part on reflection and choices (and thus on artificial selection), is to be held distinct from the realm of natural selection and from evolution of that kind.

Wallace, it should be added, discovered in 1859 the discontinuity of fauna between Borneo, Bali and Asia, on the one side, and Celebes, Lombok, New Guinea and Australia, on the other. Predominantly different animals live on either side of this line, which Huxley proceeded to name 'the Wallace Line'. (It later emerged that this line coincided with the boundaries of geological tectonic plates.) Thus Wallace was an important contributor to biogeography as well as to the theory of evolution.

Huxley was also impressed by Wallace's far-flung and perilous travels, and by the conclusions that he formed, without necessarily sharing them. Darwin was distressed at Wallace invoking a divine role to explain human powers, and wrote to him accordingly in 1869 (F. Darwin 1887/8); but Wallace persisted in his views about the limits of the scope of natural selection for the rest of his life, despite some apparent backtracking in a passage where he accepted the superiority of European intellectual and moral qualities, and the inevitable disappearance of mentally undeveloped peoples when confronted with Europeans (see Rajan 2017: 91–2). But this passage, which stands alone (and may reflect a sombre acceptance of the extinction of peoples such as the Tasmanians), seems not to have deflected him from his distinctive view of how different explanations are needed for the phenomena of nature and of culture. Perhaps this view warrants applause, in view of the dependence of culture on artificial selection, and its predominant absence (albeit not its complete absence) from the realm of nature.

Herbert Spencer and Social Darwinism

Herbert Spencer had believed in evolution well before he met with Darwin's writings. He believed that the whole universe is subject, throughout its history, to evolution; and he combined this view with belief in gradual but inevitable progress. On discovering Darwinism, he combined these metaphysical beliefs with natural selection, interpreted natural selection as involving 'the survival of the fittest', and converted this tenet into a theory of ethics. He also adopted the Lamarckian belief in the inheritability of acquired characteristics (Ruse 2001: 171), which may explain his belief that if the poor and feckless have children who survive, they will inherit poverty and fecklessness.

Evil, Spencer held, consists in the maladaptedness of an organism to its environment. Because of this, evils tend to disappear in due course, because beings eventually either adapt or die out. Adaptations are passed on to succeeding generations, and in this way evils are overcome and eliminated. However, the multitude of evils in human life points to human beings not yet having learned to adapt to human society. Humans need to adapt so that, instead of sacrificing others to themselves, they learn to be altruistic and fully social. But the process of adaptation is itself inevitable, at least eventually. 'Evolution can end only in the establishment of the greatest perfection and the most complete happiness' (Spencer 1862). Spencer based all this on his own version of the laws of history, which have proved just as unfalsifiable and ungrounded as those of his predecessors Herder, Saint-Simon, Comte and Marx. Eventually, as Passmore records, even Spencer abandoned belief in perfect adaptation, allowing that the time this would take to be accomplished was infinite (Passmore 1970: 242).

Despite Spencer's advocacy of altruism, his identification of moral ideals with adaptation and fitness to survive led others (both in Europe and America) to hold that the survival of the fittest applied to human society and to the nonhuman world alike, that competition is inevitably predominant in both realms, that the weak, being maladapted, must be allowed to suffer and die, and that the trajectory of evolution leads to the triumph of the strong. (Indeed, Spencer himself was opposed to relief of poverty by the state, as contrasted with individual charity (Ruse 2001: 172).) These views were readily merged with a commitment to laissez-faire capitalism, in a stance that came to be called 'social Darwinism'.

Meanwhile, Wallace wrote in 1900 that the progressive tendencies inherent in evolution lead not to social Darwinism but to socialism (Ruse 2006: 1036); this at least showed how open to question was the attempt to derive social Darwinism from the Darwinism of Darwin. Shortly afterwards, the philosopher G. E. Moore (1873–1958) argued that Spencer's equation of fitness to survive with goodness committed the naturalistic fallacy (Moore 2003). I have argued elsewhere that Moore's attempt to demonstrate that the concept of goodness is indefinable itself begs the question (Attfield 2012b: 172–3). But this critique of Moore's reasoning is consistent with acceptance of Moore's argument that Spencer's evolutionary ethics are grounded in a manifest fallacy; for, as Moore held, the question 'Is whatever is fit to survive good?' is beyond doubt an open question, and not a closed one, as Spencer's views entailed.

It should be added that in 1910 the novelist Thomas Hardy wrote in *The Humanitarian* that 'the most far-reaching consequence of the establishment of the common origin of all species is ethical' (Salt 1928). As Nash puts it, Hardy believed Darwinism 'logically involved a readjustment of altruistic morals, by enlarging . . . the application of what has been called "The Golden Rule" from the area of mere mankind to that of the whole animal kingdom' (1989: 43). Hardy, we might comment, had as much justification for this view as had Spencer and the social Darwinists for their contrary interpretations.

As we have seen in the previous section, the belief that 'the survival of the fittest' is the central theme of human society was also opposed by Huxley, not least on ethical grounds, and was far removed from the beliefs of Darwin himself, with his stress on the importance within human life of a moral sense and of conscience. With better understandings of society, social Darwinism gradually fell from favour in the early twentieth century, and in any case tells us little about environmental thought, except for the currency among many for several decades of the (by now long-outdated) belief that Darwinism implies unremitting competition both between species and within them. At the same time, it proved to be an impediment for several decades to recognition of the social capacities of human beings, and of those of many of our pre-human ancestors.

Another thinker influenced by Spencer was Henri Bergson (1859–1941). Bergson's study of time moved him away from Spencer's thought to a process philosophy that rejected determinism. However, he accepted evolution as a scientific fact, and in his book *L'Évolution créatrice* (Creative Evolution; 1907), he argued that it is driven by an *élan vital* ('vital impulse') which pervades the world. Bergson's work assisted the adoption of evolution in France around the turn of the century, but his metaphysics later fell from favour. Yet his process philosophy probably influenced the process theology of his contemporary, A. N. Whitehead (1861–1947), and later Charles Hartshorne (1897–2000), whose version of panentheism (see Chapter 2) can be understood as a further response to Darwinism.

The Reception of Darwinism in the Nineteenth Century

As Ruse relates, evolution was accepted as fact rapidly and readily (2001: 25). Not everyone accepted that natural selection had the importance attributed to it by Darwin, and, given Darwin's lack of a theory to explain mutations, some such as Huxley preferred a theory of large beneficial variations ('saltations'), which seemed more likely to persist across the generations, contrary to Darwin's own gradualism. These problems about inheritance could have been resolved if Darwin had recognized the significance of the scientific discovery of laws of genetics and thus of inheritance on the part of his contemporary Gregor Mendel (1822–84); but unfortunately, he left Mendel's key paper unread. Nevertheless, by 1900 or soon after, virtually all reputable biologists were adherents of Darwinism (Wilkie 1973: 241).

It is often supposed that the opposition to Darwinism, manifested by Bishop Wilberforce in his 1860 debate with Huxley, epitomized a general rejection of Darwinism among Christians. But, as we have already seen, some Christians actually endorsed versions of Darwinism from the outset; see the passage about Asa Gray and Charles Kingsley in the section above, 'Darwin's Argument'. As Owen Chadwick puts it, these people accepted Darwinism on religious grounds, because Darwinism reduced the number of inexplicable things in the universe, and therefore pointed in their eyes to its universal design. Others, Chadwick adds, either welcomed Darwin's search for truth and saw nothing in Darwinism inconsistent with God's goodness, or preferred Darwinism to the antics of those who 'sought to reconcile geology with Genesis', such as the naturalist Philip Gosse (1810–88), who held that God must have created trees with tree-rings already complete despite their not having grown, and Adam with a navel despite his not having been born. Such ingenuity struck some as unintentionally blasphemous, and made adopting Darwinism appear far preferable (Chadwick 1973: 284–5). Another supporter of Darwinism was John Henry Newman (1801–90), who wrote in 1870 explaining his support of Darwin's being awarded an honorary degree from the University of Oxford: Darwinism, in his view, did not contradict Christian teaching (Ruse 2006: 1035).

While there were some clerical opponents of Darwinism, many took the view that it was preferable to suspend judgement. These included such high churchmen as Edward Pusey and his disciple Henry Liddon, somewhat surprisingly in view of their rejection of the 'higher criticism' of the Bible around the same time (Chadwick 1973: 285). In a similar spirit, the review in *The Times* of Darwin's *Descent of Man* accepted that humanity was part of the evolutionary process, adding: 'Nor is there any reason why a man may not be an evolutionist and yet a Christian. . . . Evolution is not yet proved, and never may be. But . . . there is no occasion for being frightened out of our wits for fear it should be' (Chadwick 1973: 286).

When Darwin died in 1882, and Huxley considered the possibility of his being buried in Westminster Abbey, Canon F. W. Farrar told him: 'We clergy are not all so benighted as you suppose.' But an application was made anyway, and Darwin was buried in Westminster Abbey with Christian rites, and the anthem *Happy is the man that findeth wisdom*. What is more, despite isolated protests, churches in Britain generally took pride in this decision. A memorial fund was set up, and its committee included, in addition to leading scientists and other Darwinians such as Herbert Spencer, the Archbishops of Canterbury and York and the Bishop of London (Chadwick 1973: 286).

Chadwick goes on to recount that in 1896 Asa Gray told the Bishop of Rochester that, as he looked back on the progress of thought in Britain and America, 'he could not say that there had been any undue or improper delay on the part of the Christian mind and conscience in accepting . . . Mr Darwin's doctrines'. Chadwick adds that some church leaders, including Cardinal Manning, continued to reject Darwin's doctrines (1973: 287). It was not until the twentieth century that the Catholic Church was able to accept Darwinism; and the same probably applies to some nonconformists, while others welcomed the recognition accorded to Darwin by his burial in Westminster Abbey.

Chadwick further relates that in 1902 the Liverpool school for the blind applied for permission for mosaic glass in its chapel. The light of the world (Christ) was to be in the centre, surrounded by men and women 'deriving inspiration from him', Charles Darwin among them. In approving this application, the relevant church official (the diocesan chancellor) remarked that 'we have long ago satisfied ourselves that natural science, as represented by Darwin, is not contrariant to revealed religion', and that it was wholesome to be reminded that 'every good and perfect gift cometh from above, from the father of lights' (a quotation from the New Testament) (Chadwick 1973: 287). Thereby, he accepted that Darwinism was a 'good and perfect gift' from 'the father of lights', God the creator.

Meanwhile in Germany, Ernst Haeckel (1834–1919) popularized his own Lamarckian version of Darwinism (1876 [1868]). At the same time, August Weismann (1834–1918) defended Darwinian natural selection and sexual selection as explanations of speciation. He also rejected belief in the inheritance of acquired characteristics. Later, Ernst Mayr (1982: 698) considered Weismann the most important evolutionary theorist between Darwin and the Darwinian synthesis of 1930–40. Darwinism thus quickly took root in parts of the Continent, as well as in Britain and the USA.

Darwinism in the Twentieth Century

Asa Gray's acceptance was qualified by the phrase 'in such sense as ... they [Mr Darwin's doctrines] ought to be accepted'. This phrase was probably intended to convey tentative acceptance; for Darwin had no theory of the source of variations, nor (his Lamarckism aside) of why advantageous ones persisted across the generations rather than being gradually diluted to the point of disappearance. That these gaps in his theory were remedied by the findings of Gregor Mendel was not realized until the works of the latter were rediscovered and developed around the turn of the century and subsequently. From then onwards, Darwinism began to be regarded as scientifically established rather than just probably true.

The key figures in this entrenchment of Darwinism were Ronald Fisher (in his 1930 book, *The Genetical Theory of Natural Selection*) and J. B. S. Haldane (with his 1932 book, *The Causes of Evolution*) in Britain, and Sewall Wright (in his articles of 1931 and 1932) in the United States. Despite some minor differences between the members of this group, they jointly showed that natural selection and Mendelian genetics go well together, and were able to give 'a fuller theory and a more satisfactory causal theory than Darwin had been able to produce' (Ruse 2001: 26). They showed in particular that, given Mendel's laws of heredity, new variations need not waste away to nothing, but can rather be transmitted without attenuation to a succession of generations; and that in this way the advantageous variants selected by natural selection can persist, and in some cases give rise to new species.

The work of these mathematically minded biologists thus produced the modern 'Darwinian synthesis', which has become the prevalent stance in contemporary biology. Julian Huxley, the grandson of Thomas Henry Huxley, published a key book in 1942 with 'synthesis' in its title (*Evolution: The Modern Synthesis*). This emerging theory was further corroborated by the work of more empirically minded biologists such as Theodosius Dobzhansky in the United States, who in 1937 published *Genetics and the Origin of Species*. As Ruse (1996) has shown, this further group of writers sought to provide the factual evidence to support the theoretical calculations of Fisher and the others. Another of the empirical biologists was E. B. Ford, founder of the school of 'ecological genetics', whose overview, with *Ecological Genetics* as its title, was eventually published in 1964 (Ruse 2006: 1037; but the date of 1974 given there by Ruse is incorrect).

It is significant that among the adherents of the new Darwinian synthesis, at least two were (in Ruse's words) 'ardent Christians'. Fisher belonged to the Church of England, and in a sermon given at his college explained that the new theory shows that creation 'was not all finished long ago but is still in progress'. Dobzhansky, by contrast, adhered for most of his life to the Russian Orthodox Church, but moved towards a more universalistic faith in his later years. He too was a practising Christian, who detected the hand of God in all events, both spectacular and humdrum, such as the events that shape evolution (Ruse 2001: 9).

However, a contrary view, that of Trofim Lysenko (1898–1976), was officially endorsed in the Soviet Union in the 1920s, and not officially disavowed until 1964. Lysenko accepted the inheritability of acquired characteristics, while rejecting natural selection and, at the same time, Mendelian genetics. It was only in the former respect that he was in any sense a follower of Darwin. Lysenkoism set back Russian biology by four decades, until the Darwinian synthesis could at last be adopted.

Meanwhile, since the stage in which Fisher and Dobzhansky were prominent, there has been the discovery in 1953, by James Watson, Francis Crick and Rosamund Franklin, of the double helix as the shape of DNA molecules, as well as a range of new ideas that this has led to. On one wing of evolutionary science there have been adaptationists such as Richard Dawkins, who detect adaptation (past or present) behind virtually all biological phenomena. On the other wing there have been figures such as Stephen Jay Gould and Richard Lewontin, who hold that biological phenomena can be by-products of factors other than selection, such as the homologous bone structures of birds and animals, inherited from ancestral species; they compare such by-products with 'spandrels' (triangular concave surfaces in the ceilings of churches, formed by the intersection of two rounded arches at right angles to each other), the intricate designs of which make them seem central to their architect's purpose, but which are actually the inevitable by-products of any building plan involving a dome and arches. Another possibility that they express involves the secondary utilization of parts or processes already present for other reasons; thus human blushing could be an adaptation for sexual selection in humans, but it cannot explain why blood is red, something that must have a prior and independent explanation (Gould and Lewontin 1994; Attfield 2006: 111).

Later, Gould and Elisabeth S. Vrba introduced the term 'exaptation' for features that are well-adjusted to their current role, but not selected for it, such as lactation in mammals (granted that lactose-like fluids probably evolved not for nourishing a mother's young, but to kill bacteria). Another example is the supportive role of bones, originally selected as stores for phosphates rather than for rigidity and their current role in the musculo-skeletal system (Gould and Vrba 1998). (For a previous mention of 'exaptation', see the passage in the above section 'Darwin and Ecology' about the hooks of climbing plants.) Yet, as Ruse remarks, Gould and Vrba remained Darwinists: they recognized both evolution from common ancestors and natural selection as the most important source of biological adaptation. Indeed, Gould had just expounded and defended such a generic Darwinist stance (Gould 1997: 138; Attfield 2006: 112).

Hence Darwinism can be adhered to without the sociobiological explanations of human behaviour adopted by Richard Dawkins in *The Selfish Gene* (1989). Like many others, Dawkins regards the basic unit of selection as the gene (although others consider the basic unit to be the species, or units of other kinds; see Lewontin 1970), and adheres to a virtually deterministic theory of the moulding of human behaviour by the genes and their self-replicating tendencies. But since our genes cannot plausibly account for our thoughts and ideas, he introduces additional basic units to account for these, and calls them 'memes' (persistent thoughts that colonize the minds of thinkers, virus-like). Human life is thus represented as largely the deterministic outcome of the interplay of genes and memes, although Dawkins acknowledges that human beings have the ability to rebel against their joint despotism.

Philosophers have rightly questioned this postulation of memes. For this theory makes people the mere containers or carriers of both genes and memes, and it is genes and memes that are supposedly the true drivers of history, and not ourselves. Nor can this stance account for human rationality and autonomy, as opposed to representing them as illusory. (But this is not the place for a full-dress debate of these issues; those interested should consult Midgley 1979b, 2000; Holdcroft and Lewis 2001; Attfield 2011a.)

Yet other Darwinians combine recognition of natural selection with the view that there is much in the realm of biology that lies beyond its scope, such as change at the molecular level, as investigated by the Japanese scientist Motoo Kimura (Ruse 2001: 31). To such theories, adaptationists reply that the very case of their opponents turns on secondary adaptation and its preconditions, and can thus be reconciled with the centrality of adaptation (Sober 1998). Ruse calls this position 'ultra-Darwinism', because it is more Darwinian than Darwin himself was (Ruse 2001: 25); see further Darwin's letter to Wagner at the end of the section above, 'Darwin on Ecology'.

Adaptationism is highly implausible unless it is at least purged of its commitment to belief in memes. Even then, its apparent belief that all biological phenomena in every possible world would be due to adaptation appears doctrinaire and exaggerated. Recognition of the possibility of other causes would greatly increase its credibility, while the representation by Dawkins of genes as 'selfish' (a term that makes sense only when used of responsible agents) is profoundly misleading. So is the tendency of biologists to describe all cooperative behaviour as 'altruism', a term ordinarily denoting love of others, and not merely acting as if one were motivated by such love. Since love of others turns out to be possible, adaptationism apparently needs to be adapted itself, so as to cease to imply that such behaviour is invariably driven by unobservable units that are themselves necessarily incapable of human motives of any kind.

Thus debates between diverse forms of Darwinism continue, with adaptationists making adaptations and natural selection do all or most of the work, while others, like de Waal, stress the pre-human origins of sociality alongside natural selection. This second approach also leaves room for group selection, and epitomizes a parallel debate about whether the units of selection include species, subspecies, communities and individuals as well as genes, or consist in genes alone.

This chapter has concerned Darwin's predecessors, his scientific contributions, his associates and his successors. Darwinism has increasingly influenced thought not only about human society but also about animal behaviour (studied by ethologists: see Chapter 6) and the science of ecology (discussed in Chapter 5). Coates seems wrong in regarding Darwin's grasp of (what would later be called) ecology as occasional and uninfluential. Instead, Darwinism (as we have seen) comprises one of the key influences on this new form of science. However, another key influence emerged in America, and the American debate (or debates) is appropriately the theme of the coming chapter.

Recommended reading

Attfield, Robin (2006). *Creation, Evolution and Meaning*. Aldershot: Ashgate. (Since 2015, London: Routledge.)

Coates, Peter (1998). *Nature: Western Attitudes Since Ancient Times*. Berkeley: University of California Press.

Darwin, Charles (1859). *On the Origin of Species*. London: John Murray.

Darwin, Charles (1871). *The Descent of Man, and Selection in Relation to Sex*. London: John Murray.

Gillispie, Charles Coulston (1969 [1951]). *Genesis and Geology*, 2nd edn. Cambridge, MA: Harvard University Press.

Gould, Stephen Jay and Lewontin, Richard C. (1994). 'The Spandrels of San Marco and the Panglossian Paradigm: A Critique of the Adaptationist

Programme', in Eliot Sober (ed.), *Conceptual Issues in Evolutionary Biology*, 2nd edn. Cambridge, MA: MIT Press, pp. 73–90.

Gould, Stephen Jay and Vrba, Elisabeth S. (1998). 'Exaptation: A Missing Term in the Philosophy of Form', in David L. Hull and Michael Ruse (eds), *The Philosophy of Biology*. Oxford: Oxford University Press, pp. 52–71.

Kropotkin, Petr (1902). *Mutual Aid: A Factor of Evolution*. London: William Heinemann.

Midgley, Mary (2014 [2010]). *The Solitary Self: Darwin and the Selfish Gene*. London: Routledge.

Passmore, John (1970). *The Perfectibility of Man*. London: Duckworth.

Pepper, David (1984). *The Roots of Modern Environmentalism*. London: Routledge.

Rajan, S. Ravi (2017). *Genealogies of Environmentalism: The Lost Works of Clarence Glacken*. Charlottesville: University of Virginia Press.

Ruse, Michael (2001). *Can a Darwinian be a Christian?* Cambridge: Cambridge University Press.

4

The American Debate

The Transcendentalists

This chapter focuses on the contributions of George Perkins Marsh and of John Muir (1838–1914) to environmentalism, forestry and environmental preservation, and then on the growth in the United States of the related protection of animals from cruel treatment.

Darwin's contemporary in America, Marsh, made a hugely important contribution to environmental thought in his book *Man and Nature*, published just after *The Origin of Species*, in 1864. Marsh, however, is regarded as one of the transcendentalists, whose founding fathers have already been briefly discussed in Chapter 2.

But in order to set the context of Marsh's work, it is worth reverting here to the pioneers of American transcendentalism, Ralph Waldo Emerson and Henry David Thoreau. Although these thinkers can be regarded as jointly a manifestation of the Romantic movement in the United States, they can also be understood as nourishing the culture there from which the future development of environmental thought was able to emerge. This chapter goes on to outline how environmentalism developed in the United States in the later decades of the nineteenth century and the early years of the twentieth.

The work of Emerson and of Thoreau has already been briefly introduced in the 'New Philosophies of Nature' section towards the end of Chapter 2. But it was not explained there how they came to be called 'transcendentalists', how Marsh's family was involved in this movement, or how it influenced Marsh himself.

Mention should first be made of Frederic Henry Hedge (1805–90), who studied in Germany before joining Harvard Divinity School. Later, he took up the task, which he felt had been performed inadequately by Coleridge, of introducing what he called 'the transcendental philosophy' of Kant to the English-speaking world. He set about explaining Kant's Copernican revolution in philosophy and his claim that, instead of our intuitions depending on the outside world, the very possibility of our understanding the world depends 'on the nature of our intuitions', and thus on a priori knowledge (knowledge, that is, not based on experience) (Myerson, 2000). In 1836, Hedge suggested to Emerson that they create a discussion group for disaffected young Unitarian clergy (of whom Emerson was already one); it lasted for four years and became known as the Transcendental Club. (Unitarians were a group of Congregationalists who detached themselves from orthodox Calvinism – see the opening section of Chapter 2 – and from belief in the divinity of Jesus Christ; Emerson was disaffected from mainstream Unitarianism through rejecting miracles as proofs of belief in God.)

Emerson later explained, in a lecture titled 'The Transcendentalist', that Kant's term for the intuitions of the mind (on which, in his view, knowledge of the world depended) was 'Transcendental forms', such as our concepts of space and time. For Kant, transcendental inquiry would have concerned study of the presuppositions of human experience. But the shared theme of the nineteenth-century American transcendentalists was the powers of the mind, its insights, and the kinds of nondoctrinal spirituality that go with it (Emerson 1990 [1836]). Like Emerson, they rejected Locke's appeal to miracles as proofs of Christianity, and appealed to an inbuilt religious sentiment, which they took Jesus to have expressed and inspired. Thus, in the first paragraph of *Nature* (1883 [1836]) Emerson wrote: 'Why should we not have a poetry and philosophy of insight and not of tradition, and a religion by revelation to us, and not the history of theirs' (that is, of religious authorities) (Goodman 2018: 2–4). An example is to be found when Emerson 'recounts an ecstatic experience in the woods: "I became a transparent eyeball. I am nothing. I see all; the currents of the universal being circulate through me"' (Emerson 1990 [1836]: 6; Goodman 2018: 3). In this way, 'using intuition, rather than reason and science, human beings could transcend physical appearances and perceive "the currents of the Universal Being", binding the world together' (Nash 1989: 36, 225n.10).

This helps explain that, as Roderick Nash relates, the core of transcendentalism became the belief that a correspondence of parallelism existed between the higher realm of spiritual truth and the lower one of material objects. For this reason material objects assumed importance because, if rightly seen, they reflected universal spiritual truths. It was this belief that led Emerson to declare in his manifesto of 1836 that 'nature is the symbol of the spirit ... the world is emblematic'. (Emerson 1883 [1836], vol. I: 38; Nash 2014 [1967]: 85)

This influential movement employed Kant's terminology, but its emphasis on the spiritual significance of nature was in fact a far cry from the main themes of Kant and of Kantianism.

This is where James Marsh (elder cousin and companion of George Marsh) enters the story. James, who eventually became president of the University of Vermont, had no doubt that German philosophy held the key to a reformed theology. In 1829, he edited and published Coleridge's *Aids to Reflection*, which introduced Kant's terminology, much used in Emerson's early work, for example on the subject of the imagination; he also translated and published in 1833 Herder's *Spirit of Hebrew Poetry* (originally published in 1782), which cast doubt on the authority of the Bible, and suggested that texts with equal authority could still be written (Goodman 2018: 2). It was through intuition or imagination that the human mind could transcend material existence and 'penetrate to spiritual truths' (Nash 2014 [1967]: 85).

From 1840 to 1844, the transcendentalists organized and published *The Dial*, whose editor was Margaret Fuller, later the author of *Woman in the Nineteenth Century* (1845). These were among the elements of the culture in which the young George Perkins Marsh was brought up.

But as we have seen in Chapter 2, the full flourishing of transcendentalism came with Henry Thoreau, for whom nature attained even greater prominence in *Walden* (composed at Walden Pond in 1845–7, but not published until 1854) than in Emerson's *Nature* (1836). For Thoreau, nature 'becomes particular: this tree, this bird, this state of the pond on a summer evening or winter morning become Thoreau's subjects' (Goodman 2018: 5). In the opening chapter of *Walden*, titled 'Economy', Thoreau asks what life's real necessities are, and concludes in favour of 'a life of simplicity, independence, magnanimity and trust' (1989 [1854]: 15). He favoured both frugality and the prodigality of 'a spending of what you have in the day that shall never come again. This is true frugality ...' (1989 [1854]: 17; Goodman 2018: 5). Other chapters were called 'Solitude', 'Winter' and 'Spring', and another was called 'Reading', commending great books that both demand and inspire 'reading, in a high sense' (1989 [1854]: 102), among which *Walden* itself has often been included by others. However, it attracted little attention in the United States until the English animal welfarist Henry Salt (1851–1939) popularized this seminal work in the United Kingdom early in the next century. In connection with the theme of animal welfare, it should be remarked that Thoreau stopped using guns in 1852 (Egerton 2012: 155).

Later, Thoreau recognized, unlike Emerson, that the wild is not always either consoling or uplifting. Thus in *Cape Cod* (1865) he remarked on the foreignness of nature: the shore is 'a wild, rank place, and there is no flattery in it' (1988 [1865]: 577; Goodman 2018: 6). Yet he also wrote: 'The earth I tread on is not a dead, inert mass; it is a body, has a spirit, is organic and fluid to the influence of the spirit' (1906, vol. 3: 165; Nash 1989: 37).

Elsewhere, Thoreau (1973) wrote in condemnation of slavery, and advocated civil disobedience grounded in conscience. The citizen, he held, 'has no duty to resign his conscience to the state, and may even have a duty to oppose immoral legislation', such as the law requiring 'all citizens to assist in returning fugitive slaves to their owners' (Goodman 2018: 7). It is also worth remarking that in 1860 Thoreau read Darwin's *Origin of Species* and endorsed Darwin's theory as implying 'a greater vital force in nature' (Egerton 2012: 155).

One of those influenced by Emerson and Thoreau was Frederick Law Olmsted (1822–1903), who inherited their belief that nature should be treated with respect and awe. Olmsted later 'worked with the naturalist John Muir to secure the protection of the Yosemite Valley and the Mariposa Grove of redwood trees in California' (Thompson 2014: 52: on Muir, see later in this chapter). Another was George Perkins Marsh.

George Perkins Marsh: Regenerating the Earth after Human Disruption

Marsh, who was influenced among others by his cousin James, by his younger contemporary Thoreau as well as by Emerson, became a transcendentalist, albeit one with distinctive emphases of his own. From his transcendentalist heritage, his key emphases were on free will and the centrality of human agency. His upbringing, in rural Woodstock, Vermont, and later at Dartmouth College, was a mixture of strict Calvinism and authoritarian schooling, which long immunized him against both these tendencies. Readers eager to trace his biography in greater detail are recommended to peruse Lowenthal's *George Perkins Marsh* (2000 [1958]).

Marsh was more at home in the woods than most transcendentalists (Thoreau included); but, unlike Thoreau, he was far from being a consistent biocentrist. His central tenet in *Man and Nature* (1864) was that nature was and remained in balance until humans interfered in its processes. The diversity produced by geological and astronomical forces, operating gradually over long periods, led to stability and balance, which nature set about repairing where its stability was damaged. This understanding of nature, while out of favour currently, was widely held for at least a century (Lowenthal 2000 [1958]: 292).

But it was a related theme that made most impact, expressed more emphatically in his second book, *The Earth as Modified by Human Action* (1874), but already present in the subtitle of *Man and Nature*: *Physical Geography as Modified by Human Action*. It was, Marsh held, human disturbance of the equilibrium of nature that was producing unwelcome changes such as deforestation, loss of fertility, loss of watersheds (which regulated flows of water to the lowlands beneath them) and of topsoil, and the transformation of streams in winter into raging torrents. Thereby Marsh launched a reversal of American attitudes of optimism about the inexhaustible advance of industry and agriculture, towards a new awareness of the unintended impacts of human action on the natural world (Lowenthal 2000 [1958]: 303). Parallel remarks about the vulnerability of nature were later to be made by Friedrich Engels in *Dialectics of Nature* (1883; see Parsons, 1978).

While Marsh's work is seldom at the centre of attention in our own day – John Passmore's recognition of its significance (1974: 23–5) is an exception – it was, alongside Darwin's *Origin of Species*, one of the most influential texts of its time, particularly in the United States. (His relation with Darwin is discussed in the next section.) After a career as a lawyer, Marsh became a far-travelled diplomat, writing *Man and Nature* in his spare time. He wanted people to learn 'how we affect the environment, and restore and husband it as long as we tenant the earth' (Lowenthal 2000 [1958]: 267). While the problem of human impacts on nature had been noticed by Theophrastus (see Chapter 1), by Albert and by John Evelyn (Chapter 2), none of Marsh's predecessors had grasped its scale, centrality or moral significance.

Nash writes that, unlike Thoreau, Marsh did not challenge anthropocentrism (Nash 1989: 38), but this verdict calls for some qualification (as we shall shortly see). Certainly he did not object to belief in human dominion over nature, as long as it was 'careful and far-sighted' (Nash 1989: 38). But importantly, as he recognized, humanity had failed woefully in these regards. 'Man has forgotten', he wrote, 'that the earth was given to him for usufruct alone, not for consumption, still less for profligate waste' (Marsh 1965 [1864]: 45; Nash 1989: 38. 'For usufruct' means 'on a leasehold basis'). Here we find a clear expression of the stewardship tradition of Calvin and Hale (see Chapter 2), but one illuminated with an up-to-date grasp of natural history. 'The interrelatedness of "animal and vegetable life is too complicated a problem for human intelligence to solve, and we can never know how wide a circle of disturbance we produce in the harmonies of nature when we throw the smallest pebble into the ocean of organic life"' (Marsh 1965 [1864]: 46; Nash 1989: 38). For example, many of the lands around the Mediterranean have been degraded as a result of the destitution of the peasantry (Lowenthal 2000 [1958]: 283). The corrective proposed by Marsh was 'geographical regeneration', requiring 'great political and moral revolutions' (Marsh 1965 [1864]: 91–2; Nash 1989: 38).

The kind of regeneration favoured by Marsh was as much about initiating or sustaining the diversity to be found in a well-tilled garden as it was about sustaining the lesser diversity (in his view) of a primeval forest (Lowenthal 2000 [1958]: 299), although he also favoured (and was successful in fostering) the planting of forests. Here Marsh was effectively the heir of Basil the Great (see Chapter 1) and of John Ray (Chapter 2). Yet he also took delight in untamed nature, 'loving better' the venerable oak tree than the casks whose staves are cut from its wood (Lowenthal 2000 [1958]: 299). There again, he condemned cruelty towards 'subordinate species', and censured lack of sympathy for those 'humble creatures' whom people treat as lacking 'rights and interests of their own' (Lowenthal 2000 [1958]: 299–300), thus distancing himself from the stance of Calvin and moving closer to that of Thoreau. Earlier, he asserted (in language that echoes both St Francis and Thoreau):

> He whose sympathies with nature have taught him to feel that there is a fellowship between all God's creatures, he who has enjoyed that special training of the heart and intellect which can be acquired only in the unviolated sanctuaries of nature . . . will not rashly assert his right to extirpate a tribe of harmless vegetables, barely because their product neither tickle his palate nor fill his pocket. (Marsh 1965 [1864]: 248–9; Lowenthal 2000 [1958]: 300).

Thus Nash's charge (1989: 38) that Marsh did not challenge anthropocentrism proves to be inaccurate. In a note, Lowenthal goes so far as to claim that the passage just quoted 'foreshadows such reformers as Albert Schweitzer, Aldo Leopold and Arne Naess' (Lowenthal 2000: 507n.30). Marsh's distancing of himself from Calvin emerges further, when, in a letter of 1871, after disagreements and delays ascribable to his publishers, he asked, in jest: 'Did Calvin get his notions of total depravity from his dealings with his booksellers?' (Lowenthal 2000 [1958]: 302). Yet

Man and Nature proved to be a publishing success from the very outset, one reviewer designating Marsh as 'our American Evelyn' (Lowenthal 2000 [1958]).

Indeed, Marsh's second work, *The Earth as Modified by Human Action* (1874) led to a considerable reversal of American environmental attitudes. There followed a tree-planting craze and the establishment in 1876 of a national forestry commission. Franklin B. Hough, who became its first chief of forestry, had led a petition of the American Association for the Advancement of Science in 1873, in which he drew extensively on Marsh's work of 1864 (Lowenthal 2000 [1958]: 303).

Meanwhile in Europe, Marsh's work had already begun to exercise an influence. The leading British geologist, Charles Lyell, acknowledged that Marsh had disproved his own view that man's geological impact was no greater than that of animals (Lowenthal 2000 [1958]: 302). In France, Élisée Reclus (1830–1905) was much influenced by Marsh in the publication of *La Terre* (1868), a book that Marsh welcomed for treating 'the conservative and restorative, rather than ... the destructive effects of human industry' (1970 [1874]: viii). A translation of *Man and Nature* into French was begun soon after its publication, but was lost when the translator was killed in the Franco-Prussian War of 1870–1. It may not have been a coincidence that in Germany in 1866 the word 'Oekologie' was devised by the Darwinian, Ernst Haeckel. In Italy, *Man and Nature* was twice translated as *L'Uomo et la natura*, and published at Florence in 1869 and again in 1872. The Italian forest laws of 1877 and 1888 embody passages quoted from Marsh, favouring ecological restoration (Lowenthal 2000 [1958]: 304, 509nn.31–32; for Haeckel, see Nash 1989: 55).

Lowenthal further supplies evidence of Marsh's influence in India, and of its impact on legislation in New Zealand. His insights also influenced conservationists in Australia, South Africa and Japan (Lowenthal 2000 [1958]: 304–5, 509n.33). In view of its influence on the United States, Europe, Asia and Autralasia, *Man and Nature* came to be regarded (even by Marsh himself) as succeeding in its aims of bringing anthropogenic environmental problems to widespread attention and of initiating ways of confronting them.

Yet for decades, *Man and Nature* and revised editions thereof remained 'the only general work in the field' (Lowenthal 2000 [1958]: 305), at least in English. Lowenthal relates that the third edition of 1884 was last reprinted in 1907, 'on the eve of the White House Conference that led Theodore Roosevelt to create a national conservation commission under Gifford Pinchot' (2000 [1958]: 305) (For Pinchot, see the last section of this chapter). This was a further part of its legacy.

But Marsh's legacy lived on. Lewis Mumford, who became aware of

Marsh's work in the 1920s, led a scholarly reassessment of his 'role in changing the face of the earth' at a Marsh Festival in Princeton in 1955. Marsh's *The Earth as Modified by Human Action* was further updated (as *Earth Transformed*) at a Clark University symposium in 1987, which stressed the accelerated pace of anthropogenic change.

Marsh's boyhood home in Woodstock, Vermont was designated a National Historical Landmark in 1967, and in 1998 the Marsh-Billings National Historical Park was inaugurated there (Lowenthal 2000 [1958]: 309). His twin projects of conservation and regeneration have enjoyed fluctuating fortunes, but (despite partial oblivion in the first two decades of the twentieth century) have never been entirely forgotten.

Marsh and Darwin

Marsh and Darwin, authors of the most influential texts on the relations of nature and humanity, never met and never corresponded. Nor is there any evidence that Darwin either ever read *Man and Nature* or was aware of Marsh's environmental investigations, with one possible exception, shortly to be mentioned.

Yet Marsh's work, including *Man and Nature*, has plentiful references to Darwin, and Darwin's study of orchids of 1862 contributed to Marsh's recognition of mutual dependence among and between flora and fauna. Importantly, Marsh was persuaded of Darwin's main theory about the origin of species. But Marsh took the view that Darwin's work on earthworms and their role in aerating soils, while valuable, neglected their role in supplementing the fertility of the soil through their own decay. In Darwin's 1881 book on earthworms, he made good this omission, but without any acknowledgement of Marsh, and without the detail of Marsh's account of how worms and wormcasts enrich soils (Lowenthal 2000 [1958]: 307–80).

Marsh, however, rejected Darwin's account of the role of natural selection in cultural history, and in particular of the supposed evolution of languages (a field that lies outside the concerns of this book). Marsh's emphasis here was on voluntary selection as opposed to natural selection.

He also played up the role of voluntary selection in the form of the human breeding of domesticated plants and animals. He paid tribute to Darwin's work in this field (which he acknowledged Darwin to have 'virtually created'), but considered that Darwin's estimation of the pace and scope of human domestication of species as 'fleeting' hugely underestimated the difference made by selective breeding in comparison with natural selection. Thus, where Darwin emphasized the new species that had colonized Staffordshire heathland after the human introduction of

Scotch fir, Marsh suggested that the seeds of these species had been deposited when this heathland had long before been an ancient forest. Where Darwin played down possibilities such as the creation of heaths through Neolithic deforestation, Marsh traced longstanding human agency as a key element in the story (Lowenthal 2000 [1958]: 308). Similar recent findings about the human role in shaping the Amazon rainforest have lent some degree of support for Marsh in this debate.

Lowenthal traces the differences of emphasis of Darwin and of Marsh to their different philosophical and religious stances. 'Darwin's agnosticism made it congenial for him to stress human affinities with other living beings; Marsh's Christian faith spurred him to stress their differences. While no biblical fundamentalist, Marsh felt more at home viewing man as an angel, however fallen, than an ape, however risen' (Lowenthal 2000 [1958]: 308). Certainly, Darwin at one point alleged 'no fundamental difference between man and the higher animals in their mental faculties' (1871: 70). Yet, as we have seen in Chapter 3, Darwin asserted later in the same work:

> These several inventions, by which man in his rudest state has become so pre-eminent, are the direct results of the development of his powers of observation, memory, curiosity, imagination and reason. I cannot, therefore, understand how it is that Mr. Wallace maintains that 'natural selection could only have endowed the savage with a brain a little superior to that of an ape'. (1871: 432; Rajan 2017: 77)

Thus the passage selected by Lowenthal about Darwin recognizing affinities with other species hardly supports his point about Darwin emphasizing such similarities, even in the matter of mental and moral traits. The two passages could no doubt be reconciled (for example, by ascribing to Darwin the view that humanity shared the faculties that he lists with other relevant species, but that in the case of humanity they have been developed in an unparalleled manner). We also need to remember that Darwin needed to counter the widespread view that there was little or nothing in common between humanity and other species. Yet if we consider the passage just quoted, the distance between Darwin and Marsh that Lowenthal ascribes to their different religious outlooks turns out to be much slighter than he suggests. Indeed, Marsh's stress on the far-reaching impacts of human agency could in principle have been shared by Darwin if he had not adhered to different factual assumptions about, for example, the geographical spread and impact of human agency in the period following the Ice Age.

It was, however, to Marsh's credit that he challenged these assumptions. More importantly, he was able, because of his stress on human agency (deriving ultimately from his transcendentalism), to grasp the extent of the human impact of his own day on the planet. Darwin's findings strengthened his case, but it was Marsh, rather than Darwin, who brought to attention the vastness of the human ecological impacts of an age of industrial and agricultural expansion, and at once the possibility and the need to counter them.

John Muir, Yosemite and Preservation

Discovering transcendentalism removed the doubts of John Muir concerning possible conflict between religion and the study of the natural world (Nash 2014 [1967]: 124). Muir had been brought up in Scotland in a form of Calvinism that virtually precluded any linkage between Christianity and nature. His family emigrated to America when he was eleven, to a farm in Wisconsin. Leaving his father's farm, his skills as an inventor took him to Madison, and at the University of Wisconsin he encountered geologists, botanists and theologians, who began to disabuse him of his father's attitudes towards nature and religion. He turned to the writings of Asa Gray for a contemporary expression of the argument from design and the compatibility of design with Darwinism. He also discovered the writings of Wordsworth, and of Emerson and Thoreau, and thus the transcendentalism that resolved his remaining doubts.

In 1866 he was able to write to his mentor, Mrs Jeanne C. Carr, that the Bible and nature were 'two books which harmonize beautifully', continuing: 'I will confess that I take more intense delight from reading the power and goodness of God from "the things which are made" than from the Bible' (Nash 2014 [1967]: 124). 'The things which are made' is an allusion to Paul's epistle to the Romans 1:20; Muir found in this biblical passage an authorization to study and delight in God's other book, that of nature. Relatedly, Mark Stoll has shown how Presbyterian upbringings were associated with subsequent environmentalist commitment in many American environmental campaigners, Muir included, and how the Reformed theme of God's presence in nature may have contributed to such commitment (2015: 8–21).

The belief that God has presented humanity with two books, one of which is the book of nature, has been encountered already in different characters from Bacon to Byron (see Chapter 2). Bacon used this theme to justify the inauguration of natural philosophy (science), while at the same time arguing that there was no sacrilege in investigating nature, any more than in studying the Bible. Much later, Byron's *Childe Harold* seems to have found more illumination from the book of nature than from that of scripture. Muir, however, used this trope of over two hundred years to convey the ecstasy that nature gave him, and how it formed more of a revelation than the Christian scriptures, even though he had earlier learned a large part of the latter by heart.

However, a key revelation had taken place two years earlier, in 1864. To avoid being drafted into President Abraham Lincoln's army to defend the Union, Muir left Wisconsin and fled to the Canadian wilderness north of Lake Huron. There he found a cluster of rare white orchids, miles from human habitation. Beside them he sat down and wept for joy. Later he reflected that his response arose from the realization that the orchids had not the slightest relevance to human beings. From this he concluded that nature must exist primarily for itself and for its creator, and had value as such, independently of human interests (Nash 1989: 38–9). This is the stance that others have called 'biocentrism' (see Chapter 2).

The basis of respect for nature, Muir held, was recognition of it as part of the community of life created by God. Both animals and plants, and rocks as well, were 'sparks of the divine soul'. So he sought to counter the disparagement of nonhuman creatures on the part of conventional Christianity, and in a diary entry of 1867 affirmed the rights of fellow-members of the community of creation. Nash regards this passage as the first use of the language of rights in an environmental context (1989: 39–40). Others had written of the rights of individual animals, including the American Henry Bergh (see later in this chapter), as well as many Europeans. For Muir, however, respect was due to all creatures partly because they were all linked. As he later wrote: 'When we try to pick out anything by itself, we find it hitched to everything else in the universe' (Nash 1989: 40).

It is worth mentioning that, at least in this period, the humanitarian tradition (see Chapter 2) and the new environmentalist tradition were profoundly intermingled. The language of rights was characteristic of the former, but in Muir's writings spilled over into writings that were increasingly focused on preservationism. Some twentieth-century environmental ethicists, such as J. Baird Callicott (1980), have set these two movements in opposition to each other, and there have certainly been differences of emphasis between them. But at least in Muir's day, the two movements needed to work in tandem, rejecting (with Muir) the view that rattlesnakes were valueless because they did not serve human purposes, and that alligators were vermin, rather than 'filling the place assigned to them by the great Creator of us all' and 'beautiful in the eyes of God'. 'The rights of animals' was a favourite phrase of Muir (Nash 1989: 40).

An accident early in 1867, in which Muir temporarily lost his sight, made him determined to lose no more time in search of wilderness. Thus began his walk of a thousand miles from Indiana to the Gulf of Mexico (Muir 1992 [1916]: 113–83). Muir's book *A Thousand Mile Walk to the Gulf* (published posthumously) pours scorn on the view that the Earth was made for our own species alone, rather than for the creatures that preceded us, or for contemporary creatures, or for their successors; and goes as far as to ascribe sensation to rocks (1992 [1916]: 160–1). The same book describes how, after a stay in Cuba, he reached California 'by a crooked route', and thus the Sierra Nevada (1992 [1916]: 175–83).

Thus began Muir's lifelong association with the mountains of the High Sierra of California, which he traversed with a copy of Emerson's *Nature* in his backpack. Through his essays he became famous among his contemporaries, much more so than Thoreau, and was celebrated for championing wilderness and its preservation, not least because of its spiritual benefits. In 1871 he was briefly joined in a visit to the Sierra by the elderly Emerson, but was disappointed that Emerson's companions insisted in his staying at a hotel, rather than camping with Muir. Later, Emerson invited him to forsake the mountains and become a professor at Harvard, but Muir declined the invitation (Nash 2014 [1967]: 126)

At this point, we need to turn our attention to events elsewhere in the United States. For in 1872, partly as a result of the ideas of Thoreau, Marsh and others, President Ulysses S. Grant designated more than two million acres of north-western Wyoming as Yellowstone National Park (a clear case of ideas exercising an influence on the course of history). Yet the advocates of this turning point were not concerned with preserving wilderness, or its spiritual or aesthetic qualities. They were concerned instead to prevent the geysers, hot springs and waterfalls of the area becoming privately acquired and exploited. Then, in 1885, the State of New York declared a 'Forest Reserve' of 715,000 acres in the Adirondacks. This time, the motives of the legislators turned on the need to preserve forested land for the sake of an adequate and reliable water supply. So in both places, the preservation of wilderness took place unintentionally, and almost by accident (Nash 2014 [1967]).

Nevertheless, in 1883 the defenders of Yellowstone in Congress resisted later proposals to sell it off on the grounds that this 'mountain wilderness' was 'aesthetically important in counteracting America's materialistic tendency', following here the stance of the French and English Romantics. It was also argued that the exploding population of the United States needed 'a great breathing place for the national lungs' (Nash 2014 [1967]: 113–14). And more explicitly transcendentalist arguments were employed in the mid-1880s to prevent a railroad from securing a right of way across park lands. The application was defeated by 107 to 65, an emphatic vindication of wilderness values (Nash 2014 [1967]: 114–15).

To return now to Muir; his writings during this period nourished the growing awareness of the spiritual benefits of wildness. Americans were to be immersed 'in the beauty of God's mountains' (Nash 2014 [1967]: 129). He also supported the conservation movement, initially in alliance with advocates of the planned use of natural resources, but eventually coming down in favour of a preservationist interpretation of conservation. At this stage, he came under the influence of the economist Henry George (1839–97) concerning the evils of the private ownership of land, and in 1876 wrote an article in the Sacramento *Record-Union* titled 'God's First Temples: How Shall We Preserve Our Forests', suggesting that governmental control of the forests was the solution (Nash 2014 [1967]: 130). In this period, Muir also became aware of the adverse effects of sheep on mountain wilderness, despite his earlier sympathy for these animals, expressed in his chapter 'Through the foothills with a flock of sheep' (1992 [1916]: 191–201). By now, they were 'hoofed locusts', and Muir wrote that 'As sheep advance, flowers, vegetation, grass, soil, plenty, and poetry vanish' (Nash 2014 [1967]: 130).

Then, in 1889, Robert Underwood Johnson, associate editor of the leading monthly *Century*, joined Muir in a wilderness trip above the Yosemite Valley. When Muir told Johnson about the impacts of overgrazing on the formerly luxuriant meadows of that region, Johnson suggested the declaration of a national park around the Yosemite Valley, on the model of Yellowstone, to which Muir agreed, consenting to write two articles in *Century* to publicize this plan (Nash 2014 [1967]: 130–1). These articles appeared in 1890, receiving a larger readership than any previous preservationist writings. Muir made it clear that the objective was the protection of wilderness, describing the nobility of the Yosemite Valley and surrounding mountains. He adduced some of the arguments of Marsh about preserving soil and forests as watershed cover, but made it clear in his final sentence that his central concern was to prevent 'the destruction of the fineness of wilderness' (Nash 2014 [1967]: 131).

Meanwhile, Johnson lobbied in Washington for a Yosemite national park, based on Muir's proposal to designate 1,500 square miles of the Sierra. In September 1890, a bill along these lines passed both houses of Congress, and the next day President Benjamin Harrison signed it into law (Nash 2014 [1967]: 131–2).

The next year, Muir welcomed Johnson's idea for a Yosemite and Yellowstone defence association, and when professors at the University of California at Berkeley and Stanford proposed an alpine club, he rapidly noticed the connection, and took the lead in planning for such an organization. Thus, in June 1892 in San Francisco, the Sierra Club was formed, dedicated to 'exploring, enjoying and rendering accessible the mountain regions of the Pacific Coast' (Nash 2014 [1967]: 132). Their aim was, in Muir's words, to 'do something for wildness, and to make the mountains glad' (Sierra Club, n.d.). Muir was unanimously appointed president, and occupied that office for the remaining 22 years of his life.

Muir, Gifford Pinchot and Forests

By now, Muir was advocating preservation for the sake of people, on the basis of their need for aesthetic satisfaction, rest and recuperation. Nash suggests that such arguments were necessary once Muir had turned to politics, for the only way to persuade Americans to preserve wilderness was to emphasize its use to them. Thus he 'tempered his biocentricity ... under the cover of anthropocentrism' (Nash 1989: 41). But his basic beliefs remained unchanged.

In 1891, Muir's and Johnson's plea for a national park around King's Canyon, California, led Harrison's Secretary of the Interior, John W. Noble, to draft a Forest Reserve Act, with a view to the region around King's Canyon becoming a forest reserve, which was comprehensively successful. However, the function of forest reserves was not specified. Muir took it to be the protection of undeveloped forests. But a cluster of officials in the federal Division of Forestry, led by the Yale graduate Gifford Pinchot, saw matters otherwise. Pinchot had undergone graduate training in Europe, where forests were managed on the principle of maximum sustainable yield. This policy allowed both harvests of timber in the present and the ongoing sustainability of forests into the indefinite future – as Mary Williams (1978) has more recently argued. Initially, even Muir agreed, writing in *Century* in 1895 that preservation was not enough, and that the nation needed timber as well as the spiritual benefits of enduring forests.

But in 1896 an advisory commission, led by Charles Sargent and including Pinchot in its membership and assisted by Muir, toured the western woodlands. Initially, Muir and Pinchot became close friends, both enjoying the outdoor life. While Sargent and Muir hoped to persuade the government to reserve more forests for permanent protection, Pinchot and others favoured all reserves becoming subject to scientifically managed development. It thus emerged that while Muir's priorities were wilderness and preservation, those of Pinchot were forestry and society (Nash 2014 [1967]: 135–6).

At one stage in early 1897, President Grover Cleveland sided with

Sargent and Muir, and approved more than 21,000,000 acres of forest reserves, with no mention of human use. (Nash here says 'with no mention of utilitarian objectives' (2014 [1967]: 134), but he recurrently misuses 'utilitarian' to mean 'instrumental', which gives him problems whenever he has to represent the stance of opposition to animal suffering held by utilitarian sentientists such as Bentham and John Stuart Mill.) However, this decision was rapidly challenged, and Sargent recommended Muir to write for *Atlantic Monthly* in defence of forest reserves. In the first of two articles, besides arguing that clearing had gone far enough, he actually went along with the concept of sustained yield, and the maximum harvesting of timber consistent with sustainability, even though this stance was incompatible with the wilderness ideal. Meanwhile in mid-1897 Congress passed the Forest Management Act, which made it clear that the reserves would be used for continuous harvesting and grazing (Nash 2014 [1967]: 136–7), and conveyed that they would nowhere remain wilderness.

This led to an arranged meeting between Muir and Pinchot at Seattle, after Pinchot had written in support of grazing in forest reserves, despite having agreed the previous year that sheep caused great damage. When Pinchot refused to back down, Muir declared that he would have nothing more to do with him. Muir then wrote a second article for *Atlantic Monthly*, published early in 1898, with a celebration of wilderness, no mention of the 'wise use' of forests, and a rejection of the Pinchot approach (Nash 2014 [1967]: 137–8). From this stage onwards, Muir lost hope for the forest reserves and focused on protecting the National Parks – see for example, *Our National Parks* (1901) and *The Yosemite* (1912) (Muir 1992 [1916]: 453–605, 607–716). In 1903, President Theodore Roosevelt, who had sought out Muir's companionship, joined him beside a camp fire, and, despite a four-inch snowfall, and being persuaded by Muir to give up hunting, Roosevelt declared it 'the grandest day of my life'. Not much later, Muir's campaign to include the Yosemite Valley in the adjacent National Park was successful, and in 1906 Roosevelt designated the Grand Canyon as a national memorial.

Muir, Pinchot and the Hetch Hetchy Valley

Most of Muir's remaining energy went towards resisting the damming of the Hetch Hetchy Valley, part of the Yosemite National Park, for a water supply for San Francisco. The San Francisco authorities had formed the idea of deriving water for their dry city from the Hetch Hetchy Valley as early as 1882, but in 1890 it was designated as part of the Yosemite National Park. Nevertheless, the mayor applied for permission for the valley to be used as a reservoir site soon after 1900, but this application was rejected by the Secretary of the Interior who stated that the sanctity of a national park would be violated. However, after San Francisco was devastated by an earthquake and a fire in 1908, a new application was immediately put forward, which was approved by the Secretary of the Interior, James R. Garfield (Nash 2014 [1967]: 161–2).

This led to a national debate that lasted for five years. President Theodore Roosevelt was a close friend of Muir, but regarded forests as primarily resources, and only secondly as refuges for wild creatures. Also, Gifford Pinchot had been (since 1905) Chief Forester, the champion of scientific forestry and of the use of Hetch Hetchy as a reservoir. Besides, he too was a close friend of Roosevelt, who declared that 'in all forestry matters I have put my conscience in the keeping of Gifford Pinchot' (Nash 2014 [1967]: 163). Nevertheless, Muir wrote to Roosevelt, reminding him of their joint trip of 1903 into the Sierra, suggesting that a water supply could be had from elsewhere and claiming majority support for refusing the San Francisco plan (Nash 2014 [1967]: 163). For the present, Roosevelt held firm; but although he was supported later in 1907 by a letter from Pinchot, he also asserted that he was uncomfortable about the decision (Nash 2014 [1967]: 163–4).

Muir struck back with an article in *Outlook*, stressing the aesthetic grounds for preservation. Robert Johnson also wrote an article, protesting on behalf of lovers of beauty against the materialistic pursuit of profit. Their protest was further joined by the president of the American Civic Association, J. Horace McFarland, who argued in the presence of the Secretary of the Interior that undeveloped places would become increasingly valuable for recreation as Americans increasingly lived in cities, and that national parks were needed for the sake of their health. Likewise, Lyman Abbott, the editor of *Outlook*, used this journal in defence of wilderness and against an emphasis on business values (Nash 2014 [1967]: 164–6).

The cause of preservation was further supported on religious grounds. In 1912, Muir published his popular book *The Yosemite*, in which he called his opponents 'temple destroyers'. 'Dam Hetch Hetchy!', he concluded. 'As well dam for water tanks the people's cathedrals and churches, for no holier temple has ever been consecrated by the heart of man' (1912: 261–2; see also Muir 1992 [1916]: 716). And by now, Theodore Roosevelt had retracted his earlier support for using the valley as a dam, maintaining that Yellowstone and Yosemite should be preserved, their creatures protected and their scenery left unspoilt (Nash 2014 [1967]: 167–8).

The Committee on Public Lands now approved the dam proposal, but a strong minority report supported the protestors, whom it listed as 'scientists, naturalists, mountain climbers, travellers and others'. In consequence, the House of Representatives shelved the proposal, until the administration of Woodrow Wilson came to power in 1913.

San Francisco responded by claiming that human needs and human life itself were at stake, winning some degree of support even within the Sierra Club. They also argued that a reservoir would not spoil the valley's scenic beauty. Thus in 1913 the issue returned to the Committee on Public Lands. Gifford Pinchot, as a leading witness, admitted that the idea of preserving a wilderness was appealing if nothing else were at stake, but held that the policy of using resources for human benefit indicated that meeting the needs of San Francisco was imperative. The argument about loss of beauty spots from a preservationist was countered by a former mayor of San Francisco, who undertook that the city would construct picnic places and trails around the reservoir. So the Committee submitted a report unanimously approving the proposal. This unanimity included the support of Congressman William Kent, whom Muir had assumed to be a supporter of preservation (as on past occasions). But Kent actually helped draft the bill authorizing the building of the reservoir, and telegraphed his support of it to Pinchot (Nash 2014 [1967]: 169–74).

The final debate in the House was hard-fought, but the Hetch Hetchy bill was overwhelmingly approved. Before the Senate could debate the matter, hundreds of newspapers published editorials, mostly favouring preservation. Similarly, Johnson returned to the fray, holding that the issue was one of 'worship and sacrilege', and that San Francisco could have its water supply from elsewhere. But San Francisco had lobbied well, and the proposal was convincingly carried. Johnson then urged the new president to defend the park, but in December 1913, Wilson signed the bill into law, declaring that the fears and objections of the bill's opponents were not well founded (Nash 2014 [1967]: 175–80).

John Muir was deeply disappointed, but took comfort from the fact that 'the conscience of the whole country has been aroused from sleep'. The controversy had amassed considerable support for the National Parks, and this resulted in legislation in their support, the National Park Service Act of 1916 (Nash 2014 [1967]: 180). As Nash remarks, 'One hundred or even fifty years earlier a similar proposal to dam a wilderness river would not have occasioned the slightest ripple of public protest' (2014 [1967]: 181). But Muir, Johnson and, arguably, Marsh before them had by the early twentieth century generated what amounted to nothing less than a national wilderness cult.

Thurman Wilkins rightly claims that Muir's aim was to challenge humanity's 'enormous conceit', and adds that in so doing he moved beyond transcendentalism to a 'biocentric perspective on the world', by describing the natural world as a 'conductor of divinity' (1995, 265). Granted that he did describe it thus, there is room to doubt that in so doing he moved beyond transcendentalism. Thoreau, after all, was both a transcendentalist and a biocentrist; these two stances are therefore compatible. Yet Muir's understanding of himself as 'John the Baptist', and the panpsychism that he showed in detecting sentience even in rocks, suggests that his sense of the revelation of divinity in nature and particularly in the mountains of the Sierra marks him out as unusually prophetic even among transcendentalists. It is as if, despite the Calvinism of his upbringing, he were rediscovering the panentheism of Luther unawares.

American Humanitarians

A distinctive strand in the history of American attitudes to nature is to be found in American humanitarianism. We have traced humanitarianism in Europe (with its concern to prevent cruelty to slaves, factory-workers, children and nonhuman animals) in Chapter 2 up to the foundation of the Royal Society for the Prevention of Cruelty to Animals (RSPCA) in Britain in 1824, and this sets the scene for the founding of its American counterpart.

Now, in 1865, Henry Bergh (1813–88) visited London following his retirement as secretary of the United States legation to Russia, and there conferred with leaders of the RSPCA, with a view to organizing an equivalent American Society. The RSPCA of this period was an upper-class organization, which disregarded behaviour such as fox-hunting among its own members; this was the basis on which John Stuart Mill, the utilitarian philosopher who hated cruelty to slaves, children and animals, declined an offer to become its vice-president. Its initial successes, as Nash remarks, support Mill's analysis – for example, its securing the banning of such lower-class pastimes as bear- and bull-baiting (1835) and cock-fighting (1849). Nevertheless, in 1876, the RSPCA secured the wider-ranging Cruelty to Animals Act, which restricted vivisection to licensed medical centres using anaesthetics (Nash 1989: 26). It was this broader conception of animal welfarism that Bergh set out to emulate in America.

Like Mill, Bergh took the view that, with the abolition of slavery, the next ethical goal was to terminate the abuse of animals, or, in his own terms, to affirm animal rights. Bergh began his struggle with several public meetings in New York. His arguments included John Locke's view that cruelty to animals was liable to spill over into cruelty to humans, and to the brutalization of those who participated or stood by; but he also believed that animals have rights, whether their treatment affects human beings or not. Thus in April 1866 he secured a charter for the American Society for the Prevention of Cruelty to Animals, including a Declaration of the Rights of Animals. Shortly afterwards, he pushed a law through the New York legislature that forbade cruelty to all animals, wild as well as tame (McCrea 1910: 33–4). Domestic draft animals were in practice the main beneficiaries; wild animals, including the victims of the ongoing fur trade, were little affected.

Then in 1868, following a horse race in which two horses, each carrying two men, were ridden to death, George T. Angell formed the Massachusetts Society for the Prevention of Cruelty to Animals, which pressed for humane legislation in matters of the care, transport and slaughter of animals. And in 1882 he founded the first American Band of Mercy for schoolchildren, which taught 'kindness, justice and mercy to every living creature'.

Other adherents of the new humanitarian movement included Harriet Beecher Stowe, the author of *Uncle Tom's Cabin*. Stowe wrote to Bergh in 1877 about her distress at the treatment of Florida's animals and birds, calling the cages in which the birds were transported 'veritable slave ships' (Nash 1989: 47). Later, Congressman John F. Lacey gave his name to legislation designed to prevent shipments of plumage from Florida to New England: the Lacey Act of 1900 made the transport across state boundaries of illegally killed wildlife a federal offence (Nash 1989: 49). In addition, Harriet's brother, Henry Ward Beecher, a minister, publicized ASPCA from 1873, describing the 'humane mission' as advancement of 'the rights of animals'. Adopting a broader view than Bergh, he exhorted his congregation to teach children not to abhor insects, worms and 'harmless reptiles' (Nash 1989: 47).

While these humanitarians lacked a concern for ecosystems, they took seriously the human kinship with animals implicit in Darwin's work, and stressed the feelings of sentient animals in ways that even biocentrists such as Thoreau and Muir did not. In these ways, they broke new ground in the formation of American attitudes to nature, and contributed to worldwide awareness of the sufferings of creatures both domestic and wild.

Henry Salt Rediscovers Thoreau

The influence of Henry George on Muir has already been mentioned. George's book *Progress and Poverty* (1879), which challenged traditional attitudes to land ownership, also attracted the English advocate of animal rights, Henry Salt. Salt explicitly acknowledged the connection between the abolition of slavery and improved treatment for animals, writing in *Cruelties of Civilization* (1897) 'The emancipation of men from cruelty and injustice will bring with it in due course the emancipation of animals also. The two reforms are inseparably connected, and neither can be fully realized alone' (Nash 1989: 29). He also believed that the spread of democracy would advance both these causes. His admiration for Thoreau, of whom he wrote a biography in 1890, was based as much on Thoreau's advocacy of the release of humanity from economic and political oppression as on his role as a naturalist. Salt took the view that capitalism victimizes both nature and people.

Salt played a large part in generating Thoreau's modern reputation. Although Thoreau's work was known to Marsh and Muir, he did not become an environmental hero in America until well into the twentieth century, largely as a result of his popularization by Salt of the first complete edition of his unpublished work in 1906, and of another biography by the American environmentalist Joseph Wood Krutch in 1948 (Nash 1989: 38, 74–5). Salt sought to foster Thoreau's belief in including fellow-creatures in our ethical system, expressing his own ideas in *Animals' Rights* (1894 [1892]), which went through several editions, and became well known in the United States. While this could not have been achieved without his humanitarian predecessors, Salt in these ways played a part himself in the development of American attitudes to nature.

It should be added that it was only because of Salt that Thoreau joined the galaxy of American environmental pioneers. Emerson, Marsh and Muir were already well known and influential, but Thoreau's influence was confined to just a few readers such as Marsh and Muir. But with Salt, the American transcendentalist quartet of Emerson, Thoreau, Marsh and Muir became complete, and subsequently Thoreau's influence spread gradually to the rest of the world.

This chapter has surveyed several related American debates, involving Marsh (including debates about forestry and about Darwinism) and Muir (and his debates with Pinchot and others about forests and about preservation), and also involving Bergh and the other campaigning founders of American humanitarianism. In the next chapter we consider the origins and development of ecological science, both in Europe and in America. While some 'proto-ecologists', such as Linnaeus and von Humboldt have been discussed already, the discoveries of Darwin made it possible for natural history to be studied more scientifically, and for the ecological implications opened up by Darwinism to become a new focus of study.

Recommended reading

Emerson, Ralph Waldo (1990 [1836]). *Nature*, in Richard Poirier ed., *Ralph Waldo Emerson* (The Oxford Authors). Oxford: Oxford University Press.

Goodman, Russell (2018). 'Transcendentalism', in *The Stanford Encyclopedia of Philosophy*, ed. Edward N. Zalta. https://plato.stanford.edu/archives/fall2018/entries/transcendentalism/.

Lowenthal, David (2000 [1958]). *George Perkins Marsh*. Seattle: University of Washington Press.

Marsh, George Perkins (1965 [1864]). *Man and Nature: Physical Geography as Modified by Human Action*, 1st edn, ed. David Lowenthal. Cambridge, MA: Harvard University Press.

Marsh, George Perkins (1970 [1874]). *The Earth as Modified by Human Action, A New Edition of Man and Nature*. St. Clair Shores, MI: Scholarly Press.

Muir, John (1992). *The Eight Wilderness Discovery Books*. London: Diadem Books / Seattle: The Mountaineers.

Nash, Roderick Frazier (2014 [1967]). *Wilderness and the American Mind*, 5th edn. New Haven, CT: Yale University Press.

Nash, Roderick Frazier (1989). *The Rights of Nature: A History of Environmental Ethics*. Madison: University of Wisconsin Press.

Salt, Henry (1890). *The Life of Henry David Thoreau*. London: R. Bentley.

Sierra Club (n.d.). *John Muir: A Brief Biography*. https://vault.sierraclub.org/john_muir_exhibit/life/muir_biography.aspx.

Stoll, Mark (2015). *Inherit the Holy Mountain: Religion and the Rise of American Environmentalism*. Oxford: Oxford University Press.

Thompson, Ian (2014). *Landscape Architecture: A Very Short Introduction*. Oxford: Oxford University Press.

Thoreau, Henry David (1989 [1854]). *Walden*. Princeton, NJ: Princeton University Press.

Wilkins, Thurman (1995). *John Muir: Apostle of Nature*. Norman, OK: University of Oklahoma Press.

5

Foundations of the Science of Ecology

The Field that Haeckel Named

As we saw in Chapter 4, the Darwinian Ernst Haeckel invented the term 'Oekologie' in 1866. Shortly afterwards, he defined it as 'the study of all those complex interactions referred to by Darwin as the conditions of the struggle for existence'. Prior to Haeckel's time, this subject had been pursued by the Swedish scholar Carolus Linnaeus (1707–78), in his studies of the interactions of animals and plants (which he called 'the economy of nature'), and by the German biogeographer Alexander von Humboldt, in his studies of the distribution of plant communities, particularly in South America. Shortly before Haeckel gave ecology its name, Alfred Russel Wallace, as we have seen in Chapter 3, discovered in 1859 the discontinuity between the fauna of Borneo, Bali and Asia and those of Celebes, Lombok and Australasia. Another contributor of the nineteenth century was Edward Forbes (1815–54), a British marine biologist who studied marine communities, and who introduced quantitative methods into this area of study, thus initiating the process by which natural history transformed itself into a recognizably scientific subject (1991 [1887]). Long before this, the relation of climate to human communities had been studied by Hippocrates (see Chapter 1). But the discipline was not fully recognized as a distinctive science until the British geologist Charles Elton (1900–91) defined it in the twentieth century as 'scientific natural history'.

This chapter studies the origins, development and influence of ecology.

While modern self-styled 'ecologists' (or 'environmentalists') often claim to hold a certain kind of worldview, one reason why they are taken seriously lies in the existence of a body of scientific study that also goes by the name of 'ecology', and which influenced some of the pioneers of preservationism, such as Aldo Leopold and Rachel Carson, who were both also participants in the study of ecological science. Leopold and Carson are the main focus of the next chapter; the origins, development and influence of mainstream scientific ecology from August Grisebach to Eugene Odum and J. P. Grime are studied in this one.

Pioneers, from Grisebach to Warming

While Darwin was still pondering his Galapagos findings, August Grisebach (1814–79), a follower of von Humboldt, working at Göttingen, was investigating why a physical environment produces a forest rather than grassland. In 1838 he gave the name 'formation' to assemblages of plants generated by similar climates, such as the rain forests of Africa, South America and the Indonesian archipelago. Grisebach took the view that categorizing these major types of plant communities and discovering the laws they obey should supersede the study of identifying species and explaining their distribution. In his view, climate was one of the most important determinants of life-forms and of plant communities (Worster 1985 [1977]: 194–5). As we have seen, Darwin disregarded this factor, but later came to recognize that he may have underplayed it (Chapter 3). In the period following Grisebach's investigations, the climate factor became foregrounded again, as it had been for von Humboldt, associated initially with global temperature belts, but eventually contextualized to take account of other climatic elements and soil conditions.

The most influential proposal for biogeography of this kind was put forward by C. Hart Merriam (1855–1942), who was chief of the federal Division of Economic Ornithology and Mammalogy and later of the Bureau of the Biological Survey. His work was conducted independently of continental geographers, but it shows the continuing influence of von Humboldt. In the late 1880s, Merriam ventured into the Painted Desert of northern Arizona, and found that as one ascends from the basin where this desert lies and climbs San Francisco Mountain, the air rapidly becomes much colder and more humid. Extrapolating from this discovery, he produced a classification of seven 'Life Zones', which he applied to North America as a whole, differentiated according to their place on the spectrum of temperature, as experienced by climbing a mountain or travelling towards the North Pole (Hunter 2018).

This classification was widely taught to the public, but scientists came to regard it as too simplistic, some contending that Merriam's belief in abrupt spatial succession only works for the American south-west. It does not work, they objected, for the American grasslands, where transitions are much more gradual, and operate not so much from south to north as from east to west (Worster 1985 [1977]: 196–7; Hughes 1994).

Back in Europe, the most important of the plant geographers to secure recognition for ecology as a scientific discipline was the Danish scholar, Eugenius Warming (1841–1924). His main work, *Plantesamfund*, was published in 1895 and translated into English in 1909 under the title *Oecology of Plants: An Introduction to the Study of Plant Communities*. Warming had earlier studied the plant communities of Greenland, but later applied his theories to countries such as Venezuela. He devised the term 'epharmosis' for the structural and physiological adjustments that plants make to adapt to their various habitats. Sometimes the adjustments are independent of species, as when the American cactus and the South African euphorbia respond alike to arid environments by developing fleshy, succulent stems, and spines in place of leaves, as ways of conserving moisture (Warming 1909 [1895]: 5, 360–70, 373).

However, his main emphasis was on the communal life of organisms, and the many relations between the plants and animals that form a single community. So interdependent are these different life-forms that change at one point may bring significant changes at other points (Warming 1909 [1895]: 83, 91, 94, 140, 366). The most common form of interdependence is 'commensality', where several species 'sit down at one table' and take what the others do not want, as when a tree provides nesting sites for birds and squirrels and shade for flowering plants at its base (Worster 1985 [1977]: 199; *Encyclopaedia Britannica* 1998b). Other forms of interdependence can take the form of mutualistic symbiosis, as in lichens, where an alga and a fungus cooperate, and also parasitic symbiosis, as when cuckoos lay eggs in the nests of reed warblers, and the young cuckoos then evict the young warblers and dominate the energies of the parent birds. Warming's work on interdependence showed that, as Darwin would have recognized, nature does not operate as a struggle of all against all, since alongside the pursuit of self-interest there is also much cooperation.

This was also a theme of the anarchist and biologist Petr Kropotkin, whose *Mutual Aid: A Factor of Evolution* was published in 1902. Slightly earlier, in 1899, Kropotkin published his proposal for a countryside with agriculture and industry based on cooperatives, *Fields, Factories and Workshops*, which (as Pepper remarks) anticipated *A Blueprint for Survival* (*Ecologist* 1972) in numerous particulars (Kropotkin 1991

[1899]). Whether Warming knew the work of Kropotkin or arrived at his theme of interdependence independently is unclear.

Warming also introduced a new system of classification (which contrasted with that of Merriam) based on the need of plants for water. Plants needing plenty of water were called 'hydrophytes', those able to grow in dry areas 'xerophytes' and those living in habitats of moderate rainfall 'mesophytes'. Other classifications related to plants' toleration of salinity. Once again, plants of different species were found to display convergent patters of root structures, transpiration and water storage (Worster 1985 [1977]: 200–1).

Additionally, Warming also described processes of the dynamics or succession from one kind of community to another in a given habitat, and this theme proved to be his most influential. On the one hand, he was clear that community formations may abruptly disintegrate, whether through external pressures or the action of humans or of animals such as beavers. On the other hand, he held that in every habitat the process of succession moves in a definite direction, involving maximal diversity, stability and balance. In retrospect, Grisebach and Merriam could be understood as describing the end-states of millions of years of successional development towards a climax equilibrium. With this (apparently secure) theory of climax formations, ecology entered into its mature period, and attained increasing recognition as the science of the development of communities. And at the same stage, the epoch of the amateur naturalist began to decline (Worster 1985 [1977]: 201–4).

Towards the end of Warming's life, in 1920, the journal *Ecology* was founded in America by Barrington Moore, who became its first editor, and was also president of the Ecological Society of America at the time. For Moore, ecology was 'a point of view' or integrating outlook, whose participants sought to bring together the various specialisms into which natural history was becoming divided (Worster 1985 [1977]: 203). The new journal succeeded *Plant World*, and many of its readers will have had a scientific orientation, as well as a systems-based outlook. Many will also have sympathized with Warming's forceful approach, carried forward in the dynamic ecology depicted in the coming section.

Dynamic Ecology: Cowles and Clements

Many of the new ecologists went out into the field, and generated new findings. These included Henry Chandler Cowles (1869–1939), who undertook graduate studies at the University of Chicago (Hagen 2019: 1–3). Cowles is best known for his studies of the sand dunes on the southern shore of Lake Michigan. As well as chronological succession, he discovered that succession can be spatial, as dunes develop and become more stable the further inland they are (Nash 1989: 56; Worster 1985 [1977]: 207). Closest to the lake was a limited number of hydrophytic (water-tolerant) plants, buffeted by the lake's waters. Further inland were rolling dunes, many of them unstable, but others anchored by xerophytic plants. Finally, further back still, there were oak woods, a mesophytic community that formed the climax vegetation of that district. Cowles published this research in two journal papers of 1899, including 'The Ecological Relations of the Vegetation on the Sand Dunes of Lake Michigan'.

After these significant contributions, Cowles focused on teaching. But several of his students, including Victor Ernest Shelford, became leading contributors to ecology, establishing Cowles's role as America's first professional ecologist (Worster 1985 [1977]: 206–8; see also Cassidy 2007).

The other major contributor to dynamic ecology was Frederic Clements (1874–1945). 'Vegetation is essentially dynamic' was one of the themes of his *The Development and Structure of Vegetation* (1904): plant communities are never static and always changing. His belief in the persistence of flux is regarded by Worster as being 'Darwinian or perhaps Heraclitean' (1985 [1977]: 209), after the ancient philosopher Heraclitus, who believed in perpetual and universal change. Clements's other central theme was that landscape eventually reaches a more or less stable climax stage of relatively permanent equilibrium after passing through a 'sere', or system of developmental stages from an unbalanced plant assemblage to a more balanced one, driven first by soil conditions and later by climate. Subsequent writers have ascribed to Clements the theory that for each broad climatic region there is just one possible formation, or 'monoclimax', although unusual soil conditions can instead produce 'subclimaxes' (Worster 1985 [1977]: 210). This directional feature of landscapes encouraged him to compare landscapes with organisms. These themes were further elaborated in his most influential book *Plant Succession: An Analysis of the Development of Vegetation* (1916). There is, of course, a tension between belief in perpetual change and belief in even partial eventual equilibrium, as subsequent developments were to bring out.

In adopting an 'organicist' (or organism-like) view of plant communities, Clements displayed the extent to which he was influenced by Herbert Spencer. (For more on Herbert Spencer, see Chapter 3.) Spencer claimed to detect evolution throughout the universe, not least in human societies; to Spencer, Darwinism appeared to be a vindication of his evolutionism, even though it concerned the evolution of living organisms only.

Under the influence of Spencer, Clements claimed that plant communities were 'complex organisms' that evolve, and can be studied experimentally with the same rigour as physiologists apply to individual organisms in laboratories. He presented this organismic idea and this understanding of how ecological research should be conducted in *Research Methods in Ecology* (1905), which became a manifesto for the new science of plant ecology (Hagen 2018: 2). His organismic view of plant communities as superorganisms may have influenced James Lovelock in later representing the entire biosphere as a superorganism. (For more on Lovelock, see Chapter 8.)

But there are many disanalogies between plant communities (also known as 'biocoenoses') and organisms (particularly those with annual cycles). Besides, the very notion of plant communities generated resistance in Clements's day from Sir Arthur Tansley, a leading Oxford ecologist (1871–1955). Tansley (1935) objected to the anthropomorphic connotations of the term, and in 1935 proposed instead the concept of 'ecosystem' which later became widely adopted (and included fauna as well as flora, and nonliving entities such as rocks and soils as well as flora, fauna and bacteria) (Nash 1989: 57–8). Tansley's objection was later presented with greater clarity by the leading Australian philosopher John Passmore, as follows:

> Ecologically, no doubt, men [sic] form a community with plants, animals, soil, in the sense that a particular life-cycle will involve all four of them. But if it is essential to a community that the members of it have common interests and recognise mutual obligations then men, plants, animals and soil do *not* form a community. Bacteria and men do not recognise mutual obligations nor do they have common interests. In the only sense in which belonging to a community generates ethical obligation, they do not belong to the same community. (1980: 116; see also Attfield 1991 [1983]: 157).

Passmore perhaps exaggerated in claiming that bacteria and human beings do not have common interests, but he was right about plant communities not generating internal ethical obligations of themselves, although his criticism was probably targeted directly at Aldo Leopold, who attempted to derive ethical implications from the ecological notion of community, rather than at Clements, who did so at most indirectly, with regard to the obligation to conserve climax communities. But this too was shortly to prove controversial.

A different problem with the concept of plant communities was explained to Clements by his co-writer Victor Ernest Shelford as they jointly wrote *Bio-Ecology* (1939). Shelford objected that since Clements's idea of the climax of plant communities excluded animals, it was too narrow. So they adopted instead the concept of 'biotic community' or 'biome' (Nash 1989: 57), a term that remains in widespread use today.

Nevertheless, the success of Clements's *Plant Communities* led to his appointment as a research associate of the Carnegie Institution in Washington, a post he held from 1917 to 1941. Each summer, he would work at the Pikes Peak laboratory in Colorado, which he had founded in 1900. Later he claimed that he had experimentally generated new species there, in support of his (by now heterodox) belief that new plant species arise through the inheritance of acquired characteristics. But he never fully documented this claim; and from the 1940s his non-Darwinian approach was superseded by the Darwinian perspective of his former collaborator Harvey Monroe Hall, which combined genetics, ecology and taxonomy to study local adaptation (Hagen 2018: 4).

Much earlier, Clements's first publication, his doctoral thesis, *The Phytogeography of Nebraska* (1898; jointly composed with his fellow-student Roscoe Pound), covered the plant distribution and plant communities of this prairies state. As we shall later see, his theories about the plant communities and climax vegetation of such states led him into further controversies when, in the 1930s, much of America was affected by the 'dust bowl'. First, however, some British contributions to ecology, some of them from earlier in the twentieth century, should be mentioned.

British Developments: Arthur Tansley and Charles Elton

Arthur Tansley has already been mentioned in connection with his resistance to regarding plant groupings as communities or as holistic organisms, and with his introduction of the concept of ecosystem (1935). Long before, however, he had helped found the British Ecological Society (1913), and served as editor of *Journal of Ecology* (the journal of the BES) from 1917 to 1938. With these developments, the new science of ecology was now equipped with journals and with institutions on both sides of the Atlantic. Earlier still, he had founded in 1902 the journal *New Phytologist*, which he also edited. In 1927 he accepted the Sherardian Chair of Botany at the University of Oxford.

Besides contributing the concept of ecosystem, his most lasting work was his 1939 book *The British Islands and Their Vegetation*, the fourth edition of which was published in 1965. This was the first major work to employ the ecosystem concept, receiving admiring reviews from ecologists in several countries. It also won the Linnean Gold Medal. Across his many decades of activity as an ecologist, Tansley wrote lucidly for many audiences, and encouraged the wider public (including schoolchildren) to apply ecology in the conservation of British landscapes. Here we can trace how the science of ecology began promoting an ecological and conservationist worldview.

In 1926, in collaboration with T. F. Chipp, assistant director of the Royal Botanical Gardens, Kew, Tansley published *Aims and Methods in the Study of Vegetation*, with a view to management and conservation in the British Empire. Thus his influence was not confined to Britain, but extended to much of Asia, Africa, the Caribbean and the Pacific. From the 1930s onwards, he also worked in psychology, and assisted the work of Sigmund Freud in Freud's later years; but that history does not belong to this book. More relevantly, the BES continues to support the Tansley Lecture, established in his honour (Cameron 2017: 1).

We have already encountered Charles Elton in the introductory section of this chapter. At heart a naturalist, Elton regarded naturalists and their fieldwork as preparing the ground for ecologists, who follow up the work of naturalists with more quantitative and more experimental methods. He was particularly impressed by the methodology of the American Victor Ernest Shelford (1877–1968), illustrated particularly in his book *Animal Communities in Temperate America as Illustrated in the Chicago Region* (1913), which is regarded as the first monograph in animal ecology. (We have already encountered Shelford, over his collaboration with Clements and his devising of the concept of 'biome'.)

Elton spent his career at the University of Oxford (not at Cambridge, as Worster relates (1985: 294)), and had the good fortune, while studying under Julian Huxley (grandson of Thomas Henry Huxley, discussed in Chapter 3), to take part in no fewer than three expeditions to Spitzbergen (1921, 1923 and 1924), and later in another to Lapland (1930). He was given a free hand to study animal ecology there, choosing to use the methods of Shelford, and taking a particular interest in fluctuations of animal populations.

In 1927, Elton published *Animal Ecology*, a short textbook that became a classic, describing his subject as 'the sociology and economics of animals'. (In part, this was a deliberate echo of Linnaeus' phrase 'the economy of nature', but increasingly Elton came to regard ecology as related to economics more than metaphorically, and as concerning how best nature should be managed.) In this book he wrote about many subjects, using detailed natural histories of species to explain how natural systems operate. Another theme was biological invasions, which he regarded as uncontrolled experiments, showing how one invasive species affects others. He also initiated the concepts of food chains, and of ecological niche, understood as where a species fits into the web of interactions. Over the next few years, Elton produced three short books for lay readers, all based on *Animal Ecology*. One of these, *Animal Ecology and Evolution* (1930) addresses the role of evolution (at the time a newly accepted concept) in ecology, without giving it the central role that it would later receive.

In 1932, Elton established at Oxford the Bureau of Animal Population. In its early years, the bureau focused largely on population cycles (such as those of the lynx and its main prey, the snowshoe hare in Canada). Successful predation by the lynx leads to a reduction of the hare population, followed by a crash of the lynx population and a recovery of that of hares. Yet Elton was never satisfied that he had grasped all the key factors (toying with and then abandoning his interim hypothesis that the fluctuations coincided with sunspots). However, during the Second World War, the bureau's efforts were refocused on researching four pest species, to assist the war effort in an unsuccessful attempt to eliminate them; by this stage, Elton was combining invasion ecology with anthropocentric management of unwanted creatures. After the war, much of the bureau's attention was devoted to the study of Wytham Woods (a woodland near the north-west fringes of Oxford), on issues such as the population numbers of the different animal species, and how the species there interacted. But on Elton's retirement in 1967, despite his objections, the bureau was closed down (Simberloff 2013: 3).

In 1931 the BES accepted a recommendation from Elton and Tansley that a new journal, *Journal of Animal Ecology*, be set up, while its longstanding *Journal of Ecology* would limit itself to the study of plants. This development meant that there were now journals of both zoological and botanical ecology, an innovation that much better entrenched the new discipline of ecology. Elton held the position of editor of the new journal for nineteen years, and in that role encouraged the study of population cycles, of introduced species and of conservation. And he contributed as many as sixty-two book reviews, using them to discuss the various ecological issues that concerned him.

One of Elton's persistent themes is that the dynamic nature of populations means that tracts of nature cannot simply be made into reserves and left alone, but that conservation requires management, which itself needs to be based on research on the populations in the reserve. In 1942, he sent a memorandum to Tansley (now Sir Arthur), who was chairing a BES committee on 'Nature Conservation and Nature Reserves'. The eventual outcome was the establishment by the British government of the Nature Conservancy to select and manage reserves and advise on conservation. Elton, despite his antipathy to committees, served as a founder member of the Conservancy, and is credited with adding to it a research branch and establishing surveys as pivotal to reserve management. Another of his contributions to conservation was his hypothesis that biological diversity promotes stability, an influential (albeit controversial) tenet of much contemporary conservation (Simberloff 2013; 12). This tenet, however vulnerable, suggests a slight dilution of the implicit anthropocentrism of much of Elton's work; implicitly, biodiversity was treated as an independent value.

Though Elton published few books, one that had a major impact was *The Ecology of Invasions by Animals and Plants* (1958). This book followed through the ecological consequences of the ongoing global rearrangement of species caused by human activities, and proved to be Elton's most famous work, often regarded as founding the new field of invasion biology. It studied the impacts of more than one hundred introduced species of animals, plants and microbes all over the world. It also reflects the ongoing influence of George Perkins Marsh (see Chapter 4). After the rapid expansion of the field of invasion biology, this book was reprinted by the University of Chicago Press in 2000.

Elton, however, viewed another book, *The Pattern of Animal Communities* (1966) as the culmination of his research life, and a guide to the methods needed for conducting ecological research. But in fact this book wielded little influence compared to his textbook of 1930. By this time, ecology had become dominated by quantitative frameworks, statistical tests and the kind of ecosystem ecology that was preoccupied with energy flows and materials cycling, subjects far removed from Elton's central interests, albeit increasingly related to the model of ecology as a branch of economics. However, after his retirement, Elton travelled to the tropics, and produced papers with new insights into forest invertebrate communities of those regions, which advanced the basis of tropical forest conservation (Simberloff 2013: 6).

Thus, the ecological study of both animals and plants became established across the first six decades of the twentieth century in Britain as well as America. But it is time to return now to a practical problem and the involvement of American ecologists, Clements included.

Challenges to Clements: The Dust Bowl

There had been dust storms in prairies in America in 1886, 1894, 1913 and 1932, but these had local rather than national significance. Then in 1934, a 'black blizzard' advanced towards Texas, and a month later was affecting Chicago, Washington and even ships out in the Atlantic. Such storms continued with similar ferocity until 1937, and the combination of storms and drought lasted in places until 1940 (Worster 1985 [1977]: 221–2). One consequence was the migration of former farming families from Oklahoma, Texas and Kansas to California between 1935 and 1939, to the number estimated at some 300,000 people. This migration was immortalized by John Steinbeck in *The Grapes of Wrath* (1939), where the author also advances a related ecological ethic.

While the drought was a contributing factor, others included overcultivation and poor land management (*Encyclopaedia Britannica* 1998a: 1). Thus the Mexican government had encouraged the ranching of its prairies, while in USA the Homestead Act of 1862 encouraged the development of wheat-cropping, and a substantial surge of 'sod-busters' migrated by the 1890s to Kansas, Texas, New Mexico and Oklahoma, despite the advice of scientists of the United States Geological Survey that livestock ranching was the only safe use of shortgrass country (Worster 1985 [1977]: 227–8). This advice becomes understandable in view of the fact that the annual rainfall of the western part of this region is less than twenty inches. Poor land management was exacerbated by the widespread introduction of the tractor after the First World War, and the encouragement of US presidents at that time to states such as Oklahoma to increase their wheat crop as part of the war effort.

By 1936, the federal Great Plains Committee concluded that at least 15 million acres should immediately be returned to their pre-settlement condition, and should never be ploughed again. More strikingly, they blamed the problems on the pioneering culture of the desire to conquer nature, and criticized the assumption that 'Nature is something of which to take advantage and to exploit'. Instead, farmers needed to take into account periods of deficient rainfall, and the destructive influence of wind blowing over dry and loose soil. Farmers needed to learn greater humility, and conform to nature's economy rather than seeking to make nature conform to our own. At the same time, conservation began to change from a sectoral focus that treated water, soil and forests separately, to one seeking a coordinated and more ecological approach. In the course of a few short decades, the science of ecology moved from being encapsulated in the isolated works of Cowles and Clements to having a position of influence over government policy (Worster 1985 [1977]: 231–3).

Several of the leaders of this new movement of ecological conservation were either students of Clements or scientists inspired by his writings. In 1935, ecologist Paul Sears published *Deserts on the March*, which concerned in part other continents, but also focused on the way that his own state of Oklahoma was adopting a Sahara-like situation, partly through human agency. The general view of Sears and other contemporary ecologists was that, in the light of Clements's climax theory, the aim of land-use policy should be to leave the climax (for example, of the grasslands) as undisturbed as possible (Sears 1935: 233–4). They held this view not out of belief in any intrinsic value being attached to wilderness, but because of the stability and reliability of climax vegetation, and of the way that it best served human interests.

Two other ecologists, both at the University of Nebraska, were followers of Clements: John Weaver and Evan Flory. They jointly wrote in 1934 of the potential role of prairie in stabilizing temperature and humidity, and thus indirectly the soil. The human culture of the prairies, they held, needed to conform to the natural environment, if this could be understood, so as best to utilize it prudently, and this should be done as early as possible before the natural vegetation was irrevocably destroyed (Weaver and Flory 1934). Clements himself was in full agreement, having long held that when homesteaders destroyed the Nebraskan sod, they were risking ruination. This is a message that he had long since conveyed in *The Phytogeography of Nebraska*.

But in the 1930s, Clements's detailed position changed. Hitherto, he had been advocating the preservation of the biological community. Now he was urging research to predict the occurrence of droughts, so that humanity could deflect or retard the successional process more skilfully, and, both in forests and in prairies, could manipulate nature for human purposes more successfully. He even went so far as acknowledging that 'the climax dominants are not necessarily the most valuable to man' (Worster 1985 [1977]: 236–7; Clements and Chaney 1949 [1935]: 49).

Nevertheless, Clements's climax theory remained famous and was not to be disavowed. Accordingly, criticisms began to be raised. One significant criticism was contributed by Herbert Gleason of the University of Michigan, in his essay, 'The Individualistic Concept of the Plant Association' (1991 [1926]). Gleason there rejected Clements's treatment of plant communities as organisms, remarking that the same plant can be found in many different associations, many of them accidentally formed, and more haphazard and co-incidental than the kind of organization that an organism might be expected to manifest. Gleason was rejecting the rigid and deterministic claims of Clements about there being a precise succession leading to the climax state. A less formal concept of ecological dynamics was needed, which allowed for shifting forms of organization, in which humanity might sometimes reasonably play a part.

Another critic was Tansley, who accepted many of Clements's findings, but objected, for example, to his idea of a monoclimax. In any given climatic region, there were many possible kinds of apparently permanent ensembles of vegetation, each of which can be regarded as climax vegetation. Where there has been heavy grazing by sheep (as in many fields and meadows in England) there is a biotic climax; where fires have recurrently affected an area, there is a fire climax; nor can it be claimed that human activity is alien to biotic sequences, since humanity frequently generates a new (and lasting) equilibrium state, to which Tansley gave the name 'anthropogenic climax'. Accordingly, the primeval climax vegetation of an area was not the only model for that area, nor was the outcome of the unaided local climate. Civilization can change the course of natural succession, as it had done in most of Britain and much of Europe. Hence, Tansley (1935) argued, the natural climax theory need not be treated as a check on human interactions with nature, which were sometimes disruptive, but need not always be. It was in this same paper that Tansley proposed the concept of 'ecosystem': see the two previous sections. An ecosystem is to be regarded as an open system (and not an organism or superorganism), often with no clear boundaries, and with no single clear direction or culmination.

More of a direct challenge to Clements was presented by James Malin of the University of Kansas, who in 1956 republished *The Grassland of North America* (originally self-published by Malin in 1947). By 1956 there had been another drought and more dust storms during the early 1950s, often ascribed to policies of 'all-out production' during the Second World War and the Korean War, and yet a disaster comparable to that of the 1930s had been averted (through measures such as growing wind brakes). Contesting the stance of climax conservationists, Malin claimed that agriculture and mechanization had benefited the plains, which had actually needed to be ploughed. In support of this conclusion, he claimed that the prairies were almost nowhere in a condition of equilibrium when the white farmers arrived, and that it was farming that gave them some kind of stability. Dust storms had been recurring on the plains since at least 1830, and had played their part in fertilizing the soil of states such as Nebraska.

Malin also contested the model of humanity as the despoiler of nature, whether the Indians or the white immigrants. Since the first arrival of humanity, people had been disrupting the plains, and – as Carl Sauer (1925) asserted – the habit of the Indians in setting fire to the grasses each year to assist hunting had played a part, something that even Clements had much earlier admitted. But if human activity had helped mould the grasslands to be as the white immigrants found them, then policies of returning them to their pre-human condition or climax were apparently undermined as meaningless. Many of Malin's claims have more recently been refuted by scientists, and it was never claimed by Clements that climax vegetation was stable for ever, whatever climatic changes might bring. Malin was in fact seeking to defend the role of humanity as conqueror of the vast storehouse of nature (rather like Pliny the Elder: see Chapter 1), and his stance on the grasslands can be seen as having the same vulnerability as that questionable ideology (Worster 1985 [1977]: 242–6). Indeed, Aldo Leopold had already managed to argue impressively for contrary conclusions well before Malin's work was published (for more on Leopold, see Chapter 6).

Earlier, American historian Walter Webb had published *The Great Plains* (1931). His rather different stance was that ranching had been much better suited to climax grassland than ploughing and harvesting wheat, and that human beings should modify their behaviour and adapt to the environment of the grasslands. Humanity was not inevitably a disrupting influence; whether it was or not depended on human choice. But his message (while much more sympathetic to Clements than that of Malin) might have had more influence if it had appeared after rather than before the dust bowl of the 1930s. At the time, if made little impression on the adherents of progress and mechanization.

Nevertheless, Worster shows how Malin himself disclosed an underlying acceptance of Clements's message. In *Grassland*, Malin wrote a passage that Clements himself might have written: 'The degree of success in the occupation by man of any of these land regions could be measured in terms of his ability to fit his culture into conformity with the requirements of maintaining rather than disrupting environmental equilibrium' (1956: 154–5). Thus the importance of upholding rather than subverting nature's systems, in which Malin here concedes that there is reason to believe, was after all a limit to human initiative, and supplied alternative guidelines to the pursuit of productivity and market forces. This limit had almost certainly been transgressed by agricultural policy, by the sod-busters and by mechanization. And although Malin's central message pointed in a contrary direction, the climax school was not seriously shaken by his criticisms, nor by those of Gleason or Tansley, and continues to be influential in ecological thought on both sides of the Atlantic (Worster 1985 [1977]: 247–9).

The New Ecology and Eugene Odum

However, there was already a trend, as Worster claims, towards the development of what he calls the 'New Ecology', implicit already in the work of Elton and Tansley, but taken further by subsequent ecologists. For example, Elton's notion of a 'food chain' (possibly based on the great chain of being, but fundamentally different in function, as roles within food chains were modelled on the relations of human beings within an economy) was developed in 1926 by the German ecologist August Thienemann so as to redescribe the various plants, animals and bacteria as either producers (the plants), consumers (animals), reducers (funguses, etc.) or decomposers (often bacteria). These notions were then applied by Elton to the many food chains of nature, from the simple chains of regions like Spitzbergen to the complex ones of the tropics.

Next, Elton added the notion of food size (since each animal can only live on food of a certain size), and population size (because plants and animals near the bottom of a food chain must be more numerous than other creatures and must reproduce more rapidly). And he further added the notion of 'niche', the role that a species carries within a biological community, claiming that no two species can occupy the same niche. (When it was argued that, for example, all species of warblers in spruce woods can eat the same food, Elton described niches more specifically as involving the characteristic level in the trees at which particular species of warbler make their nests, thus keeping the niches of his theory distinctive.) This whole system portrays nature as organized into multiple integrated bioeconomies. As we shall see in Chapter 6, Aldo Leopold, who held discussions with Elton, was to use this understanding of food chains and trophic pyramids to correct current understandings of nature and propose a new ethical approach (1966 [1949]: 230–6).

To this understanding, Tansley's ecosystem approach added an emphasis on energy flow within each ecosystem. The second law of thermodynamics, according to which energy tends to disperse and become unavailable for use, had been formulated by German physicist Rudolf Clausius in 1850. By collecting solar energy, plants retard this process, and make energy available for animals, although at all stages energy leaks away, as the second law predicts. Tansley's concept of ecosystem in principle allowed the flow of energy through each system to be quantified (Worster 1985 [1977]: 295–304).

Already in 1926, American botanist Edgar Transeau (1875–1960) had begun studying the generation of glucose (and thus food) by a wheatfield in Illinois, and the number of kilocalories of energy needed to produce each kilogram. His findings were that, in its use of the incoming solar energy, cornfields use just 1.6 per cent of the energy available. Then, in 1940, limnologist Chancey Juday studied the efficiency of the plant-making activity of the phytoplantons and other bottom flora in Lake Mendota in Wisconsin, and found it to be as low as 0.35 per cent.

Influenced by these findings, in 1942 ecologist Raymond Lindeman (1915–42) published 'The Trophic-Dynamic Aspect of Ecology', foregrounding the possibilities for studying all ecological processes in energetic terms. Lindeman was studying the food and energy cycles of an ecosystem (Cedar Bog Lake in Minnesota was his selected example), and he classified its organisms into different 'trophic levels'. For example, plants, which synthesize their own food, were regarded as 'autotrophs', and animals and bacteria, which feed on other organisms, as 'heterotrophs', which could be divided into herbivores, carnivores and decomposers. At each level, Lindeman encouraged ecologists to calculate the energy consumed and the living matter generated, as well as the energy used up in respiration. He found that the primary producers (the phytoplankton, etc.) used up only 0.1 per cent of the available energy, while the herbivores consumed 17 per cent of the plants, and the carnivores consumed 28.6 per cent of available food energy, of which they used up 60 per cent on respiration. Thus energy extraction becomes 'more efficient' the higher an organism is situated in the food chain, while the proportion used on respiration increases on the same basis.

Lindeman also discovered that, in the early stages of succession, productivity is high, but later decreases as organic matter accumulates and as the system reached senescence. At the same time, with eutrophication, the oxygen supply (in ponds and rivers) gradually decreases. This helps account for the difference between the 0.1 per cent efficiency of Cedar Bog Lake, which had reached senescence, and the 0.35 per cent of Lake Mendota. Effectively, Lindeman was bringing together the ideas of Elton, Tansley, Transeau and Juday into a theory of the energy-based study of nature and its efficiency (Worster 1985 [1977]: 304–10).

Although Lindeman died young, his energy-economic approach has increasingly been employed in subsequent and post-war ecology, with contributions from a cluster of prominent ecologists, including in particular Eugene Odum (1913–2002). In 1953, Odum published *Fundamentals of Ecology*, with ecosystems understood to be the fundamental units; and in 1964, as president of the Ecological Society of America, he explicitly proclaimed the establishment of a 'new ecology', bringing all the ecosystem sciences together. Odum had studied the Eniwetok Atoll in the South Pacific, and concluded that, despite atomic weapon tests nearby, the coral reef was maintaining itself in equilibrium because of the symbiotic relationship between the coral and the associated algae. His key tenets of the new ecology were that biological diversity (and symbiosis in particular) increase system stability, that homeostasis is important at all biological levels, and that since 'the whole is greater than the sum of the parts', reductionist methods for doing science are unequal to the task of understanding living systems. Together with students at the University of Georgia, he also played a successful part in preserving the threatened wetlands of coastal Georgia (Craige 2002: 102).

On the one hand, Odum was resisting some of the reductionist tendencies upheld by Lindeman and his followers. On the other, Odum's work could be seen as a vindication of their new quantitative, energy-flow approach, combined with Tansley's concept of ecosystem. The new approach followed Tansley in rejecting the organism-based model of Clements, but took over Clements's beliefs in the importance of biological diversity, and upheld the view that there is more to biological communities than a mere chance assemblage of organisms haphazardly thrown together. However, these issues continue to be contested and debated; for, as Worster remarks, ecology lacks a unified approach (1985 [1977]: 346), and is itself almost as diverse as the ecosystems that it studies, ranging from evolutionary ecology with its microecological focus to systems macroecology and resilience theory.

Some More Recent Work in Ecology

It remains to present examples of more recent work in ecology, to illustrate the way in which the subject has continued to develop since the days of figures such as Odum. In 1971, T. R. E. Southwood published *Ecological Methods: With Particular Reference to the Study of Insect Populations*, which intended to show how to distinguish and to estimate insect populations. This was the kind of work needed for a clearer understanding of the role of insects within ecosystems, and was much used in other studies. Southwood also encouraged the new role of women scientists within the new ecology.

The other example to be mentioned is J. Philip Grime's *Plant Strategies and Vegetation Processes*, first published in 1979, and revised in 2002, with a reassessment of these concepts, as *Plant Strategies, Vegetation Processes and Ecosystem Properties*. Grime depicts three kinds of plant strategies for adaptation. 'Competitors' thrive in areas of low-intensity stress and low disturbance, and excel in competition by tapping into available resources, and deploying rapid root growth and high productivity in terms of height and lateral spread. 'Stress tolerators', however, live where there is high-intensity stress but low disturbance, using slow growth rates, long-living leaves, and high rates of nutrient retention. 'Ruderals', by contrast, thrive where there is high-intensity disturbance but low-intensity stress. They grow and complete their life-cycles rapidly, and produce large amounts of seeds, and are thus able to colonize recently disturbed land. This pattern illustrates the different strategies by which plants both compete and cooperate with others and with their surroundings, enabling the vegetation of ecosystems to develop and be renewed (Jones 2019).

Thus, the work of recent decades has made it possible for the research of leading theorists such as Clements, Tansley, Elton, Lindeman, Malin and Odum to be developed and tested further. Theories about stable climaxes, about diversity promoting stability or about coral reefs being preserved by symbiosis have not remained unchallenged, but theories about succession and about ecosystems remain central to ongoing research. Important distinctions have been made between communities (biocoenoses) and ecosystems, not least by Robert H. Whittaker (1975 [1970]: 354).

Nevertheless, the last word about the science of ecology should be given to Aldo Leopold:

> Ecology is an infant just learning to talk, and, like other infants, is engrossed with its own coinage of big words. Its working days lie in the future. Ecology is destined to become the lore of Round River, a belated attempt to convert our knowledge of biotic materials into a collective wisdom of biotic navigation. (1966 [1949]: 176)

An explanation of the meaning of 'the lore of Round River' is now needed. This phrase emerges from earlier passages in the same essay:

> One of the marvels of Wisconsin was the Round River, a river that flowed into itself, and thus sped round and round in a never-ending circuit... Wisconsin not only *had* a round river, Wisconsin *is* one. The current is the stream of energy which flows out of the soil into plants, thence into animals, thence back into the soil in a never-ending circuit of life. (1966 [1949]: 175)

This chapter has presented the origins, development, debates and influence of the science of ecology in the nineteenth and twentieth centuries, and its increasing grasp of ecological systems. We return to the significance of ecosystems in ethics in Chapter 8. But we turn first, in Chapter 6, to one figure whose work (when rediscovered in the twentieth century) prefigured the new environmental consciousness, Gerard Manley Hopkins, and to three figures who inaugurated it, Aldo Leopold, quoted above, Rachel Carson and Edward O. Wilson.

Recommended reading

Clements, Frederic, E. (1916). *Plant Succession: An Analysis of the Development of Vegetation*. Washington, DC: Carnegie Institute of Washington.

Clements, Frederic E. and Shelford, Victor E. (1939). *Bio-Ecology*. London: Chapman & Hall.
Elton, Charles S. (1927). *Animal Ecology*. London: Sidgwick and Jackson. Reprinted (2001). Chicago: University of Chicago Press.
Elton, Charles S. (1930). *Animal Ecology and Evolution*. Oxford: Clarendon Press.
Elton, Charles S. (1958). *The Ecology of Invasions by Animals and Plants*. London: Methuen. Reprinted (2000). Chicago: University of Chicago Press.
Gleason, Herbert (1991 [1926]). 'The Individualistic Concept of the Plant Association', in Leslie A. Real and James H. Brown (eds), *Foundations of Ecology: Classical Papers with Commentaries*. Chicago. IL: University of Chicago Press, pp. 98–117.
Grime, J. Philip (2002 [1979]). *Plant Strategies, Vegetation Processes and Ecosystem Properties*. Chichester: John Wiley.
Kropotkin, Petr (1902). *Mutual Aid: A Factor of Evolution*. New York: McClure, Phillips and Co.
Leopold, Aldo (1966 [1949]). *A Sand County Almanac with Other Essays on Conservation from Round River*. New York: Oxford University Press.
Odum, Eugene P. (1953). *Fundamentals of Ecology*. Philadelphia, PA: Saunders.
Steinbeck, John (1939). *The Grapes of Wrath*. New York: Viking Books.
Tansley, Arthur G. (1935). 'The Use and Abuse of Vegetational Concepts and Terms'. *Ecology* 16(3): 284–307.
Tansley, Arthur G. (1965 [1939]). *The British Islands and Their Vegetation*, 4th edn. Cambridge: Cambridge University Press.
Whittaker, Robert H. (1975 [1970]). *Communities and Ecosystems*, 2nd edn. New York: Macmillan.
Worster, Donald (1985 [1977]). *Nature's Economy: A History of Ecological Ideas*. Cambridge: Cambridge University Press.

6

Further Origins of Conservation

This chapter brings onto the stage two very different pioneers of environmentalism and conservation, Aldo Leopold (1887–1948) and Rachel Carson (1907–64), together with the sociobiologist and conservationist, Edward O. Wilson (born 1929), and two other conservationists who became well known on television. However, it is important to make mention first of a poet, little heeded in his own day, whose writings emerged in the twentieth century and prepared the way for environmentalism: Gerard Manley Hopkins (1844–89). All these were exceptional people, and strikingly different from one another. But such, as this chapter shows, were the roots of environmentalism and of the new environmental activism of the late twentieth century.

Gerard Manley Hopkins

Hopkins, while a student at the University of Oxford, converted to Roman Catholicism, then became a Jesuit, and was later appointed Professor of Classics at University College Dublin. Unlike his near contemporary Alfred Lord Tennyson, who in *In Memoriam* (1849) wrote of nature 'red in tooth and claw', Hopkins seems to have ignored evolution and Darwinism, or perhaps, like his mentor John Henry Newman (see Chapter 3), he regarded Darwinism as unobjectionable. His letters concern issues of faith, family and verse, for he was steeped in English literature from Shakespeare and Milton to Wordsworth and Tennyson, and himself reinvented 'the Sprung Rhythm' (Gardner 1953: 151–217). His poetry was almost entirely unknown in his own century, partly because of censorship on the part of his order, but it became widely known in the early twentieth century through his friend Robert Bridges (1844–1930; poet-laureate 1913–30).

Hopkins's appeal to environmentalists becomes immediately clear from poems such as 'Binsey Poplars' (1879). The village of Binsey is a short walk from Oxford (closer even than Wytham Woods: see Chapter 5), and this poem conveys Hopkins's distress at the felling of its trees, and related themes. His message can be conveyed through three short extracts (Gardner 1953: 39–40), the first from the opening stanza.

> My aspens dear, whose airy cages quelled,
> Quelled or quenched in leaves the leaping sun
> All felled, felled, are all felled.

The second stanza begins like this:

> O if we but knew what we do
>   When we delve of hew –
> Hack and rack the growing green!

It continues (concerning nature):

> Where we, even when we mean
>   To mend her we end her,
>   When we hew or delve:
> After-comers cannot guess the beauty been.

Hopkins did not object to agriculture in general (see his poems about ploughmen and harvest). But his concern at the loss unknowingly suffered by future generations already marks him out as a proto-environmentalist, as does his sorrow at the felling of trees.

Another of his poems ('Inversnaid', 1881), a four-stanza poem about a Scottish burn, concludes with a final stanza that could serve unamended as a rallying cry for many environmentalists (Gardner 1953: 51):

> What would the world be, once bereft
> Of wet and of wildness? Let them be left,
> O let them be left, wildness and wet;
> Long live the weeds and the wilderness yet.

Hopkins lived well before the debates about the centrality or otherwise of wilderness for environmentalism, but this stanza speaks readily to many, even those unaware of his central preoccupations.

But lest a superficial impression be given of Hopkins's verse, it should be made clear that his poetry was an expression of his profound Christian faith, the relation of which to his appreciation of nature emerges in the poem 'God's Grandeur' (1877; Gardner 1953: 27):

> The world is charged with the grandeur of God.
>   It will flame out, like shining from shook foil;
>   It gathers to a greatness, like the ooze of oil
> Crushed. Why do men then now not reck his rod?
> Generations have trod, have trod, have trod;
>   And all is seared with trade; bleared, smeared with toil;
>   And wears man's smudge and shares man's smell: the soil
> Is bare now, nor can foot feel, being shod.
>
> And for all this, nature is never spent;
>   There lives the dearest freshness deep down things;
> And though the last light off the black West went
>   Oh, morning, at the brown brink eastward, springs –
> Because the Holy Ghost over the bent
>   World broods with warm breast and ah! bright wings.

Hopkins was not committed to a primitivist rejection of culture, any more than he was to a rejection of agriculture. Rather, he requires a poetic contrast between nature as trodden and transformed by humanity and the irrepressible nature that can be resurrected because of God's presence within it. It is as if he has stumbled unawares on the panentheism of the Protestant pioneer, Martin Luther (see Chapter 2).

Another poem in which Hopkins's theological beliefs are explicit is 'The Windhover' (1877), subtitled 'To Christ our Lord', although the entire poem is about his catching sight of a falcon. Hopkins later described this as 'the best thing I ever wrote' (Gardner 1953: 30, 227). But the poem that perhaps best relates Hopkins's faith to his appreciation of diversity is 'Pied Beauty' (1877; Gardner 1953: 30–1):

> Glory be to God for dappled things –
>   For skies of couple-colour as a brinded cow;
>   For rose-moles all in stipple upon trout that swim;
> Fresh-firecoal chestnut-falls; finches' wings;
>   Landscape plotted and pieced – fold, fallow and plough;
>   And all trades, their gear and tackle and trim.

> All things counter, original, spare, strange;
>   Whatever is fickle, freckled (who knows how?)
>   With swift, slow; sweet, sour; adazzle, dim;
> He fathers forth whose beauty is past change;
>   Praise him.

Admittedly praise of diversity is not praise of biodiversity, and could equally be focused on the diverse products of human technology, although biological diversity was in fact pivotal for Hopkins. Yet Hopkins here contrives to recapture the advocacy of praise in Psalms 145–150, and in St Francis's *The Canticle to Brother Sun*, and at the same time Augustine's thoughts about beauty (see Chapter 1).

Hopkins's poetry, then, stems from profound religious convictions, but brings everyday experience to life, particularly experience of the natural world. Even those who resile from his theology can share in his vivid depictions of the world as he saw it and as it might be. His was not the scientific path of ecology, but that of aesthetic experience, and concern that this experience should be available to his successors.

While the rediscovery of his work did not of itself initiate the environmental movement, it predisposed many to the quality of experience that was widely to motivate it.

Influences on Aldo Leopold and Some Early Stances

In complete contrast, we turn now to the Yale Forest School, founded by the family of Gifford Pinchot (1865–1946) in 1900, and to Aldo Leopold, a graduate of that institution. The school, as Worster relates, was the leading academic centre for 'the productivity outlook on nature' (1985 [1977]: 271). It developed the ideas of Pinchot, who had written: 'The purpose of Forestry, then, is to make the forest produce the largest possible amount of whatever crop or service will be most useful, and keep on producing it for generation after generation of men and trees' (Worster 1985 [1977]: 267). Pinchot had also long advocated the application of this policy to all the national forests, of which the productivity was to be maximized over time; and had organized the US Forest Service on this basis (see Chapter 4). It was a policy far superior to the irresponsible deforestation characteristic of the previous century.

This policy involved resource management, so that productivity could persist into the future (or the pursuit of sustainability, as we would now call it), and thus a considerable degree of conservation. Within this policy, selective cutting of trees was to be matched by natural regeneration.

Such policies of 'wise land use' involved, for example, preventing soil erosion and, where possible, removing species liable to compete with the intended crop. Pinchot and his followers ignored Marsh's recommendation to foresters (see Chapter 4) that they proceed with caution with the aim of preventing the eradication of species that might later prove beneficial; they also ignored the principles of humanitarians such as Congressman John F. Lacey (again see Chapter 4). Indeed, ecological considerations went unheeded except where ignoring them brought risks to productivity. All this was regarded as 'scientific management'.

Foresters of this persuasion were prepared to include game management among their aims, regarding game such as deer as a resource and potentially a crop for hunters to harvest. Predators, on the other hand, were regarded as competitors and were to be exterminated. So, while many forests were set aside as reserves for the breeding of game, government hunters trapped or shot all the predators they could find (coyotes, wolves, grizzly bears and mountain lions included), despite the resulting overpopulation of deer in places such as the Kaibab Forest in Arizona, designated as the Grand Canyon National Game Reserve. Yet even when overpopulation of this kind became noticeable, the official view was that predators were unnecessary, because human hunters could carry out their role just as well (Worster 1985 [1977]: 270–1).

These were the policies and the practices that Leopold inherited. They explain why, in his first years of employment, he focused on the management of game, and attempted to introduce to it the kind of scientific management already described above. Indeed, in 1933 he published a book titled *Game Management*, which advocated treating game as a crop, the productivity of which was to be fostered by controlling those environmental factors that biological science disclosed as threatening it. The control of predators was central to this approach, but there was also an acknowledgement of their ecological role, and a long-term approach was commended. At least in this respect, Leopold was already calling for a new ethic. His book is widely regarded as founding the enterprise of game management.

As is well known, Leopold eventually changed his mind about predator control, and about the whole related approach to managing forests and wilderness. He had, in any case, long been advocating the establishment of wilderness reserves, to ensure that untouched areas remained relatively untouched, as in an article of 1921 with regard to part of the Tila National Forest in New Mexico (Nash 2014 [1967]: 186–7), and he had, several years earlier, been organizing hunters and fishermen into groups to protect game (Nash 2014 [1967]: 183). All the same, it is important to grasp the milieu in which he was educated and to which he significantly contributed, despite his inner reservations deriving from some quite different influences.

One very different influence was the work of Thoreau, whose writings were included in Leopold's favourite boyhood reading, and whose fourteen-volume *Journal*, published in 1906, was given to him by his mother as a wedding present (Egerton 2012: 156). So he was acquainted from his early years with Thoreau's belief in the value of all creatures and sense of oneness with nature as a whole, despite the strong contrast of all this with the teachings of the Yale Forest School.

Another influence was Liberty Hyde Bailey, who in 1915 published *The Holy Earth*. According to Bailey, the natural world is divine because it is God's handiwork. (This conclusion goes well beyond the usual stance of Protestants, whether Lutheran or Calvinist, and of Catholics too.) Hence, abuse of the earth is morally wrong. While Bailey did not reject belief in the human dominion of the earth, he interpreted dominion as a status requiring moral righteousness (Nash 2014 [1967]: 194–5). Leopold will have come across this book as a young adult, but, while it may have instilled doubts about the Pinchot approach, at least to the extent of his believing that harmless animals (other than game and the predators of game) should be left alone, it does not seem to have undermined his support for a long-term productivity approach to forests.

Yet a further influence was Albert Schweitzer (1875–1965). While serving as a medical doctor in equatorial Africa, Schweitzer came to the conclusion that the true foundation of all morality was 'reverence for life'. Ethics, he held, should not be restricted to interhuman dealings, but should include the preservation, as far as possible, of all animals and plants as well; the unnecessary killing or injuring of any of them was wrong. While Schweitzer's autobiography was not published until 1933, Leopold could well have seen a translation of a part of it as early as 1923 (Nash 2014 [1967]: 195n.48). Schweitzer's ethic leads more directly to the biocentrism of Paul Taylor (see Chapter 8) than to Leopold's approach, even in its mature form; but it could well have led Leopold to reflect further on the value of fellow-creatures. With his continuing advocacy of the control of predators, Leopold cannot have adopted Schweitzer's beliefs in full, but they may well have added to his developing doubts about this matter, and strengthened his conditional support for nature preservation.

Another influence, this time closer to Leopold's professional concerns, was the development of the new science of ecology (see Chapter 5). At least in the view of Clements, land and the living community that shared it formed a complex organism, which functioned through a nexus of interactions. Leopold regarded the work of Clements and also of Elton (with whom he held discussions) as 'the outstanding discovery of the twentieth century', comparable in its import to Darwinism (Leopold 1953: 147; Grober 2007: 27; Nash 2014 [1967]: 195). Studying the findings of ecology enabled Leopold to regard nature as 'an intricate web of interdependent parts, a myriad of cogs and wheels each essential to the healthy operation of the whole' (Nash 2014 [1967]: 195). This understanding was once again at odds with the teachings of Pinchot, as usually understood, and gradually and eventually enabled Leopold to revise his view of the role of humanity. 'We are', he later wrote, 'only fellow-voyagers in the odyssey of evolution', with the difference that technology had given us the 'whip-hand over nature', with the ability to change it extensively (Leopold 1966 [1949]: 109–10; Nash 2014 [1967]: 195–6). We may imagine Leopold moving through stages of reflection, initially believing in preserving everything but game and its predators, while conserving game for hunting, and later realizing that even this stance was unacceptable in the light of the ethic of Thoreau, Bailey and Schweitzer, and the scientific discoveries of ecologists such as Clements.

The Russian philosopher Peter D. Ouspensky (1878–1947) was yet another influence. Ouspensky's book *Tertium Organum* (a title implying that it bears comparison with the works on scientific method of Aristotle and of Francis Bacon) was published in 1912, and translated into English in 1920; Leopold probably read it shortly afterwards. Ouspensky maintained that 'there can be nothing dead or mechanical in Nature ... life and feeling ... must exist in everything', and went on to hold that mountains, trees, rivers and even fire must each possess a mind of its own. Ouspensky also believed that interacting organisms, together with the air, water and soil with which they interacted, each formed a superorganism. These beliefs inclined Leopold towards organismic thinking, to which the theories of Clements may have already predisposed him, and they may well have influenced his choice of title for an essay of the 1940s, 'Thinking Like a Mountain' (Nash 1989: 65–6). Leopold explicitly quotes Ouspensky (a rarity) in his essay 'Some Fundamentals of Conservation in the Southwest', composed in 1923 and unpublished until it appeared in *Environmental Ethics* in 1979. His organismic tendencies could further have been strengthened by the Chicago school of ecologists, led from 1921 to 1950 by Walter Allee, whose influential (coauthored) book *Principles of Animal Ecology* was eventually published in 1949, too late to influence Leopold (Worster 1985 [1977]: 326–7).

At the same time, there was a development of Leopold's understanding of the meaning of wilderness, which he came to see as vital for the quality of American life. Thus by 1926 he took the view that the achievements of civilization were valuable, but in danger of going too far. 'While the reduction of the wilderness has been a good thing', he wrote, 'its extermination would be a very bad one' (1926: 63; Nash 2014 [1967]: 187). And he went on to employ a metaphor about the compromise that he at this stage favoured:

> What I am trying to make clear is that if in a city we had six vacant lots available to the youngsters of a certain neighbourhood for playing ball, it might be 'development' to build houses on the first, and on the second, and on the third, and on the fourth, and even on the fifth, but when we build houses on the last one, we forget what houses are for. The sixth house would not be development at all, but rather ... stupidity.

In other words, a new criterion was needed to recognize that a progressive civilization was one that preserved its remaining wilderness (Nash 2014 [1967]: 187–8). Leopold later took these matters forward in *A Sand County Almanac* (1966 [1949]: 241–56; see the next section).

Leopold's mature stance

Leopold, then, had been advocating wilderness preservation since the 1920s, not least on the grounds of American traditions and culture. 'Is it not a bit beside the point', he wrote in 1925, 'for us to be so solicitous about preserving [American] institutions without giving so much as a thought to preserving the environment which produced them and which may now be one of our effective means of keeping them alive?' (1925: 401).

Then, early in the 1930s, around the time that he accepted a post at the University of Wisconsin as a specialist in game management, he went on several hunting expeditions in the wilderness of the Sierra Madre in northern Mexico. Later he wrote, in a foreword intended for *A Sand County Almanac* (but not included there): 'It was here that I first clearly realized that land is an organism, that all my life I had seen only sick land, whereas here was a biota still in perfect aboriginal health' (Nash 2014 [1967]: 192). This response will have increased his doubts about the extermination of predators; yet it was around this time that he wrote and published the much more Pinchot-like *Game Management* (depicted in the previous section).

Further reflection on the ethical implications of ecology eventually led Leopold to regret his earlier contributions to campaigns against predators. As far back as 1909 – as Lance Richardson (2015) discloses – Leopold had an experience that began his eventual change of stance.

He and a companion had shot a wolf and its cubs. Leopold much later recounted what followed: 'We reached the old wolf in time to watch a fierce green fire dying in her eyes. I realized then, and have known ever since, that there was something new to me in those eyes, something known only to her and to the mountain.' It had seemed that each dead wolf meant a better environment for hunters; but 'the wolf and the mountain knew better' (1966 [1949]: 129–30). But the claim 'I have known ever since' in fact telescopes a long period of transition, lasting thirty-five years from the day the wolf was shot to the day Leopold wrote about it. This episode, however, led Leopold (no doubt still influenced by Ouspensky) to conceive the phrase 'thinking like a mountain', first presented in *A Sand County Almanac* (1966 [1949]: 132). As Nash puts it, his campaigns against predators were newly seen as misguided not merely because the elimination of predators removed a desirable check on the growth of the population of prey species, but also because the very notion of an undesirable species was perverse, involving a failure to recognise such a species as part of that community which he came to call 'the land' (2014 [1967]: 196).

A further example of Leopold's new attitude to the extermination of predators concerns his response to the shooting of a grizzly bear on the Escudilla Mountain in Arizona. 'The government trapper who took the grizzly knew he had made the Escudilla safe for cows. He did not know he had toppled the spire off an edifice a-building since the morning stars sang together' (1966 [1949]: 136). The reference is both to the science of ecology (the edifice being the ecosystem of the mountain) and to a passage about creation in the book of Job; and the whole quotation shows what a fine stylist Leopold was, as well as his passionate commitment to his new message.

Leopold's changed view of the role of humanity was accompanied by his new understanding of ethics; like Schweitzer, he now maintained that the scope of ethics should be enlarged. The first stage of ethics, in his account, dealt with the relation between individuals. He gives the Mosaic Decalogue as an example; morally relevant individuals are limited to humans (and God), with nonhumans not included. At this stage, he claims, slaves were mere chattels, and beyond the scope of morality. The second stage brought in the relation between human and society; his examples are the Golden Rule and democracy. But land remained and remains property. The third stage is the extension of morality to include 'land and the animals and plants which grow upon it'. He allows that thinkers since the days of Ezekiel and Isaiah have asserted that the despoliation of land is not only inexpedient but wrong, but that society has not yet affirmed their belief. Extending ethics to cover land is 'an evolutionary possibility and an ecological necessity'. Indeed, 'the present conservation movement is the embryo of such an affirmation' (Leopold 1966 [1949]: 218).

Leopold proceeds to write about the community concept and the ecological conscience. He begins with the claim that all ethics so far evolved rests upon the single premise 'that the individual is a member of a community of interdependent parts'. Even if we allow 'ethics' to be a synonym of 'morals', this is not strictly true, since traditional morality (including 'the Mosaic Decalogue') includes concern for future generations, and the current generation is in few, if any, respects dependent on the generations of the future. But a stress on interdependence strengthens the case for enlarging 'the boundaries of the community to include soils, waters, plants and animals, or collectively, the land'. A land ethic cannot prevent the 'use of these "resources"' (Leopold's inner quotation marks), but it affirms their right to continued existence, and 'at least in spots, their continued existence in a natural state' (1966 [1949]: 219). There is of course a tension here between the kind of use that involves consumption and selective preservation; but Leopold's statement clearly differentiates him from his earlier stance that he inherited from Pinchot.

A 'land ethic', he now asserts, 'changes the role of *Homo sapiens* from conqueror of the land-community to plain member and citizen of it. It implies respect for his [sic] fellow-members, and also respect for the community as such.' Ecologically interpreted, he goes on to claim, history bears out the fact that 'man' (*sic*) is only a member of a biotic team (Leopold 1966 [1949]: 219–20). We might ask whether respect for fellow-members of the biotic community need imply either respect for its inanimate components or for the community as such. This question can for the present be left open.

What is equally important is that Leopold here seeks to derive ethical conclusions from interdependence and ecological succession, and thus from his concept of the land community. Yet interdependence is neither sufficient for moral standing (think of houses and roofs) nor necessary (we are not interdependent with our great-grandchildren). As we shall see in Chapter 8, Holmes Rolston later saw the need for a different way of deriving ecological 'oughts'.

More cogently, Leopold writes of the difference made by the ecological conscience. Standard attitudes, he held, rely on education, and on individual property-owners complying with incentives and exhortations in causes such as maintaining the soil. The result, however, is that farmers select practices of conservation that are to their advantage and ignore the rest. Leopold cites recent experience in Wisconsin in support of this interpretation. Indeed, as he memorably states: 'The farmer who clears the woods off a 75 per cent slope, turns the cows into the clearing, and dumps its rainfall, rocks and soil into the community creek, is still (if otherwise decent) a respected member of society . . . still entitled to all the privileges and emoluments of his Soil Conservation District.' Such public programmes are falling short because 'obligations have no meaning without conscience, and the problem we face is the extension of the social conscience from people to the land' (1966 [1949]: 224–5). It is actually untrue that obligations have no meaning without conscience; but in these circumstances they have little effect, unless others can bring their holders to observe them.

What is required for this important change in ethical consciousness, Leopold continues, is 'an internal change in our intellectual emphasis, loyalties, affections and convictions'. He adds: 'The proof that conservation has not yet touched these foundations of conduct lies in the fact that philosophy and religion have not yet heard of it' (1966 [1949]: 225). This was, perhaps, an exaggeration, as the transcendentalist Thoreau had earlier advocated measures of conservation, while John Stuart Mill had sought to preserve wild flowers; and there were religious elements in the thought of earlier conservationists such as Marsh and, more obviously, Muir, as well as in the longstanding stewardship tradition, expressed by figures such as the biocentric John Ray, and in many Eastern traditions too. But where mainstream contemporary philosophy and majority contemporary Western religious beliefs were concerned, his case was more or less secure.

This is the stage to introduce some of the themes that Leopold derived from ecologists such as Clements and Elton. In a section of his essay 'The Land Ethic', titled 'The Land Pyramid', Leopold explains the flow of energy through the layers of the biotic pyramid. The bottom layer is the soil, on which rests a plant layer, then an insect layer, then a layer of birds and rodents, and so on through other animals up to the apex layer of the larger carnivores. There are numerous food chains, and the whole pyramid is apparently a tangle of these chains, but its stability shows it to be a 'highly organised structure'. Originally the pyramid of life was 'low and squat', but evolution has added layer after layer (one of which is humanity); and science tells us that 'the trend of evolution is to elaborate and diversity the biota' (1966 [1949]: 231). Further, the circuit through which energy flows is not a closed circuit, with much of the energy stored in soils, peats, forests and seabeds, from which, in the course of geological time, new lands and new pyramids will arise (1966 [1949]: 231–2).

Leopold derives three conclusions from all this. '(1) That land is not merely soil. (2) That the native plants and animals kept the energy circuit open; others may or may not. (3) That man-made changes are of a different order than [sic] evolutionary changes, and have effects more comprehensive than is intended or foreseen' (1966 [1949]: 234). While he could not have foreseen the implications of these conclusions, they serve to throw considerable doubt on the central thesis of the anthropocentric ecologist James Malin, as presented in the following decade (see Chapter 5).

For his own part, Leopold surveys different continents with regard to the sturdiness and viability of their biotic circuits. Both Western Europe and Japan have undergone radical conversions, but show 'no visible stoppage or derangement of the circuit' (1966 [1949]: 234). This verdict appears rather lenient; for example, the River Thames at that time lacked fish in its lower reaches, and was widely compared to a sewer; since then, however, it has largely recovered. With respect to Asia Minor and North Africa, Leopold speaks of advanced wastage in connection with climate change, an early recognition of this worldwide problem. As for the United States, he finds varying degrees of disorganization, worst in much of the South. But disorganization is never complete. 'The land recovers, but at some reduced level of complexity, and with a reduced carrying capacity for people, plants and animals.' Indeed, 'the less violent the man-made changes, the greater the probability of successful readjustment in the pyramid'. This, he adds, is a conclusion that runs counter to widely prevalent current assumptions (1966 [1949]: 235–6).

There follows an interesting survey of the implications for forestry, wildlife management and agriculture. In each case, one attitude regards land as soil and its function as the production of commodities, whereas another regards land as biota, and takes a (variously) broader view of its functions. In forestry, adherents of the first view grow trees like cabbages, and cellulose is 'the basic forest commodity'. Those of the second approach prefer natural reproduction, worry about loss of species, and are concerned for a range of 'forest functions', including wildlife, recreation, watersheds and wilderness areas. It is among these that 'the stirrings of an ecological conscience' are felt.

As for wildlife management, proponents of the first approach regard the basic commodities as sport and meat, and artificial propagation (even of a permanent kind) is acceptable where unit costs permit. By contrast, adherents of the second approach are additionally concerned about 'the cost in predators', recourse to exotic species, restoration of shrinking species like prairie grouse, and threatened species such as trumpeter swans, whooping cranes and threatened wildflowers. Leopold's verdict is the same (1966 [1949]: 237). It is, however, notable that the second approach is in stark conflict with that of his own work *Game Management* (1933), which had become the bible of game managers.

Where agriculture is concerned, modification of the biota is inevitable, more so than in forestry and wildlife management. Adherents of the first approach measure food value by poundage or tonnage, using imported fertilizers where they are economical, whereas those of the second recognize that the products of fertile soil may be superior in quality as well as quantity. Organic farming is an example, 'particularly in its insistence on the importance of soil flora and fauna'. 'In all of these cleavages', Leopold adds, there are the same contrasts: 'Man the conqueror *versus* man the biotic citizen . . . land the slave *versus* land the collective organism.' It is important here to recognize that Leopold had a place for agriculture, and was not advocating comprehensive rewilding; but that he favoured 'biotic farming', or farming with a biotic-oriented conscience (1966 [1949]: 238).

This led him to put forward his land ethic. One element of this was that people must abandon thinking of decent land use as solely an economic question; this was perhaps his most important contribution. He then proceeded to spell out his proposed ethic as follows: 'A thing is right when it tends to preserve the integrity, stability and beauty of the biotic community. It is wrong when it tends otherwise.' This proposed general criterion of rightness warrants assessment. Where the context is limited to issues about land use, there is some merit in this proposal, although the intersection of such issues with issues of interhuman ethics such as promise-keeping raises doubts even here. But where the proposal is presented as applicable across the board, it is potentially disastrous. For example, murder is wrong, even when its impact on the biotic community is minimal, because its impact on the human community must not be ignored; and the same goes for promise-keeping, which is usually neutral with regard to the biotic community and its prospects, but is still in almost all circumstances right, and not wrong or neutral, as the land ethic implicitly represents it.

Leopold was not alone in proposing an overgeneralized ethic; a similar verdict may well be in place, for example, on Schweitzer's ethic of 'reverence for life'. Ethicists (professional or otherwise) need to exercise caution in seeking to replace received ethical rules and principles with such sweeping proposals, even when received principles provide insufficiently for future generations and for nonhuman interests. However, before leaving Leopold, we should return to one of the areas where his expertise offered guidance of an enlightened kind: that of policies concerning wilderness, guidance that has rightly proved influential.

His main proposal is that a representative series of wilderness areas can, and should, be kept (1966 [1949]: 246). Some areas, such as the long-grass prairie, have gone for good. But where there are remnants, of kinds such as short-grass prairie, coastal flatwoods and southern hardwood swamps, samples of each should be preserved, so that people can be aware of the origins and context of the development of their cultures. Also, enough of the Arctic should be preserved (among other reasons) so as to preserve its fauna (1966 [1949]: 241–6).

Leopold proceeds to go through the various functions of wilderness. Recreation is among them, but does not justify the construction of roads liable to damage flora and fauna. Wilderness is also needed for the sake of science, and also lends itself to the development of a science of 'land health' (1966 [1949]: 251) – a science currently developed among conservation biologists. Unfortunately, he writes here of 'how healthy land maintains itself as an organism', borrowing from Clements the organismic approach rightly criticized by Tansley (see Chapter 5). Then he turns to the central function of habitat for wildlife. But this requires sufficient ranges of wild country for species such as wolves and grizzlies to survive. Sufficient contiguous stretches of wilderness are required for this (1966 [1949]: 255–6); and this theme has become important since Leopold's day (for example) in Asia, with a view to the preservation of tigers in India and pandas in China.

'Even in Britain . . . there is a vigorous if belated movement for saving a few small spots of semi-wild land', Leopold remarks, perhaps alluding to plans for National Parks where farming is allowed to continue (1966 [1949]: 255). It was a mark of his common sense that, sooner than take the purist line that the cause of wilderness in Europe was lost west of the Carpathians, he implicitly endorsed the preservation of working landscapes like the South Downs, Exmoor and the Lake District, manifestly modified as they are by human husbandry, but presenting biodiverse regions and cultures, often because of this very factor.

Leopold's *Sand County Almanac* was published posthumously (he died in 1948), but went on to exercise enormous influence both on the conservation movement and on environmental ethics. Dave Foreman (of the notorious group 'Earth First!') regarded this work as 'the most important book ever written', while others honoured Leopold as a patron saint of the modern environmental movement. In several paperback editions, *Sand County Almanac* went on to sell a million copies (Nash 1989: 63). We shall return to its further influence in later chapters.

Rachel Carson

Rachel Carson (1907–64) was a biologist and marine scientist, who was 'enormously fond of Thoreau's writing, [and] kept a copy of *Walden* by her bedside' (Egerton 2012: 156; Lear 1997: 509n.7). She also harboured a strong respect for Schweitzer's principle of 'reverence for life', as she disclosed on being awarded the Schweitzer Medal in 1963, although for the most part her writings could be construed as overtly anthropocentric, and did not present any explicit environmental ethic (Nash 1989: 79-80). While writing about maritime ecosystems, Carson was in many ways a natural historian, but one whose writings were 'colored in every respect with something many modern ecologists had forgotten: love of nature' (Nash 1989: 78). Worster associates her with being one of the last voices of the Chicago school of organicist ecologists (Worster 1985 [1977]: 331), but organicism seems at most peripheral to her concerns, and Worster appears to underestimate and/or ignore her importance in bringing scientific ecology to public attention, and in initiating a related crusade that her understanding of it inspired.

In 1935, by which time Carson had been awarded her master's degree in biology, she joined the US Bureau of Fisheries as a writer and editor, and began writing books. Her first work, *Under the Sea Wind* (1941), aroused little attention (Nash 1989: 78), but later became one of a widely read trilogy of her works about the sea (later published by Penguin Classics). This was partly because of the bestselling status of her next book, *The Sea Around Us* (1951), which was used after her death to introduce the trilogy; this book was translated into thirty-two languages and generated enough royalties to enable Carson to retire from her government post. It presented an overview of the natural history of the oceans, including their origins, the creation of volcanic islands and the evolution of life within them. It was followed by the third book of the trilogy, *The Edge of the Sea* (1955), which depicts creatures such as barnacles, ghost-crabs and corals. While these books present no explicit ethic, they express on almost every page, as Nash remarks, 'the author's awe in the face of the vast community of life centered on the oceans' (Nash 1989: 79). (Indeed, they could be said to serve to complement Leopold's delight in the community of the land; it is strange that he so neglected the seas.)

Wonder was the explicit subject of another of Carson's books, *The Sense of Wonder* (published posthumously in 1965). Carson here describes adventures with her young nephew Roger, as they enjoyed walks along the rocky coast of Maine and through forests and fields, observing wildlife, strange plants, moonlight and clouds, and listening to the percussive sounds of insects in the undergrowth. 'If a child is to keep alive his inborn sense of wonder,' she wrote, 'he [sic] needs the companionship of at least one adult who can share it, rediscovering with him the joy, excitement and mystery of the world we live in.' *The Sense of Wonder* supplies a formidable antidote to indifference, and a guide to retrieving the sense of discovery that Carson viewed as essential to human life. There can be little doubt that Thoreau would have endorsed this verdict.

Carson had plans for a longer and more thematic book on wonder, sadly never written, but left notes and headings for its structure. Subsequently, Kathleen Dean Moore reconstructed some of Carson's thinking in an article in *Environmental Ethics* titled 'The Truth of the Barnacles: Rachel Carson and the Moral Significance of Wonder' (2005). This article is discussed in turn in my book *Wonder, Value and God* (Attfield 2016).

Once liberated from her job, Carson became free to study the impacts of insecticides on food chains, and in particular DDT, a poison that had concerned her since 1945. While DDT is often classified as a pesticide, Carson objected to this particular term as being anthropocentric, for creatures are pests from a human perspective only; her preferred term was 'biocides' (killers of life). She also realized early on that insecticides seldom stopped short at poisoning insects, but were prone to infect or even kill other creatures within their ecosystems, or, as Nash calls them 'unintended victims of indiscriminate sprayings'. DDT was often used to eradicate *anopheles* mosquitoes, the carriers of malaria and other diseases. But the unintended effects could possibly include a 'silent spring', where no birds sang (Nash 1989: 79). And such a 'silent spring' could spread from the northern hemisphere, where the spraying was done, to the Antarctic, where DDT was actually found in the flesh of penguins.

Carson, who was suffering by now from breast cancer, realized that her remaining span of life was limited, and, rather than proceeding with her thematic book on wonder, she decided to concentrate on educating the public about the hazards of insecticides, herbicides and radioactive substances. This decision led to the publication in 1962 of *Silent Spring*, a book that was to change the world, and which was described later in the twentieth century as 'arguably the most important book published this century' (Carey 2005: 345).

While ultimately Carson rejected anthropocentrism, *Silent Spring* focuses on harms and threats of harm to humanity. Chemicals intended to kill insects get into food chains, and soon affect most creatures; they are even found in mothers' milk. There are parallel dangers from strontium 90, a radioactive by-product of nuclear tests, which is also found in the cow's milk that used to be given to schoolchildren, and is still given to babies. Carson was also concerned about monocultures in agriculture, and quotes Elton (on whom, see Chapter 5) on the importance of conserving biodiversity (Carson 2000 [1962]: 112). Ecosystems are also mentioned (hence the book's title, concerning places where there might no longer be birdsong in spring), but the urgency of the book is based on the potential undermining of human life. An early chapter is called 'The Obligation to Endure', but, rather than containing ethical proposals, it concerns the threats to the future of humanity, concluding with a quotation from Jean Rostand: 'The obligation to endure gives us the right to know.' So its focus was on bringing to attention knowledge already available (but often concealed) about the threats of chemicals and of intensive agriculture to the health of both ecosystems and human beings. It was also implicitly a call to action grounded in this knowledge.

Its impact was made more forceful through the preface, written by Julian Huxley (grandson of Thomas Henry Huxley, discussed in Chapter 3). Huxley relates that his brother, the novelist Aldous Huxley, had said, after reading the book: 'We are losing half the subject-matter of English poetry' (Carson 2000 [1962]: 20). This passage also serves to explain the importance of the references above in this book to the metaphysical and the Romantic poets (Chapter 2) and (in the current chapter) to Gerard Manley Hopkins. To take further examples, in the kind of world saturated with what Carson preferred to call 'biocides', there would be no room for Shakespeare's 'Hark, hark! the lark at heaven's gate sings', or for Keats's 'Ode to Autumn' or his 'Ode to a Nightingale'.

Silent Spring was serialized in three editions of the *New Yorker* prior to publication; it became a publishing sensation and is widely held, not least by Linda Lear in her afterword to the 2000 edition, to have initiated the contemporary environmental movement (Carson 2000 [1962]: 258). Carson wrote at a time when McCarthyism was still a recent memory, and the public were expected to trust their government and its scientific experts in the overall cause of resistance to communism. (This attitude may have been exemplified in the findings of Eugene Odum of 1964 about the harmlessness of atomic testing: see Chapter 5.) Carson explicitly set out to undermine this trust, and to demonstrate that these people and agencies were withholding crucial information affecting human health. (In other writings she also drew attention to the danger of dumping radioactive materials in the oceans, the diversity and wonder of which she had depicted in her ocean trilogy.) Not surprisingly, she was 'vilified by persons, corporations and government agencies engaged in agriculture' (Nash 1989: 81), and also by the chemical industry. But she also became a heroine for millions of Americans, and implicitly an ethical pioneer. For, besides her message about the dangers to human health, she also conveyed that in nature everything is connected to everything else; and effectively drew all forms of life into the circle of ethical concern, insects included (Nash 1989: 82). Additionally, she conveyed some of the insights of scientific ecology, and of its importance, to a public that had been slow to grasp them.

As Lear relates, Carson's book 'so impressed President John F. Kennedy that he ordered an investigation of the subject of pesticide misuse by his President's Science Advisory Committee' (Carson 2000 [1962]: 259). This committee substantially sided with Carson's scientific and ecological conclusions. Further, in 1963 the Secretary of the Interior, Stuart Udall, published *The Quiet Crisis* (1963), a title that gave rise to the much-used phrase 'the environmental crisis'.

Before long, such harmful chemicals as DDT were banned both in America and in many other countries, and a number of others were subjected to critical scrutiny. It may also be no coincidence, in view of the concerns raised by Carson and others about the radioactive fallout from nuclear tests, that a Nuclear Test-Ban Treaty was agreed by President Kennedy in August 1963. What made it possible for Carson to have such an impact was due partly to the influence of Thoreau, Muir and the other transcendentalists, partly to the solid achievements of the early exponents of ecological science, and partly to the increased influence of the media. The fact that the USA was no longer engaged in a world war gave her ideas a popular audience that was more ready to heed anti-establishment warnings of threats to their well-being. Pitted against Carson were the amalgamated forces of big business and its many allies in government (both in the USA and overseas); but (as political activist Ralph Nader was later to demonstrate) it proved possible to combat these forces, and for ideas, supported by scientific findings, liberal traditions and campaigning alliances, partially to overcome them. Agribusiness and the chemical industry did not, of course, surrender or give up their activities, but from this time onwards they were subject to public scrutiny, and required to desist from manufacturing and disseminating at least their most blatantly poisonous products.

Edward O. Wilson, Sociobiology and Biophilia

Edward O. Wilson, a professor at Harvard, has attempted to apply studies of the social insects to the study of human society. Since his writings have contributed to environmentalism, they warrant a brief section here.

His major book *Sociobiology: The New Synthesis* (1975) takes it for granted that everything in nature is to be explained in evolutionary terms. So social cooperation must be programmed in our genes, and ethics is to be explained in terms of survival value. Along lines such as these, he founded the new discipline of 'sociobiology', or the evolutionary study of social practices. He also fostered the new discipline of ethology, the study of animal behaviour (founded by Konrad Lorenz and Nikolaas Tinbergen, and taken forward more recently by scientists such as Frans de Waal: see Chapter 3).

Wilson's primary ethical concern was the threat to biological diversity, due to human technology. Against the relevant practices and the resulting biodiversity loss he originally argued on the basis of 'selfish reasoning', holding that our descendants were unlikely to forgive us if the extermination of species is allowed to proceed, because of losses of sources of food and medicine.

However, Mary Midgley argued, in *Beast and Man: The Roots of Human Nature* (1979a), that Wilson's explanation of altruism is underlyingly self-interested, and his appeal to 'the selfish gene' unnecessarily introduced the language of (selfish) motivation. Midgley praised the recognition of the sociobiologists that human beings have a nature, but disputed the implicit assumption that this nature was no less egoistic than had been propounded long ago by Thomas Hobbes. She also contested the genetic determinism implicit in the work of Wilson and his followers, and implied (in *Animals and Why They Matter*, 1983) that there are deeper arguments against the extermination of species than those presented by Wilson.

Subsequently Wilson presented a further rationale for conservation, in his book *Biophilia* (1984). He named 'biophilia' the psychological tendency of the human mind to 'affiliate' with other forms of life, and with life processes, and thus to crave green vistas. The suggestion is that we need the various life-forms for the continued survival of 'the human spirit'. While this rationale for conservation is again grounded by Wilson in human self-interest, and is open to some of the same objections from Midgley, the existence of this psychological need remains open to empirical investigation, and continues to supply a serious possible ground (alongside others) for environmentalism.

However, Wilson wanted the natural sciences to be united with the humanities through the latter being absorbed by the former (Wilson, 1999; Deane-Drummond 2008: 13). But as Deane-Drummond points out, although Wilson employed the language of wonder, his stance about the humanities conflicts with that of Carson, who wrote: 'A child's world is new and fresh and beautiful, full of wonder and excitement. It is to our misfortune that to most of us that clear eyed vision, that true instinct for what is beautiful and awe inspiring is dimmed and even lost when we reach adulthood' (cited in Deane-Drummond 2008, 14). Carson, without retrenching from commitment to science, remained persistently committed to fostering the sense of beauty, as cultivated by many of the humanities as well as the sciences, and understood these forms of appreciation too as sources and springs of care for nature and its conservation.

Two Television Personalities

Another well-known figure who cultivated an aesthetic appreciation of nature was Peter Markham Scott (1909–89), whose fame derived in part from his paintings of wild birds. After a distinguished wartime career in the British navy, he founded the Severn Wildfowl Trust (now the Wildfowl and Wetlands Trust) at Slimbridge in Gloucestershire, England in 1946. He also took part in several worldwide ornithological expeditions.

He used his role as a television personality to foster the conservation of endangered species, and was knighted in 1973 for his contributions to this field. While he did not have the world-changing impact of Rachel Carson, his frequent broadcasts (and his fame as the sole surviving child of the Antarctic polar explorer, Captain Scott, and as a friend of the Duke of Edinburgh) prepared the British public to appreciate the wild geese and swans of their skies and increasingly to sympathize with the objective of wildlife conservation.

The other television personality to be mentioned here is David Bellamy (1933–2019), who was a whole generation younger than Peter Scott. He came to fame in 1967 as one of few experts able to broadcast on pollution and its impact on marine life, at the time of the oil-spill off Cornwall from the wrecked tanker *Torrey Canyon* (treated at the time as a national emergency). He went on to spread understanding and appreciation of insects and sphagnum bogs through his idiosyncratic and frequent broadcasts. His fame if anything increased when he was imprisoned in Tasmania for his part in protests at the proposed damming of the Gordon River there. By this stage, he was one of the best-known environmental campaigners.

His opposition to the siting of wind-farms in wild or undeveloped areas appeared to some as a legitimate strand of environmental activism. But when his initial acceptance of global warming (1989) was replaced by a change of mind, and he publicly called such theories 'poppycock' (even figuring in a debate with George Monbiot, in which he denied that glaciers were retreating), he fell from favour, and his television career came to an end. After that, he retired to private life, except for an ill-fated attempt in 1997 to stand for Parliament for the Referendum Party. Yet his eccentric earlier appearances had served to inculcate a widespread appreciation of pond and bug life, inducing the British public to look beyond the charismatic wildfowl presented by Scott, and many to join him knee-deep in wetlands and related preservationist activism.

As this chapter has shown, those who have influenced or instigated environmental activism have been extremely diverse (and often eccentric), rather as environmental activism itself has been. The next chapter presents an equally diverse spate of influential environmentalist writings of the 1970s and 1980s, which collectively contributed to the momentum of the new environmentalist movement.

Recommended reading

Carson, Rachel (1951). *The Sea Around Us*. Oxford: Oxford University Press.
Carson, Rachel (2000 [1962]). *Silent Spring*, London, UK: Penguin Classics.
Gardner, W. H. (1953). *Poems and Prose of Gerard Manley Hopkins*. Harmondsworth: Penguin Books.
Leopold, Aldo (1953). *Round River: From the Journals of Aldo Leopold*, ed. Luna B. Leopold. New York: Oxford University Press.
Leopold, Aldo (1966 [1949]). *A Sand County Almanac with Other Essays on Conservation from Round River*. New York: Oxford University Press.
Midgley, Mary (1979). *Beast and Man: The Roots of Human Nature*. Brighton: Harvester Press.
Midgley, Mary (1983). *Animals and Why They Matter*. Harmondsworth: Penguin.
Moore, Kathleen Dean (2005). 'The Truth of the Barnacles: Rachel Carson and the Moral Significance of Wonder', *Environmental Ethics*, 27(3): 263–277.
Nash, Roderick Frazier (2014 [1967]). *Wilderness and the American Mind*, 5th edn. New Haven, CT: Yale University Press.
Nash, Roderick Frazier (1989). *The Rights of Nature: A History of Environmental Ethics*. Madison: University of Wisconsin Press.
Schweitzer, Albert (1923). *Civilization and Ethics: The Philosophy of Civilization Part II*, trans. John Naish. London: A. & C. Black.
Wilson, Edward O. (1975). *Sociobiology: The New Synthesis*. Cambridge, MA: Harvard University Press.
Wilson, Edward O. (1984). *Biophilia*. Cambridge, MA: Harvard University Press.
Worster, Donald (1985 [1977]). *Nature's Economy: A History of Ecological Ideas*. Cambridge: Cambridge University Press.

7

Early Environmentalism

The 1960s saw widespread demonstrations, from civil rights marches in the USA, via antinuclear marches in Britain, to a student rebellion in Paris in 1968 that all but toppled the government of General Charles de Gaulle, and the Prague Spring of that year that seemed poised to overthrow the Communist government until suppressed by the armies of the Warsaw Pact. There were also protests against herbicides, pesticides and avoidable radioactive fallout, both in Britain and America, inspired by Carson's *Silent Spring* (1962).

In the USA, the incipient environmental movement was boosted by the first Earth Day, held on 22 April 1970 (founded by the Wisconsin Senator Gaylord Nelson), and marked annually on that day ever since. The campaign movement Friends of the Earth was founded in the USA by David Brouwer in 1969, and the more activist movement Greenpeace, with its Thoreau-like commitment to civil disobedience, and its opposition to nuclear testing, in Vancouver in 1971. This new wave of demonstrations and campaigns contributed to the first stirrings and the subsequent mainstreaming of the environmentalist movement. At the same time, international concern and a resolution of the UN General Assembly were aroused following evidence of the American use of the defoliant agent orange (which contained dioxin) during the country's participation in the Vietnam War (1961–71). The health of an estimated three million Vietnamese was affected; furthermore, more than 3,100,000 hectares of forest (31,000 square kilometres, or 11,969 square miles) in Vietnam, Laos and Cambodia were defoliated, and their plant and animal species were decimated (National Academy of Sciences 1994). Some of the more prominent resulting campaigns and publications expressive of environmental concern are traced in this chapter, together with the advocacy (WCED 1987) of the key concept of sustainable development, and its widespread endorsement at the Rio Summit of 1992.

'Overpopulation', Pollution and Parables

American ecologist Garrett Hardin (1915–2003) had long been campaigning for population control, in a context of environmental concern, expressed in his first 'law of human ecology': 'We can never do merely one thing. Any intrusion into nature has numerous effects, many of which are unpredictable.' This claim about anthropogenic impacts on nature warrants greater attention than his dire warnings about overpopulation, echoing as it does the themes about unforeseen human impacts on nature of Theophrastus (Chapter 1), Evelyn (Chapter 2) and Marsh (Chapter 4).

At this stage, however, Hardin produced two parables, the first in an article titled 'Tragedy of the Commons' (1968), in criticism of shared resources (including the opportunity to reproduce). Each herdsman of a herd using common land, Hardin claims, has a self-interested incentive to add one cow or sheep or goat to graze there, and will do so until it becomes overgrazed. Hence the communal ownership of resources is disastrous, or a 'tragedy'. Hardin's remedy is the enclosure or private ownership of shared resources, and, as for population, 'mutual coercion, mutually agreed upon'. In reply, many writers pointed to the successful communal ownership of common lands – for example, in many places in Switzerland and in Africa – and how their success discloses the error in Hardin's assumption of universal egoism. As for the suggestion that many countries have outstripped their carrying capacity in terms of human numbers, William Aiken (1996 [1977]) replied that the concept of carrying capacity does not apply to human society, since trade, aid and travel make human life different in kind from the societies of other mammals.

Hardin's parable did, however, influence many countries to conserve biodiverse locations, with strong rules against poaching. Besides, some shared resources have undoubtedly been exploited to excess; a clear example is the overfishing of the Grand Banks off Newfoundland. Remedies include international agreements, with fishing quotas, which, however, have not always been as well monitored as they might be.

Shortly afterwards, Hardin presented a second parable, in 'Living on a Lifeboat' (1974). Ten men drift in a lifeboat with supplies for ten people and no more, in a sea of drowning men crying out for help. If they admit even one more person into the lifeboat, all will starve. Their situation is held to mirror the situation of the developed countries, with developing countries pleading for aid. In this situation, lifeboat ethics forbids the sharing of either food or funds. To this neo-Malthusian conclusion, Jesper Ryberg (1997) replied that the analogy fails, since assistance delivered on a sustainable basis could raise the capacity of developing countries to support their populations without causing an increase in starvation or environmental destruction, either for the donors or for the recipients. Further, the demographic transition to lower birth rates across much of Asia and Latin America has invalidated Hardin's comparison of developing countries to drowning mariners.

Thus, lifeboat ethics has no valid place either in environmentalism or in international relations. Barry Commoner wrote in his 1971 book (see the next section) of the 'new barbarism of the lifeboat ethic' (cited in Pepper 1984: 20). Hardin was, indeed, listed by the Southern Poverty Law Center as a white nationalist, whose publications were 'frank in their racism'; some supportive evidence for this view emerged when, in front of a largely African audience in Cardiff, Wales, he once ridiculed the very notion of justice in international dealings. (Fortunately, the audience just laughed.) Yet his 'tragedy of the commons' parable has remained influential, particularly in cases where resources are unarguably scarce and at risk of overexploitation.

Another campaigner against population growth is Paul Ehrlich (born 1932), who founded a movement for Zero Population Growth, and published a book titled *The Population Bomb* (1970). He also campaigned against toxic pollutants and against metals found in food chains, claiming that they were threats to the Western quality of life. Ehrlich, as Pepper remarks, was an alarmist, claiming in an address of 1969 that 'we [sc. his own generation] are already dead' (Pepper 1984: 20). Subsequently, he presented a more scientific overview, together with his wife Anne Ehrlich, called *Population, Resources, Environment* (1972).

The Ehrlichs were right to draw attention to the dangers of various chemicals beyond those publicized by Rachel Carson, or newly generated since her death, including the herbicides and insecticides introduced to facilitate the so-called Green Revolution, aimed to boost agricultural productivity in developing countries, as well as the herbicides deployed in Vietnam. But as for population growth, their claims now seem exaggerated, particularly with regard to the populations of developing countries, whose environmental footprint is often inconsiderable. Besides, as Hans Rosling has argued in his posthumous book *Factfulness* (2018), most developing countries have now reduced rates of reproduction to replacement levels, and this transition is beginning to affect those countries, mainly in Africa, where family size has remained large. It is true that population grows for a time even when population rates have reached replacement levels, before stabilizing. But the real problems are those of sustainably feeding the increased human population, preserving the habitats of other species, dealing with problems of stress on the countryside adjacent to large cities, and the challenge of fostering female education and opportunities, which prove to be by far the most effective of contraceptives.

Subsequently, Paul Ehrlich joined Carl Sagan in presenting the likely ecological impacts of nuclear war and in particular of a 'nuclear winter'. This they did, together with a number of other scholars, in an article in *Science* called 'Long-term Biological Consequences of Nuclear War' (Ehrlich et al. 1983), and in the book *The Cold and the Dark: The World after Nuclear War* (Ehrlich, Sagan et al. 1985), which included a dialogue between Soviet and American scientists on this theme. These works were widely taken seriously, and may have contributed eventually to the ending of the Cold War. But the dangers of a nuclear winter (a year or more of no crops and little light for at least the Northern hemisphere) have not gone away, and are, if anything, more threatening as a result of the recent proliferation of nuclear weapons.

Barry Commoner's *The Closing Circle* (1971)

Barry Commoner (1917–2012) was a cellular biologist, whose horizons (and concerns) were broad enough to write a book in 1966 titled *Science and Survival*. His concerns about toxins covered similar areas to those of Rachel Carson and of Paul Ehrlich, but increasingly he became aware of the dangers of post-1945 technology in general, and its threats to life, both human and nonhuman.

In 1971, he published *The Closing Circle*, in which he attempted to understand the causes of ecological problems and their most cogent solutions. He rejected the theory of Paul Ehrlich that the cause was population, remarking that the areas of maximum population density did not correspond to those of the greatest pollution (nor vice versa), and also rejected the very different theory that the cause was affluence, a theory at odds with readily available statistics. Instead, he argued that the immediate cause was high technology, which replaced fibres like wool and cotton with synthetic fibres, manure with fertilizers, steel with aluminium and plastic, and so on, with side-effects including chemical effluents and other unhealthy waste products. One solution would be a return to lower technology.

However, the driving force behind the adoption of high technology was, in Commoner's view, capitalism. Capitalist corporations had an inbuilt drive to increase profitability, on pain of the capital invested in them moving elsewhere; and pressures of this kind led to an ever-expanding search for higher technology, applied to wider and wider geographical areas, and for subjecting ever more remote regions into supplying commodities for world markets, regardless of losses to their human inhabitants, and to their wildlife and habitats. Thus alternatives to capitalism, possibly involving communitarian socialism, were needed. There was much to be said for this diagnosis of the causes of ecological problems; yet ecological problems were also to be found within the communist system of the Soviet Union, where the Aral Sea had been caused to shrink, as a result of perverse planning and attempts to expand the cotton industry beyond what the two rivers feeding that sea could sustain. Such criticisms did not show Commoner to be wrong, but rather that some of the alternatives to capitalism were potentially just as harmful. Perhaps the real objection was to large organizations and economies and to the pursuit of growth, to whichever political system they (or it) might be harnessed.

Commoner also presented four 'laws of ecology'. His first 'law' we have already encountered, as propounded by Rachel Carson (see Chapter 6): 'Everything is connected to everything else.' There is one interconnected biosphere, and given unintended side-effects, virtually all actions have unlimited repercussions. While this is hardly a testable law (and reads more like a metaphysical claim than a scientific one), it was a salutary maxim for people and organizations with a technocratic and reductionist outlook, and confident in definitive solutions, to bear in mind.

His second 'law' was that 'Everything must go somewhere.' This claim (despite its hyperbole) is particularly important with respect to unintended after-effects like the spread of DDT from continent to continent, or like plastics, discarded batteries and packaging, just then beginning to be exported to countries such as Bangladesh and those of West Africa, or like chemicals, such as those that were already contributing to the photochemical smog of Los Angeles. Subsequent developments have underlined Commoner's theme, with the oceans and sea shores bestrewn with plastics, shipping lanes contaminated with oil spills, and even interplanetary space bespattered with debris, not to mention the particulates and related diesel fumes that threaten our lungs, and the carbonic acid (and the strontium) that still falls on us each time it rains. There was little awareness of the impact of carbon emissions in 1971, but there was by the time Commoner wrote *Making Peace with the Planet* in 1990.

His third law was 'Nature knows best' (a claim reminiscent of ancient Stoicism and its modern counterparts). However, the point here is that human beings have devised technology to enhance the systems of nature, but that it is all too often prone to subvert them instead. Here Commoner again overgeneralizes. He himself was writing a book, which would be out of the question without technology. So would immunization, antiseptics and anaesthetics. Technology, indeed, must have a place within solutions. Yet his warning against the omnibeneficence of technology was worth giving, for technology certainly does not have answers to all the problems.

Much the same applies to his fourth 'law': 'There is no free lunch.' We may consider ourselves immune from the forces of nature, and able to mine or reprocess nature with impunity, but will all too often live to regret that we did so, and discover our vulnerability, not least to epidemics. Yet 'laws' such as this and its predecessor call to mind the Stoic injunction to follow nature; following such 'laws', however, as in the case of the Stoics, is all too likely to lead to acceptance of the status quo, and to failing to use human ingenuity to solve the problems of the day (another prerequisite of viable solutions).

Commoner, however, did not fall into this trap, and had the sense to infringe at least his own third and fourth laws and engage in activism. He founded his own political party and stood for president in 1980. He was an honest, reflective and independent-minded man, often perplexed, yet anything but resigned to forces beyond his control.

We may note that 'ecology' in the context of Commoner's 'laws' was no longer the science of ecology, as intended by Haeckel, but a nature-oriented ideology, with a distinctive set of values. Ecology (in this sense) is selectively sceptical about technology, and inclined towards simpler lifestyles and communal forms of organization, while campaigning for conservation and sustainability, which were among the themes of Commoner's 1976 book *The Poverty of Power*. Increasingly, the term 'ecology' came to be used in Commoner's sense, so much so that many contemporary environmentalists have hardly even heard of the science of ecology.

A Blueprint for Survival (1972)

In 1972, *The Ecologist* magazine devoted an entire volume to the publication of *A Blueprint for Survival*, which was reissued the same year as a Penguin Special book. The numerous authors involved were all professionals concerned with environmental problems.

The main message of the *Blueprint* was the desirability of a stable and decentralized society, where the growth of both capital and population would be halted. In support of this message, the authors quoted a long passage from John Stuart Mill's *Principles of Political Economy* (1848). There, Mill went out on a limb, castigating the more developed nations for their pursuit of profit and of population growth. Significantly, he added the following passage:

> It is scarcely necessary to remark that a stationary condition of capital and population implies no stationary state of human improvement. There would be as much scope as ever for all kinds of mental culture, and moral and social progress; as much room for improving the Art of Living and much more likelihood of it being improved, when minds ceased to be engrossed by the art of getting on. (Mill 1920 [1848]: 751–2)

Thus a steady-state society need not be a society of cultural stagnation. And to judge from Mill's other interests, it would also be one in which the genders were treated equally and in which species of (at least) wild flowers would be preserved, if he had any say in running it.

The authors of *Blueprint* decried the dreary uniformity of a profit-driven society, and presented the possibilities for diversity (not excluding biodiversity) that a stable society could facilitate. In this connection they cited René Dubos (mentioned in Chapter 1 in connection with Benedictine stewardship, and also discussed later in this chapter). Dubos was quoted as having written as follows:

> In his recent book *The Myth of the Machine*, Lewis Mumford states that 'If man [sic] had originally inhabited a world as blankly uniform as a "high-rise" housing development, as featureless as a parking lot, as destitute of life as an automated factory, it is doubtful if he would have had a sufficiently varied experience to retain images, retain language, or acquire ideas.' To this statement, Mr Mumford would probably be willing to add that, irrespective of genetic constitution, most young people raised in a featureless environment and limited to a narrow range of life experiences will be crippled intellectually and emotionally. (Dubos 1970; cited in *The Ecologist* 1972: 64)

Diversity, the authors assert, would be a characteristic of a stable society. However, it could be commented that there is no need to wait for the introduction of a stable society for the fostering of such diversity.

They went on to emphasize the distinction between economic value, as measured by Gross National Product (GNP), and real value (the kind of value that many others, myself among them, have characterized elsewhere as 'intrinsic value' (Attfield 2018a, 2018b)). The authors cite the economist Edward Mishan (1971) as highlighting the (absurd) way in which actions such as destroying a forest to produce Sunday newspapers contribute positively to GNP. Instead, they maintain, 'we should be encouraged to buy things whose production involves the minimum environmental disruption' (*The Ecologist* 1972: 65). Once again, it could be suggested that such encouragement need not await the complete fulfilment of their project.

On population, the authors were in some respects surprisingly accurate. They gave the world population in 1972 as 3.6 billion, and predicted that it would double by just after 2000 (as it has). On the other hand, they took too little account of the demographic transition, which has involved fertility rates reducing in much of the developing world. Their fear of a world population of 15.5 billion by 2072 (*The Ecologist* 1972: 15) now seems premature. However, their projections included an increased impact related both to population and rising average consumption, resulting in yet higher increases in environmental change, which a group of leading scientists at Massachusetts Institute of Technology called 'ecological demand' (measured by the product of population and material standard of living). Ecological demand, the authors assert, was doubling every 13.5 years, which would mean that by soon after 2000 it would increase by a factor of six (*The Ecologist* 1972: 16–17). In view of increases of carbon emissions and losses to biodiversity over this period, this prediction also seems not too far off target.

This led them to state that the world cannot continue to accommodate such an increase in ecological demand, since infinite growth cannot be sustained by finite resources (*The Ecologist* 1972: 17). Infinite growth, it could be replied, is not in question, since population growth is not exponential – despite their claims (1972: 17–18) – and the *rate* of increase has for some decades been *de*creasing. Yet the increase in per capita consumption remains undeniable. Commoner would say that this does not result from the individual choices of consumers, but rather from high technology, social pressures and the practices of large corporations; and this shows that blaming individual consumers is largely misguided, with deeper explanations being required. Nevertheless, the vastly increasing impact on the environment that the *Blueprint* authors brought to light was nothing less than an arresting and important wake-up call.

The authors relied on the thesis of ecologists that diversity within ecosystems promotes their stability (a thesis that has since been questioned). But they rightly pointed to the heedless release of toxins (such as insecticides) into the environment, and thus the anthropogenic threats to both diversity and stability (*The Ecologist* 1972: 19–20). They were also concerned about the possible exhaustion of resources (1972: 23), a threat that has receded in several cases, as new discoveries have been made, but which remains serious and pervasive in the case of fresh water. Their overall concern, however, was the establishment of a sustainable and fair society, and their second chapter concerned strategies for moving towards a society of that kind, building on the work of the UN Conference on the Human Environment, held at Stockholm that same year.

As already noted (see Chapter 5), some of the ideas for a decentralized society are also to be found in a work of Petr Kropotkin, *Fields, Factories and Workshops* (1899). The authors of the *Blueprint*, however, had the advantage of awareness of ecological science, and thus of the importance of ecosystems, and also of the work of Rachel Carson, and thus the dangers of toxic pollution.

The main influence of *Blueprint* was in the United Kingdom, but subsequently Ernest Callenbach wrote about a fictitious *Ecotopia* (1978), depicting a future society somewhat resembling that of the *Blueprint*, but situated in 1999 in Oregon and northern California, which had contrived to become independent of the USA and to block American immigration. As Pepper remarks, it was 'a moot point' whether this society 'was a socialist utopia or a fascist dystopia' (1984: 25).

The Limits to Growth (1972)

Also in 1972, a team at Massachusetts Institute of Technology published their report for a project of the Club of Rome (a group of business leaders) on the Predicament of Mankind, under the title *The Limits to Growth*. In this report, they attempted to present their findings from a computer model of the world human system. Parameters included resource-use and depletion, population growth, pollution, per capita income and per capita food supply, all studied against a complex map of the relationships of each of these to one other. Findings included that if current levels of resource-use continued, resource availability would fall below the needs of the (supposedly) exponentially increasing population around the end of the twentieth century. It was also concluded that even if various changes were introduced to forestall such a disaster, such as the doubling of agricultural output and the reduction of pollution by 75 per cent from 1970 levels, either industrial or agricultural output would decline, followed by a collapse of population. Combining all the remedial changes could delay this collapse by almost a century, but disaster would ensue sooner or later.

To avoid such 'overshoot and collapse' altogether, nothing but a stabilized world model would do. Such a model involved both population and pollution control, policies of recycling and an abandonment of economic growth. The report also favoured a redistribution of resources between the world's developed and developing countries. But its main recommendation was a combination of zero population growth and zero economic growth.

There have been many criticisms of *Limits*, with the first batch appearing in the Club of Rome's own commentary (Meadows 1974 [1972]: 185–97). One criticism was that the model involved a simplification of the real world, and the commentary recognized that this was, perforce, the case. Another was that scientific and technological advances might possibly defer the evil day; the reply of the commentary was that such a deferment would perforce be temporary at best. One of the technological changes mentioned was the generation of solar energy, which has not, in fact, come too late, as the commentary suggests; but it must be allowed that such technological solutions are not enough alone to avert disaster. A further criticism was that new stocks of minerals might be discovered; as already mentioned, this has in fact been the case, greatly reducing most of the problems of shortages of materials and of fuel. As the commentary predicts, such discoveries (in combination with the development of carbon-free energy sources) has provided humanity with a breathing-space, sufficient at least to discover the (then unanticipated) problem of climate change.

The final criticism is that the report is excessively 'technocratic' (Meadows 1974 [1972]: 185), focusing on material processes and limits and neglecting social values. In reply, the commentary urges that the report demonstrates the need for a change in the values of society. Strangely, though, the commentary considers that the report's conclusions, including zero population growth, do not conflict with the values of any society, ignoring the values of both the Vatican and its followers and (at that time) the Kremlin and theirs.

Finally, the commentary draws attention to a number of points where the Club of Rome endorsed (thereby) the report's conclusions. They agreed, for example, that the report had shown that there were limits to the growth both of production and of population, and that an equilibrium state of the planet was mandatory. But this, they added, required the development of developing countries, a process that would involve an overall global strategy to be generated and agreed. Here they concluded: 'The strategy for dealing with the two key issues of development and environment must be conceived as a joint one.' (It cannot be unduly fanciful to recognize here the seeds of the establishment in the next decade of the World Commission on Environment and Development, chaired by Gro Harlem Brundtland, and of the resulting Brundtland Report in 1987, discussed later in this chapter.)

The commentary went on to stress the need to redress 'the present unbalanced and dangerously deteriorating world situation', by which they seem to have meant both the lack of equilibrium in matters of production and population and also the prevailing global inequalities. This was a task for the current generation, and would require a concerted international effort. And then (in the spirit of Mill) they affirm that a brake on 'demographic and economic growth spirals' need not and must not mean a freezing of global development, adding that ensuring that it did not mean this was a task for the world's developed or wealthier countries. If social values were to change enough, then an equilibrium society could mean 'a good material life plus opportunities for limitless individual and social development', as Mill had propounded a century earlier (see the previous section). The situation, therefore, was one of very grave concern, but not of despair (Meadows 1974 [1972]: 194–55).

Further criticisms were to follow. Shortly after the publication of *Limits*, there was an attempt to replicate the world computer model on the part of a team at the University of Sussex, with very different results, which contested some of the key findings of the MIT team. It was also soon noticed that, striking as was the message about the exponential growth of population, including its severe dangers, population growth was not in fact exponential, albeit still a cause for concern; and, as time went on, the theory of a demographic transition in the developing world began to be borne out in observable fact, as family sizes began to decrease alongside increased prosperity and security. Population growth turns out not to be a geometrical curve, but rather to be 'S'-shaped (Rosling and Rosling 2018). This does not mean that the conclusions of *Limits* were all illusory, but it does mean that the problems of pollution and scarcity need to be reassessed, together with other issues relating to the environment.

Scepticism was also shown by some about the motives of a wealthy organization like the Club of Rome in sponsoring this report. Was it not, perhaps, in their interests to advocate self-restraint on population growth among the poor, and the discovery of previously undiscovered minerals that the corporations owned by the rich could exploit? Certainly, it is not known whether the individual members of the Club of Rome took steps to comply with their own recommendations; at the same time, it is unlikely that many of them were put at significant financial risk when some developed countries introduced measures of taxation designed to support the development of poor countries. However, whatever their motivation, the report succeeded in conveying the need for changes of values, and, as the commentary declared, nothing but the perception that this change was necessary for survival was likely to motivate its being taken seriously (Meadows 1974 [1972]: 196).

Small Is Beautiful (1973)

Small Is Beautiful, a book by E. F. Schumacher (1911–77) subtitled 'A Study of Economics As If People Mattered', discusses many topics. It opens with the claim that the modern world and the economists who guide it confuse capital with income, get their values wrong accordingly and thus treat nature and the land as expendable (like income), rather than in need of long-term preservation. By 'land', Schumacher means both the soil and the creatures that live on it (1973: 96), rather in the manner of Aldo Leopold. Land, he suggests, is currently treated as a means to human ends such as production, but he rejected the view that 'the living world has no significance beyond that of a quarry for exploitation', holding that it ought to be treated as an end in itself, not to be valued in the manner of economics, but treated as irreplaceable, and 'in a certain sense sacred' (1973: 103, 97).

This, however, would involve a complete change in the organization of modern societies. They need to be decentralized, and far more jobs need to be created in agriculture, with a recognition that the purposes of working on the land is to foster health, beauty and permanence, as well as food-production. This change would also involve a move away from high technology to 'intermediate technology', and the use of simpler machines, creatively invented to allow workers to be reconciled with the natural world and undertake fulfilling work, unlike the back-breaking work of pre-industrial society and also unlike the alienating mass-production of modern industry and industrialized agriculture. Besides, communities and productive enterprises should be small, for small units impact the environment much less than large ones, despite their greater number. And the methods and equipment employed must leave 'ample room for human creativity', in an attempt to overcome the dehumanising tendencies of modern production-lines (1973: 103, 105, 31, 32).

Schumacher's book also includes a broadside against nuclear energy generation (1973: 124–35). There is no known way of reducing radio-activity once it has been generated, and bequeathing the problem of containing and storing both the nuclear plants and nuclear wastes to future generations involves excessively discounting their interests, and risking the health of our children, grandchildren and their successors into the distant future. Compared with radioactive emissions, smoky air, he held, is a much less serious problem.

Schumacher goes on to advocate 'technology with a human face', following the Beatitudes of the fifth chapter of the gospel of Matthew. While much of his thought was inspired by Buddhism, encountered while he worked as a development economist in Myanmar, his work also quotes frequently from the Bible. Indeed, he translates 'Blessed are the meek, for they shall inherit the Earth' as 'We need a gentle approach, a non-violent spirit, and small is beautiful'; and it is from this translation that he derives the title of his book.

Criticisms of Schumacher's approach could focus, among other matters, on his adherence to the notion of natural capital. For while capital is standardly treated very differently from income, 'capital' is also widely used of assets that are potentially saleable. And while this may be harmless with reference to small parcels of land, it is less applicable to nature or the environment in general, or to (say) the land of a country, such as that of the Nauru Islanders or of the people of Diego Garcia, who were long deprived of their land for purposes of mineral extraction in one case and a military base in the other. Schumacher's association of capital with things regarded as ends in themselves is also problematic, for capital does not (as such) have intrinsic value, alongside the well-being of living creatures (see further Attfield 1998b), even though land (which he treats as capital) is standardly a precondition of the very possibility of such well-being. Nevertheless, within the concepts accessible to economists, Schumacher's choice to treat land as capital rather than income could still be regarded as a step in the right direction.

Further, Schumacher's stress on the need for different values, for reduced environmental impact and for work to become meaningful again was widely welcomed. However, his proposal for intermediate technology underwent criticism, as being unsuited to aspects of the modern world. Many enterprises and systems could not become small-scale, or even middling; examples include the national grid (supplying electric power), railway systems and national health systems, despite the scope for some amount of decentralization. Critics wondered whether Schumacher was calling for a reversion to the craft and cottage industries advocated by such Victorian pundits as John Ruskin (1819–1900) and William Morris (1834–96). Besides, 'intermediate technology' seemed to suggest too mathematical a mean between high technology and low technology that was far from universally appropriate.

The same problem of specifying an intermediate position between extremes had troubled Aristotle, in his account of virtue as a mean between extremes (understood as vices). Aristotle solved this problem by rejecting a mathematical mean in favour of 'the mean relative to us', or a humanly appropriate mean. Schumacher and his followers adopted much the same solution. In due course they replaced the concept of 'intermediate technology' with that of 'appropriate technology', in which the size of communities and enterprises would be adjusted to time, place, circumstances and human needs, and would not in all cases be small. However, Schumacher's ideas were widely and constructively taken up, particularly in developing countries, but also to some degree in Europe (McRobie 1982; Pepper 1984: 26); and they remain a recurrent part of the social philosophy of the Green movement to this day.

It should be noted that Schumacher was relatively untroubled by the problem of population, as perceived by Hardin, Ehrlich and others, as opposed to solving the problem of unemployment. However, his concern about quality of life was well targeted, and reflected that of the *Blueprint*. His strictures on nuclear energy were original and timely, but his apparent toleration of smoky air turned out to be misguided. He was, however, writing before climate change was widely acknowledged, and before air pollution became globally recognized. Besides, because of the enactment in British law of the Clean Air Act (1956), the problem in Britain seemed less acute than it does now, and hugely less pressing than the earlier problem of the 'smogs' of the early 1950s.

René Dubos and Barbara Ward

René Dubos (1901–82) was a French-born American microbiologist, whose work in isolating key varieties of bacteria paved the way for the discovery of antibiotics. He was also an environmentalist, whose contributions, including his celebrating the Benedictines (rather than the Franciscans) as patron saints of ecology, have already been remarked (see Chapter 1); and he was cited in the *Blueprint* (see earlier in this chapter).

Despite discovering how to kill harmful germs, Dubos came to recognize that not even 'disease-causing germs' should be 'eradicated'. For a healthy human being 'could and should rely on natural resistance to infection', and there were dangers if new strains of germs became resistant to antibiotics. Rather, germs were part of an ecosystem in which human beings and germs could coexist (Nash 1989: 77), a new idea, but one whose importance has been increasingly realized.

Subsequently, in his 1972 book *A God Within*, Dubos contrasted two forms of anthropocentrism. He rejected the form which makes humanity 'the only value to be considered in managing the world'. But he accepted what he called 'enlightened anthropocentrism', which holds that the world's good always coincides with the ultimate human good. (Always?) This (he maintained) was the true path of stewardship, which depended on loving nature 'for her own sake' (cited in Nash 1989: 78). Those of us who doubt Dubos's 'coincidence' theory can nevertheless welcome the tacit biocentrism or ecocentrism present (despite his denials) in his advocacy of loving nature for itself.

Barbara Ward (1914–81), a British economist, was also an environmentalist, who in 1966 published *Spaceship Earth* (possibly thereby inventing that phrase), a book that expressed concern for humanity to live self-sufficiently within the limits of our planet. She was also a strong advocate of international development, studying the social and economic problems of West Africa and India. Her Christian concern for people and their fulfilment directed her away from forms of environmentalism such as those of Hardin and Ehrlich that aimed to curtail or reduce the human population, with its implicit misanthropic bias. Instead, she originated the idea that developed countries should devote a fixed proportion of their GDP to development aid for developing countries, one of history's more fruitful ideas. There could hardly be a stronger repudiation of Hardin's 'lifeboat ethic', or a stronger endorsement of an ethics that is global in scope and internationalist in content.

With a view to the 1972 UN Stockholm conference on the Human Environment, Ward and Dubos were jointly commissioned by its secretary, Maurice Strong, to prepare and write *Only One Earth: The Care and Maintenance of a Small Planet* (1972). This was an important development, for at least two reasons. It marked the moment when the United Nations, and thus the international system, became officially cognizant of environmental problems. And effectively, Ward and Dubos devised between them the concept of 'sustainable development', although without using that phrase itself. Their task was in some ways harder than that of the authors of *Blueprint* and of *Limits to Growth*, because, as well as guarding against transgressions of limits, their brief included finding viable pathways towards adequate nutrition and adequate supplies of fresh water, energy, sanitation and healthcare for humanity, together with the conservation of other living creatures, which was also a profound concern for both these authors.

Their discussion of development was important, but would take us too far away from the central themes of this book. However, their remarks on the pollution of cities worldwide, and also of the distinct problems of developed and developing countries, were profound. Among the problems common to countries of both kinds, they considered the expansion of nuclear energy, and counselled extreme caution (1972: 187). They commended a convention that would forbid the dumping of toxic wastes at sea (1972: 280), something that came about in the form of the Law of the Sea Convention of 1982. They also remarked, *inter alia*, that the soils and ecosystems of developing countries were in most cases more vulnerable than those of the developed countries, and that protecting them would require aid from richer countries (as was agreed in principle at the Rio Conference of 1992, and in practice at the Nagoya Conference held in Japan in 2010).

Just as significantly, in an illuminating passage, they explained how the accumulation of carbon dioxide in the atmosphere might possibly become large enough to raise surface temperatures by 2 degrees (Celsius), enough to set in motion the long-term warming of the planet. They added that the growth of cloud cover might either lower surface temperatures, or reinforce the 'greenhouse' effect (1972: 266–8). There was no widespread acceptance of such problems at that stage (a time when some experts were envisaging global cooling rather than warming), but this passage proved to be an amazing anticipation of the recognition of global warming that became a commonplace from the early 1990s.

From this stage onwards, it was increasingly recognized that issues of environment and development needed to be considered together. There was considerable resistance to considering them at all, granted the prevailing technological optimism both in the capitalist West and the communist East. Nevertheless, in the aftermath of *Only One Earth*, the United Nations set up (during the 1980s) the World Commission on Environment and Development (also known as 'the Brundtland Commission' after its chair, Gro Harlem Brundtland, Prime Minister of Norway), which reported in 1987. That report, called *Our Common Future*, is the theme of the final section of this chapter.

Our Common Future and Its Aftermath

Advocacy of sustainability pre-dated the Brundtland Report. For example, in 1977 the economist Herman Daly and others had advocated *The Sustainable Society* (1977), a society with stabilized levels of population and production; and, as we have seen, a world society with upper limits to population and production was earlier advocated in *The Limits to Growth* (Meadows et al. 1974 [1972]). Also, as was mentioned in Chapter 4, Mary Williams (1978) had put forward a theory of how to manage renewable biological resources sustainably, through coordinated self-restraint, and similar ideas about forests had been pioneered long before by American foresters such as Gifford Pinchot and his followers (again, see Chapter 4). There again, a more radical form of preservation-based sustainability had long been advocated by ecologists such as John Muir (discussed in the same chapter).

Yet the idea of pairing sustainability and development will have seemed paradoxical, if not contradictory, when it was put forward first by the *World Conservation Strategy* (International Union for the Conservation of Nature 1980) and later by the World Commission on Environment and Development in 1987. The tensions were indeed already present when the concepts were combined in 1972 within *Only One Earth*; but the phrase 'sustainable development' did not emerge until 1980.

For those who associate development with economic growth, sustainable development will have appeared to be nothing more than an outright contradiction. However, development, or the process of satisfying unsatisfied basic human needs, needs to be carefully distinguished from growth, as not all development involves growth, and far from all growth constitutes development. The nature of development is well set out in the definition of the concept contained in the United Nations Declaration of the Right to Development of 1986, which states:

> [Development is] a comprehensive economic, social and political process, which aims at the constant improvement of the well-being of the entire population and of all its inhabitants on the basis of their active, free and meaningful participation in development and in the fair distribution of the benefits resulting therefrom. (United Nations 1986)

(This is, regrettably, a circular definition, but the circularity can easily be cured by replacing 'in development' with 'in this process'.)

If we bear in mind that the sustainability of a practice or society is its capacity to be practised or maintained indefinitely, it becomes easier to see how the process of development could be or become sustainable, whether through continual movement towards the satisfaction of needs, or through attaining that state or affairs and then maintaining it sustainably. This will have been the understanding of the World Conservation Strategy, which included the sustainable maintenance of resources and of habitats vital to both human beings and other creatures.

As for the Brundtland Report, its opening definition of sustainable development ran as follows: development that meets the needs of the present without compromising the ability of future generations to meet their own needs (WCED 1987: 43). This definition creditably implies that well-being should not decrease over time. But it also *under*defines sustainable development in at least two crucial ways. First, it refrains from implying that the present generation is to seek to enable the ability of future generations to meet their own needs, and, where possible, to plan accordingly. Second, it neglects to specify that sustainable development involves the preservation of nonhuman species and habitats. Both these themes are affirmed elsewhere in the report, but the definition allowed readers to form an unduly minimalist interpretation of its central message.

The central part of the report applies sustainable development to different sectors, including population and resources, food security, species and ecosystems, energy policy, industry (subtitled 'producing more with less') and the urban challenge. One recurrent theme is the need to take fully into account the costs of environmental damage and destruction (or to internalize externalities), and also to compare these costs with the value of relevant benefits (WCED 1987: 37; Attfield 2015 [1999]: 107–8). Another recurrent theme is the value that nonhuman species have independently of benefits to humanity, and the need to respect it (WCED 1987: 57, 147, 155, 163), although some parts of the report are written as if these passages were absent. Although the Declaration of the subsequent Rio conference (1992) proved to be anthropocentric, and to focus entirely on human needs and interests, the Brundtland Report was significantly different in this regard.

With respect to population, the report recognizes that levels will stabilize at some stage during the twenty-first century (a vast improvement on the thinking of Hardin and of Ehrlich), but that there are different levels and timings at which this could occur. Implicitly, it commends policies fostering the lower level (7.7 billion) and the earlier date (2010), as more readily compatible with sustainable development. While it is now recognized that stabilization will take longer, the relevant predictions were strikingly accurate.

The report goes on to discuss how to feed these numbers sustainably, recognizing that in order to save wild habitats, production per hectare of agricultural and pastoral land will need to increase. Subsequently, it also discusses global energy supplies, sitting on the fence on the question of whether nuclear energy generation should be included, but advocating increases in the various kinds of renewable energy. The 'serious probability' of a greenhouse effect produced by emissions of carbon dioxide is recognized, and this is one reason for the advocacy of renewables as a sustainable way of satisfying human needs.

The chapter on species and ecosystems acknowledges the danger that, given current trends, some third of current species (not to mention subspecies) will soon be lost. One reason to regret this prospect lies in human needs, for example because of the potential loss of genetic materials, some of which, found in the wild, have been known to replenish or regenerate stocks of cultivated crops: see the passage on fungus-resistant maize, found in a montane forest in Mexico (WCED 1987: 155). But a quite separate reason consists in the independent value of the species themselves (WCED 1987: 155, 163). National and international action to conserve species is commended through (what later became) the Convention on Biodiversity, initiated at Rio in 1992. Conservation of species and subspecies was recognized as requiring the related conservation of habitats. Relatedly, many countries had already acknowledged the importance of species preservation in 1973 by signing the United Nations Convention on International Trade in Endangered Species of Wild Flora and Fauna (CITES), for which the motivation was partly nonanthropocentric.

The urban environment is also considered, including the dangers of pollution and poor hygiene, and the need for provision of open spaces. Not all the dangers arising from vehicle emissions were known. But the risks of ozone depletion, as caused by CFCs (chlorofluorocarbons) and HCFCs (hydro-chlorofluorocarbons) in industrial processes such as refrigeration and also in aerosols, had recently come to light, and emergency steps to counteract this danger were on the point of being taken following the Montreal Protocol of 1987.

The Brundtland Report concluded with a call for action, which led to the United Nations Rio Summit of 1992, with close to two hundred countries participating. By then, the evidence of atmospheric climate change had become stronger, and a Framework Convention on Climate Change was initiated, as was the Intergovernmental Panel on Climate Change. The convention was taken forward in a series of conferences, but it was not until the Kyoto Conference of 1997 that any sort of international agreement was secured. The Rio Summit also agreed to a Convention on Biodiversity, developed in a separate sequence of conferences, culminating in that held at Nagoya in Japan in 2010.

As previously mentioned, the Rio Declaration, which endorsed sustainable development, was explicitly anthropocentric. But the campaigning that preceded and followed it frequently had a broader basis. Meanwhile, it became open to environmentalists of whichever country to argue that environmentally sustainable development was indispensable, since it was now enshrined in the international treaty agreed at Rio, and thus in national law as well. They could also appeal to a version of the precautionary principle endorsed in the Rio Declaration, namely that lack of scientific consensus was not to count as a reason against action where there was reason to believe that serious or irreversible harm was in prospect. This strengthened the arm of campaigners both for climate change mitigation and equally for biodiversity preservation.

With the Rio Declaration (despite its shortcomings) a version of environmentalism attained worldwide political prominence. This chapter has traced how environmentalist campaigns and publications (despite their varied emphases and variable degrees of clarity) achieved sufficient prominence for this achievement to become possible. The next chapter depicts some of the main strands of environmental philosophy, which also originated in the early 1970s.

Recommended reading

Aiken, William (1996 [1977]). 'The "Carrying Capacity" Equivocation', in William Aiken and Hugh LaFollette (eds), *World Hunger and Morality*, 2nd edn. Upper Saddle River, NJ: Prentice-Hall.
Attfield, Robin (2015 [1999]). *The Ethics of the Global Environment*, 2nd edn. Edinburgh: Edinburgh University Press.
Commoner, Barry (1971). *The Closing Circle: Confronting the Environmental Crisis*. New York: Alfred A. Knopf.
Ehrlich, Paul and Ehrlich, Anne (1972). *Population, Resources, Environment*. San Francisco, CA: Freeman.
Hardin, Garrett (1968). 'Tragedy of the Commons', *Science*, 162: 1243–1248.
Hardin, Garrett (1974). 'Living on a Lifeboat', *Bioscience*, 24.
International Union for the Conservation of Nature (1980). *World Conservation Strategy*. Gland, Switzerland: IUCN/UNEP/WWF.
Kropotkin, Petr (1899), *Fields, Factories and Workshops*. Reissued as *Fields, Factories and Workshops (Tomorrow)*, ed. C. Ward. London: Unwin, 1974.
Meadows, Donella H. et al. (1974 [1972]). *The Limits to Growth*. London: Pan Books.
Pepper, David (1984). *The Roots of Modern Environmentalism*. London: Routledge.
Rosling, Hans and Rosling, Ola (2018). *Factfulness: Ten Reasons We're Wrong About the World – and Why Things are Better Than You Think*. London: Hodder & Stoughton.
Ryberg, Jesper (1997). 'Population and Third World Assistance', *Journal of Applied Philosophy*, 14: 207–219.
Schumacher, E. F. (1973). *Small Is Beautiful: A Study of Economics As If People Mattered*. London: Blond & Briggs.
United Nations (1986). *Declaration on the Right to Development*. New York: United Nations.
Ward, Barbara and Dubos, René (1972). *Only One Earth: The Care and Maintenance of a Small Planet*. Harmondsworth, UK: Penguin.

WCED (World Commission on Environment and Development) (1987). *Our Common Future* ('The Brundtland Report'). Oxford: Oxford University Press.

8

Environmental Philosophy and Kindred Studies

The Birth of Environmental Philosophy

This chapter surveys the origins and development of environmental philosophy and of some of its more prominent strands. Environmental philosophy is usually held to have originated in the early 1970s. The early years of that decade saw the publication at a World Congress of Philosophy (held in Bulgaria) of the Australian Richard Routley's 'Is There a Need for a New, an Environmental Ethic?' (1973), of Arne Naess's 'The Shallow and the Deep, Long-Term Ecology Movement: A Summary' in Norway (1973) and, a little later in the USA, of Holmes Rolston III's 'Is There an Ecological Ethic?' (1975). I have been party to this kind of account several times over (Attfield 1998a, 2012a, 2018a, 2018b); and certainly the first conference in the field was held in 1971 (Palmer 2003), at the University of Georgia, USA, with its proceedings published in 1974 (Blackstone, 1974).

Yet environmental philosophy can be traced back to several decades earlier. As we have already seen (in two passages of Chapter 1), Lynn White published his famous (or notorious) article 'The Historic Roots of Our Ecologic Crisis' in 1967, generating controversies not only about whether Christianity was anthropocentric and about medieval attitudes and technology, but also about the acceptability of anthropocentrism itself. These controversies were already being conducted before the philosophical writings of the early 1970s were published, but have been sufficiently discussed in this book already (in Chapter 1). Yet it is worth adding that they gave rise among theologians to the influential ecotheology movement (see Chapter 9), which enabled White later to claim that it was he who had generated it (White 1973; Whitney 1993). A recent contribution to this thriving field can be found in Celia Deane-Drummond's *Eco-Theology* (2008).

Earlier still, in 1958, Henry Bugbee (1915–99), an American veteran of the Second World War, published his existentialist journal, *The Inward Morning*, although his reflections on the significance of wilderness continued until at least his essay 'Wilderness in America' (Bugbee 2017 [1974]). Bugbee warned that, despite wilderness having once been understood as a challenge to push back the frontier of civilization, there was currently a danger that unless attitudes changed and wilderness was recognized for itself, there would be no wilderness left (Rodick 2017: 84–93). Bugbee appears to have been influenced more by mystics such as Meister Eckhart, texts like the *Bhagavad Gita* and theologians like Paul Tillich than by ecologists such as Aldo Leopold; and despite his ongoing fame in Montana, where (after spells at Harvard and Penn State) he eventually settled, his work was little known until his essays (some published, most unpublished) were posthumously set before the public by David W. Rodick.

Even earlier, in an article called 'Le sentiment de la nature, force revolutionnaire' ('The sense of nature: a revolutionary force'), the French philosopher Bernard Charbonneau (1910–96) began associating nature with freedom and the project of escaping from authoritarianism; the article was published 'in an obscure French personalist newsletter' of 1937 (Cérézuelle 2018: xxi). Charbonneau was a lifelong friend of the personalist thinker Jacques Ellul (1912–94), and they are now regarded as among the founders of the French ecological movement, despite Charbonneau still being little known, even in France (Cérézuelle 2018). He continued discussing the role of wilderness in *Le Feu vert* (1980; *The Green Light*, 2018), where he warned against focusing on the preservation of 'pure nature' as just the kind of compartmentalization that suits technological society. Instead, we need to break with the kind of accelerated development which that kind of society fosters, and integrate nature and society rather than seeing them as separate (see further Charbonneau 2018 [1980]). Such teaching eventually exercised some degree of influence in France, albeit on a minority.

Nevertheless the works of Routley, Naess and Rolston initiated the application of the methods of analytic philosophy to environmental issues, and unleashed what has become a thriving new branch of philosophy. Routley (1935–96) was concerned about whether a new, nonanthropocentric ethic was needed, and perhaps already embodied in widespread judgements. While he may well have been right about likely responses to his thought-experiments (such as to the case of the Last Man, who occupies his final moments needlessly destroying both flora and fauna), Routley seems mistaken in thinking that Western traditions were uniformly anthropocentric. For his part, Naess (1912–2009) contrasted two kinds of ecology movement, one concerned with human interests of the current generation in the West (the Shallow Movement), and one concerned with the Third World, the distant future as well as the near future, and non-human interests (Deep Ecology). He thus invited readers to consider whether moral standing attached not only to all current human beings, but also to future ones, and to nonhuman organisms too. Some of the policies associated with Deep Ecology (such as population reduction) seem less acceptable, but Deep Ecology was to exercise considerable influence later in both Australia and the United States.

Rolston's concern was with how to derive an ecological 'ought' from ecological and other facts. The value of human survival allows of such a derivation, but in his view that of the integrity of ecosystems can generate an ecological 'ought' as well. Rolston (born 1932) was effectively raising not only the issue of the grounding of moral judgements (and ecological ones in particular), but also that of the location of nonderivative value, since it is in such value that obligations seem to be grounded (Rolston 1975; Attfield 2018b).

Routley had been responding to the stance of John Passmore (1914–2004), another Australian philosopher and historian of ideas, who in 1974 published *Man's Responsibility for Nature*. Passmore attempted to find within Western traditions the 'seeds' of attitudes capable of coping with problems such as pollution, desertification, loss of resources and of species, loss of wilderness, and growing populations. While his stance was largely anthropocentric, he also brought to light two ancient traditions, one concerning the human stewardship of nature, and the other the role of humanity in completing the creator's role through enhancing the landscape (which he called 'cooperation with nature'). Passmore controversially regarded these as minority traditions, and (amazingly) considered the stewardship tradition to have virtually disappeared between the period of pagan antiquity and the seventeenth century; yet his work disclosed possibilities of long-termist and inclusive ethical thought-forms (animal welfarism included), which others were able to develop. By the time his second edition was published in 1980, he told me that he already regarded the problems as more pressing, and was beginning to regard his earlier work as too conservative. Certainly, his rediscovery of the stewardship tradition, elicited from the narrative supplied by Clarence Glacken (1967), facilitated redevelopment of that approach, partly among theologians, but partly in the thinking of secular thinkers and organizations as well.

Works such as those by Routley, Naess, Rolston and Passmore led to a growth of interest in environmental thought among philosophers, and before long the first journal in the field, *Environmental Ethics*, was founded by Eugene C. Hargrove in 1979. Hargrove, having survived a dispute about his tenure at Athens, Georgia, moved to the University of North Texas, and the journal has been edited from there ever since. Later, another journal, *Environmental Values*, was established by Alan Holland of the University of Lancaster in 1992. By that stage, and in view of the pressing environmental problems of the day, there was a burgeoning interest among philosophers in environmental concepts and issues, which gradually spread from the original centres of interest, such as Australia, Scandinavia and USA, to most countries of the world. Thus I began teaching environmental philosophy at Cardiff in 1977, and began publishing in this field in 1981. In 1990 Holmes Rolston founded the International Society for Environmental Ethics, which soon included representatives of all the inhabited continents, and continues to hold conferences, some of them alongside conferences of the three divisions of the American Philosophical Association.

A spate of further journals now came into being. In 1996, *Ethics and the Environment* was launched in USA, where *Philosophy and Geography* also emerged in 1997. *Worldviews: Environment, Culture, Religion* started up in 1997 and in 1998 came *Ethics, Place and Environment*, more recently renamed *Ethics, Policy and Environment* (Palmer 2003: 16). Together with the older journals just mentioned, and the related societies, the arrival of this cluster of publications meant that environmental philosophy was now an institutionalized subfield of philosophy.

Individualism: Animal Welfare and Rights

While some environmental philosophers focused on ecosystems and species, developing the implications of ecological science and the insights of Leopold (see Chapters 5 and 6), other philosophers drew their inspiration from campaigners for animal welfare such as Jeremy Bentham and Henry Salt (see Chapter 4). Prominent among these was the Australian philosopher Peter Singer (born 1946), whose barn-storming first book, *Animal Liberation: A New Ethics for Our Treatment of Animals*, was published in 1975. Singer drew attention to the horrendous treatment of animals in factory farms, and insisted that the pain and suffering of sentient organisms needed to be taken seriously, since like interests should be given equal consideration, whatever the species of the creatures affected. This was explicitly a utilitarian position, now given a twentieth-century application. While Singer's stance was primarily targeted at practices of animal husbandry, and advocated vegetarianism on this basis, it also had environmental implications. For, although Singer rejected claims about the moral status of nonsentient creatures such as plants, funguses and bacteria, he recognized the needs of sentient wild animals for intact habitats, and favoured the conservation of woods, forests and wetlands on the basis of these interests, together with relevant human interests. (Vegetarianism has more recently been widely advocated on grounds of carbon mitigation as well as grounds of animal welfarism.)

Singer applied his position to further ethical issues in *Practical Ethics* (1979), which considered bioethical areas such as abortion and euthanasia, as well as questions about animal treatment and diet. This clear and radical text ran to three editions, and was widely used as an ethics textbook, despite the disagreement of philosophers who considered that it drew the boundaries of moral consideration too narrowly.

Shortly afterwards, Tom Regan (1938–2017) presented a quite different route from concern about animals to environmental ethics, in 'The Nature and Possibility of an Environmental Ethic' (1981). Two years later his position was stated more fully in his book *The Case for Animal Rights* (1983). Regan began by arguing that what Kant had held about persons applied also to any creature that is the experiencing subject of a life. (As we saw in Chapter 2, Schopenhauer attempted a similar extension of Kantianism in the early nineteenth century.) Any conscious creature that has a welfare important to itself has thereby 'inherent moral worth', and thus rights, including the right not to be treated as merely a resource for others (McShane 2013: 3). Hence it is because of this moral worth and these rights, and not just because of its sentience, that it should be protected from practices such as hunting and farming. For the same reasons, the habitats of wild creatures that are 'subjects of a life' should be preserved (but not those of others).

Critics, however, were free to comment that, for this approach, the limits of moral standing do not reach as far as those of sentience, since quite complex cognitive capacities are required for such consideration to be in place. Most but not all mammals appear to qualify, but few other creatures, and not even ones capable of suffering pain, unless also conscious of their own welfare. Hence the extent of environmental protection implicit in this 'animal rights' approach seems extremely limited. Objections could also be presented at the application of the term 'rights' to creatures that will never be in a position to claim them; yet it could be replied that infants have rights even though they will never be in a position to claim them while still infants. However, a different kind of objection should be considered here.

Stances such as those of Singer and Regan were classified as 'animal welfarism' and actually contrasted with an environmental ethic in J. Baird Callicott's article 'Animal Liberation: A Triangular Affair' (1980). For Callicott, pain was not intrinsically bad, but neutral; its value depended on its contribution to the functioning of an ecosystem. Nor were individuals of special concern; what mattered was the good of the relevant whole, whether a city-state, as for Plato, or an ecosystem or the biosphere, as for followers of Leopold. Later (after reading Mary Midgley's *Animals and Why They Matter*), Callicott abandoned these stances about animals. But there is also room for criticism of the gulf he was suggesting between animal welfarist and environmentalist stances. For, as we have seen in Chapter 4 on American humanitarians and British animal welfare campaigners, animal welfarists have often fostered a broadening of people's awareness of nonhuman species, their habitats and their needs. Thus it is doctrinaire to require that holding an environmental ethic requires abandoning individualism, and adopting instead some form of holistic or organismic view, whether at the level of ecosystems or of species. Besides, broader forms of individualist approach should also be considered, as is done in the next section: another is that of Hans Jonas (Attfield 2009a).

Individualism in the Form of Biocentrism

Already in 1973, Naess had defended biocentrism, the view that all living creatures (and not just sentient ones) have moral standing, and should be given consideration, adding that, in principle, they should be considered equally, and had 'the equal right to live and blossom'. He was aware that practical necessity obliged some to kill others, but treated this as an exception to his basic principle of biocentric egalitarianism. A comparable stance had previously been put forward by Albert Schweitzer, with his principle of reverence for life (see Chapter 6).

Subsequently, Kenneth E. Goodpaster (born 1944) clarified what biocentrism involved by distinguishing between moral consideration (which he too held to be due to all living creatures, as each had a good of its own), and the separate issue of moral significance, which concerned the degree of consideration, or the weight, which should be shown to a given creature. This opened the way to inegalitarian forms of biocentrism, in which Singer's principle of the equal consideration of equal interests could be observed, together with its implication of the greater consideration of greater interests and the lesser consideration of lesser interests.

Goodpaster (1978) went on to show how his position avoided standard objections to egalitarian biocentrism, such as that it made life unliveable. Despite hints that the author also favoured some kind of holistic position, this landmark paper has inspired many subsequent individualist forms of biocentrism.

Parts of Goodpaster's stance were echoed in the next decade in various papers and also in an influential book by a longstanding ethicist, Paul W. Taylor (1923–2015), *Respect for Nature: A Theory of Environmental Ethics* (1986). For Taylor, all living organisms have equal moral worth, because each has an inbuilt *telos* (goal or purpose) to fulfil the sort of life proper to its kind. He also presented practical principles, such as a principle of self-defence, as guidance for practical purposes, and claimed (rather implausibly) that they were derivable from his biocentric egalitarianism. James Sterba later adjusted some of the practical principles (1995: 191–207), and Taylor endorsed his adjustments, but the problem remained of deriving the adjusted principles from Taylor's basic version.

Most current biocentrists, however, reject an egalitarianism of creatures of different capacities, and hold that, while all have moral standing, their moral significance varies, for example in accordance with their different capacities. This kind of biocentrism was already implicit in my 1981 article 'The Good of Trees', published before any of Taylor's egalitarian writings; it became explicit in my *The Ethics of Environmental Concern* (Attfield 1991 [1983]) and was further developed in the form of biocentric consequentialism in my books *A Theory of Value and Obligation* (1987) and *Value, Obligation and Meta-Ethics* (1995). These books borrowed and revised the 'two-factor egalitarianism' of Donald VanDeVeer, which prioritized interests according to the degree of psychological sophistication of a creature's capacities and related interests, and also the place of the interest at stake in the creature's life (VanDeVeer 1979); interests equal in these regards were to be given equal consideration (as Singer's principle enjoined). By contrast, as Freya Mathews has argued, biocentric egalitarianism 'requires us to treat the life of a honeybee as on a par, morally speaking, with that of a wolf or a whale. This position strains credulity' (Mathews 2010: 361) and, as she goes on to suggest, has the potential to authorize atrocities. Other adherents of inegalitarian biocentrism have included Gary Varner, who in 1998 published *In Nature's Interests* but subsequently reverted to sentientism instead, and, more recently, the environmental virtue ethicist Ronald Sandler (see Sandler 2013).

Some criticisms have been made by Clare Palmer (2003) of consequentialist inegalitarian biocentrism. One of them suggests that prioritizing interests in terms of psychological complexity is covertly anthropocentric, as it valorizes the kind of psychological capacities characteristic of humanity. Yet this approach is consistent with placing the interests in being kept alive of a healthy adult ape, ahead of those of a severely brain-damaged human being who has less understanding of the encompassing world. So this criticism fails.

A more serious criticism is that this kind of biocentrism could authorize replaceability, or the sacrifice of any given organism for the sake of more valuable states of another; Palmer alleges that I do not acknowledge this problem at all (2003: 21), but in doing so, she overlooks the passage on how the kind of consequentialism that I defend (practice-consequentialism) upholds respect for rights, even in particular cases where greater good could apparently be done by disregarding them. Greater overall good stands to be achieved by general adherence to the rules guaranteeing the right of (say) a human being not to be sacrificed rather than by infringing them (Attfield 1995: 142–4). This right does not oblige us 'officiously to keep alive' a vegetative human being in all circumstances, but it does forbid the kind of sacrifice just mentioned. So the practice-consequentialism that underpins it is not open to the charge of implying the replaceability of human beings. It also supplies grounds for the same verdict about nonhumans that are self-conscious (such as most primates, whales and dolphins), but not about animals that are conscious without being self-conscious; here I endorse the conclusions of Singer (1979).

Another criticism might concern our limited knowledge of the capacities of other creatures, and thus our limited ability to take their capacities into account. But comparable criticisms could be made of numerous other theories and criteria concerning the capacities of different species. In all these cases it could be replied that it is far better to take into account current knowledge of capacities than to disregard them. A further criticism could concern the interdependence of clusters of natural creatures, and maintain that focusing on particular individuals rather than ecosystems risks endangering the creatures that depend on these particular individuals. (I owe these potential criticisms to an anonymous reviewer.) But this criticism assumes a selective and myopic application of biocentrism. For biocentrism requires the dependent creatures to be taken into consideration as well as those we initially focus on, together with all the other creatures directly or indirectly affected by impacts on those directly affected by our actions and policies. It does not imply that ecosystems are to be disregarded, but just that they are a derivative rather than a primary focus of ethical attention.

Thus biocentric consequentialism of an inegalitarian kind remains a viable option for environmental ethicists. For some recent objections, see Dicks (2019: 613); for earlier responses to just such objections, see Goodpaster (1978). Many, however, favour one or another holistic stance, and stances of this kind should now be reviewed.

Ecocentric and Holistic Ethics

Some environmental ethicists have long maintained that it is not only individuals or their experiences or states that have intrinsic (or nonderivative) value, but also ecological wholes such as ecosystems or species; and some, such as Callicott (in the article mentioned above) have held that what is valuable are wholes *rather than* individuals or their states. Such thinkers have been influenced by Leopold's essay 'The Land Ethic' (see Chapter 7), which locates what is directly important (and therefore of value) in the community, including soils, waters, plants and animals (as well as human beings), which, as we have seen, he calls 'the land'.

One such thinker is Rolston, whose essay 'Is There an Ecological Ethic?' we have already encountered in the first section of this chapter. Rolston holds that, as well as valuing organisms, we should value the ecosystems that make their lives possible, and the entire evolutionary process that is the matrix of life on Earth. Rolston presented these views in *Environmental Ethics* (1988) and in subsequent books. The value that ecosystems have is, he declared, *systemic* value, which should be distinguished from instrumental value, whether or not it counts as intrinsic value. He also made it clear that these values (intrinsic value included) are objective values, contending that beings that preserve their own way of life are valuers that should be regarded as having value, and that the same applies to the systems that make their lives possible. They are valuable not because of anything beyond themselves, but directly.

Callicott, by contrast, regards all value as anthropogenic, or generated by human valuations. He is opposed to anthropo*centrism*, the normative view that nothing matters but human interests and preferences, but nevertheless holds that it is human valuations that generate value, which is to be regarded as the object of valuation (see Callicott 1984). This view, however, seems mistaken to those who understand having value as equivalent to 'being valuable', or being such that there are *reasons* to value its holder. In this sense, value does not depend on human valuation, since much that is valued could fail to be valuable, and, more importantly, much that is valuable can fail to be valued. Besides, it does not seem plausible that nothing was valuable until human beings came on the scene to make valuations, nor that pain was undesirable up to that same stage. For such considerations, see Attfield 1991 [1983], 1987, 1995.

It is to Callicott's credit that he taught the first university course on environmental ethics at the University of Wisconsin, Stevens Point, in 1971 (Callicott 2016: 34), which focused mainly on Lynn White and Aldo Leopold. But there are problems with Callicott's ecocentrism, in which intrinsic value is ascribed to ecosystems in contrast to individuals and their states. For example, for something to have intrinsic value, we need to be able to grasp its identity and its interests. But there are doubts about where ecosystems start and stop, and when they start and stop (Cahen 1988; Sterba 1998a; Sagoff 2013); and there are also doubts about whether talk of 'ecosystem health' and 'ecosystem integrity' are more than metaphors, and genuinely allow us to understand the interests of ecosystems. There again, there are, as Palmer, McShane and Sandler remark, many different ways of delineating ecosystems (they give as diverse examples 'topographically, by trophic hierarchies, by nutrient budgets [and] by energy flow patterns'); and, as they add, there are many other kinds of ecological wholes ('communities, biomes, ecotopes, etc.'), and all this casts doubt on our ability to identify the relevant wholes and then work out what their interests are (Palmer et al. 2014: 428; see also Jamieson 1995; McShane 2004).

These problems go back, in fact, to the debates between Clements, with his organismic holism, and his opponents Gleason and Tansley (rehearsed in Chapter 5). Indeed, Tansley actually devised the term 'ecosystem' to avoid the organismic and holistic connotations of biological communities as understood by Clements. Despite the holism that the work of Clements inspired, and that Leopold later adopted, there is much to be said for the rival view that ecosystems are temporary, shifting and fluctuating associations, and that, while individuals may depend on them at given times as their temporary environment, ecosystems lack the coherence and the spatiotemporal constancy that can be ascribed to organisms (fleeting as some organisms sometimes are). Thus, as Palmer et al. conclude: 'The more indistinct, incoherent, rapidly changing and arbitrarily defined ecosystems . . . seem to be, the more difficult certain kinds of ecocentric ethics become to maintain, especially those that depend on the idea of ecosystems having a good or interests that can be set back or damaged' (2014: 428). And this is a problem not only for the extreme ecocentrism of (early) Callicott, which locates intrinsic value in ecosystems rather than in individuals, but also for the moderate ecocentrism of those who locate value in both (as Naess seems to have done). However, Rolston's suggestion that wholes such as the evolutionary process have systemic value (rather than either instrumental or intrinsic value) could survive this problem, for the evolutionary process could be valuable as the matrix of its valuable products, without being in any sense instrumental, and without the need to specify its good independently of the high value of its products.

A parallel question arises for the view of those other holists (or, in the case of Rolston, the same ones) who locate intrinsic value in species. For it can cogently be claimed that species have interests that do not reduce to those of their current members, and that we ought to care about these interests for reasons that are independent of the interests of current individual creatures (see Rolston 1988). Species can certainly be held to have instrumental value, providing, as Palmer, McShane and Sandler put it, 'food, medicine, shelter, recreation, enjoyable experiences, knowledge and so forth' (2014: 428). But this value at least usually consists in the value of their current populations, or in that of their populations of the present and the future. The issue is whether they somehow have value that is non-instrumental.

This is not the place to discuss the concept or concepts of species, controversial as these are. For, while there are diverse concepts of species, one or more of them could be central to questions of ethical concern; and this seems plausible in view of the widespread concern about the evil of species extinctions. Yet when we reflect on what we mean by 'species' (and thus by their value), it emerges that we either have in mind abstractions such as *homo sapiens*, which cannot as such be harmed, or else the populations that comprise their membership. And, while populations can certainly be harmed or benefited, this is already true of all the individuals that make them up, and so, apparently, there is no case for claiming that species, in the sense of populations, can have any additional interests.

However, the interests of a species bestride different time periods and generations, and so species can be held to have interests broader than those of their *current* population. Yet these additional interests still correspond to the interests of their future members (both those who can currently be identified and those who cannot). Hence critics of the holistic view of species and of belief in their intrinsic value can fairly ask whether the interests of species transcend the interests of present *and future* members, including all those future members that will live unless the species is rendered extinct in the near future or before they could come into existence. The answer to this question seems to be that there is in fact nothing to the interests of species beyond the interests of present and future members, except formal properties that happen to be irreducible to properties of members (such as temporal continuity). But formal properties such as these cannot plausibly be held to supply the basis for the kind of belief in the intrinsic value of species that holistic theorists uphold.

It should be granted that species often have symbolic value (for example, for certain religions or for certain countries or nations); and also that species can have contributory value, through contributing to biodiversity. But symbolic and contributory value, while different from instrumental value, should be distinguished from intrinsic value, since they are derivative forms of value, and their holders derive their value from that of something else, or from a whole set of other organisms. Nor is it plausible that biodiversity has value simply as an abstraction, as opposed to communities or systems of biodiverse populations, which can be held to possess aesthetic value and survival value. But survival value is a kind of instrumental value, while aesthetic value (which is admittedly not such) plausibly depends on the appreciation of perceiving subjects (human or nonhuman), and is thus a further kind of derivative value. All in all, the case for species having intrinsic value, and thus being an independent focus of ethical obligations, seems slender (Palmer et al. 2014). While we may well have obligations to prevent species going extinct, this could be due to the intrinsic value that their possibly numerous future members will or would have if they remain in being. Nevertheless, these obligations are widely regarded as calling for strong national and international preservationist policies; and, as far as possible, no species should be allowed to become extinct.

The Ethics of Gaia

Nevertheless, there is a different basis for a holistic form of environmental ethic, the suggestion that we owe loyalty to the living system of the planet, or to 'Gaia', as the originator of this concept, James Lovelock (born 1919), named it (on the advice of his friend, the novelist William Golding: see Attfield and Attfield 2016). In the early 1970s, in collaboration with American evolutionary theorist Lynn Margulis (1938–2011), Lovelock devised the Gaia hypothesis, that 'life on earth keeps the surface conditions always favourable to whatever is the contemporary ensemble of organisms' (Lovelock 1979; 2006: 208; Margulis 1998). As Lovelock acknowledges (1990: 101), the British geologist James Hutton hit on a similar intuition in 1788, holding that the Earth could only be studied properly by planetary physiology; this has led Lovelock to propose the study of Gaia as 'geophysiology'.

Nowadays Lovelock considers the Gaia hypothesis to be false, but he adheres to the Gaia theory, into which it later developed:

> [The Gaia theory is a] view of the Earth that sees it as a self-regulating system made up from the totality of organisms, the surface rocks, the

ocean and the atmosphere tightly coupled as an evolving system. The theory sees this system as having a goal – the regulation of surface conditions so as always to be as favourable as possible for contemporary life. (2006: 208)

If this theory is correct, then we might reasonably be held to have obligations (both to ourselves, to other creatures and to posterity) to prevent the subversion of this system and to promote its continuation.

Some detailed problems for variants of the Gaia hypothesis were presented by James W. Kirchner in 'The Gaia Hypotheses: Are They Testable? Are They Useful' (1992). (For discussion of Kirchner's critique, see Attfield and Attfield 2016.) To the objection that his theory was untestable (and thus no contribution to science), Lovelock replied with a whole table of tested predictions of his theory (1990: 102). These included his prediction that organisms make compounds that transfer essential elements from oceans to land surfaces, a prediction confirmed by his discoveries of the production by bacteria (mainly in estuaries and on continental shelves) of demethyl sulphide (which regulates the proportion of sulphur in oceans) and of methyl iodide (which regulates the proportion of iodine and crucially makes iodine available to land animals). The discovery of the production of dimethyl sulphide led to the further hypothesis on the part of Lovelock and others that this process facilitates a negative feedback loop which reduces the impact of the radiation that makes the process possible.

Another leading objection to the Gaia theory (from Kirchner and others) claims that it is circular. In the words of Michael Allaby, 'the existence of Gaia is introduced to explain the hospitable environment and the hospitable environment proves the existence of Gaia (1996: 7). But there is no need for Lovelock to accept the second of these claims; for he does not need to treat particular regulatory mechanisms (such as dimethyl sulphide) as proofs, and he further recognizes that under certain conditions natural cycles generate *positive* feedback loops, detrimental to current biota, and not only *negative* feedback loops as reported in the previous paragraph. Thus the Gaia theory is more nuanced than the circularity objection recognizes, and remains scientifically useful through suggesting new directly testable scientific hypotheses.

The Gaia theory eventually attained partial scientific recognition, as embodied in the Amsterdam Declaration on Earth System Science of 2001, which states: 'The Earth system behaves as a single, self-regulating system, comprised of physical, chemical, biological and human components.' However, advocates of the Gaia theory are aware that this declaration falls short of their claim that the system has an inbuilt goal, and that the planet is effectively a superorganism; the declaration limits itself to the view that the system simply behaves *as if* all this were the case. Yet it goes on to add that an ethical framework for global stewardship and strategies for Earth system management are urgently needed, in view of the dangers to mechanisms such as those that generate dimethyl sulphide (which requires protecting estuaries and shallow seas), and of global emissions of greenhouse gases disrupting many ecosystems, if not the system of ocean currents as well (IGBP 2001).

Some individual ethicists have gone further. Stephen Clark, for example, defends a form of holism in which it is not the individual but the whole that is real, a whole of which Gaia is the most magnificent subsystem. Yet individuals are to be respected as fellow-creatures, on the basis of a sense of kinship. (But here there could be dilemmas, since maintaining the system will sometimes suggest sacrificing individuals.) As elements of an ongoing community, we are urged to follow the maxim 'Take no more than your share, no more than you must to sustain the particular value that you carry for the whole' (Clark 1983). This is, however, a controversial metaphysic as well as a controversial ethic; it could lead to greater concern for planetary systems, but it could also lead to undue self-disparagement on the part of individuals uncertain of their value for the whole.

Mary Midgley's concern was to replace both egoistic individualism and resort to imaginary social contracts with Gaian thinking, taking into account systemic and planetary goods. Love of communities such as club, church or country is a widespread and significant motive, and motivations of this kind will need to be fostered if irreversible damage to the planet is to be averted or avoided. Midgley was concerned to reconcile Gaian thinking with Darwinism, quoting Tim Lenton as saying that 'A trait that brings the resulting organism closer to the optimum growth conditions will spread', as an explanation of the spread of traits such as photosynthesis that benefit both their possessors and the generality of other creatures, and thus the feasibility of systems that depend on such traits (Lenton 1998: 444). Maintaining both ecosystems and the planetary system is increasingly important now that they are under threat; and for Midgley, it takes Gaian thinking rather than traditional attitudes to grasp this importance and embody it in action (see Midgley 2001). Midgley's approach does not depend on Lovelock being comprehensively vindicated. Thus, even if he is wrong about Gaia having a goal and being a superorganism, what matters is people's mindsets being transformed towards planetary loyalties. Midgley's promising stance can be reconciled with a whole range of positions in normative ethics, and can be supported by them.

Environmental Virtue Ethics

Environmental ethics includes advocacy of a diversity of ethical positions. Some, like Singer's, VanDeVeer's, my own (see the above section, 'Individualism in the Form of Biocentrism') and probably Leopold's, turn on enhancing the outcomes of actions, rules or practices, and are known as 'consequentialist'. Consequentialists disagree about which are the valuable states we should bring about; Leopold's position, in omitting the flourishing of individuals, and focusing instead on states of the biosphere, appears to call for either supplementation or replacement. Other philosophers hold that it is not only outcomes that matter, if they matter at all, and present rival accounts of what is right and what makes it so; these philosophers are called 'deontologists'. Examples encountered already in this chapter include Tom Regan, Paul Taylor and Stephen Clark. There are also some who represent ethics as based on some kind of imaginary contract between intelligent beings; but such approaches are prone to ignore the interests of future people, and perforce neglect those of nonhuman creatures, however ingeniously some writers adapt the central contract to avoid all this (see, for example, Rowlands 1998).

A further strand of normative ethical theory is virtue ethics. The general idea is that right action is simply what a virtuous person would do, where the virtues are traits or dispositions of character that are beneficial either to the individual or to society or to both. This is the kind of stance presented long ago by Aristotle (see Attfield 2012b), and has more recently been impressively revived by Rosalind Hursthouse (1999). However, Aristotle's position in the *Nicomachean Ethics* was (as we would say) anthropocentric, and while Hursthouse struggles to interpret the virtues so that they take (for example) animal interests into account, it is less than clear, granted her view about what makes the virtues virtuous (promoting the survival of the agent and of humanity), that she succeeds more than partially.

Ronald Sandler and Philip Cafaro have sought to present an improved version of virtue ethics in their collection *Environmental Virtue Ethics* (2005). Sandler, for example, adopts a nonanthropocentric theory of value, and seeks to interpret the traditional values accordingly (Sandler 2005). However, the problem remains whether in an age of complex decisions (because of new issues posed by technology) it is even plausible to claim that what the virtuous person would do is right. It may still be wise to foster virtuous traits of character, since the overall impact of acting on these traits may well be much better than adhering to beneficial practices and, in cases where they offer little or no guidance, attempting to calculate which action makes the greatest positive difference. But some decisions are sufficiently important to make it necessary to move beyond the virtuous path and reflect deeply on which course of action produces the greatest foreseeable good and the least foreseeable harm.

Holmes Rolston makes some profound and well-judged remarks on environmental virtue ethics in his article 'Environmental Virtue Ethics: Half the Truth, but Dangerous as a Whole' (2005). Environmental virtue ethics, he suggests, puts the cart (of the value of human virtue) before the horse (of the intrinsic value of nature). It is rather nature's intrinsic value (plus, we may want to add, the intrinsic value of human flourishing) that confers on human virtue such value as it has. If, instead, we seek to derive all talk of value from the value of human virtue, we get our values the wrong way round. The value of human virtue turns largely, if not wholly, on the independent value of both the human and the nonhuman well-being that it characteristically makes possible. Besides, the world did not have to wait for the arrival of humanity and of human virtue before it could become valuable, and theories that imply otherwise are seriously misleading, even when they rightly recognize the value of virtue (Rolston 2005).

This said, there is an important place for the virtues within a consequentialist ethic. As Dale Jamieson (2007) has argued, those seeking the best overall, long-term outcomes of actions and of policies will often be best advised to foster and inculcate beneficent virtues, alongside (as I would wish to add) adherence to beneficial practices such as promise-keeping, truth-telling, and respect for human rights. This is no longer an appeal to virtue ethics, but it helps explain some of its appeal. The kind of consequentialism that calls for adherence to beneficial practices in cases where they are relevant, and for calculation of outcomes where they are not, is liable to lead to a far more unstable and erratic society than the kind that valorizes beneficial virtues alongside beneficial practices. Reflection on overall and long-term outcomes must sometimes be undertaken, but where agents standardly pursue the path of beneficial practices and beneficial traits of character, outcomes are likely to be both more predictable and more satisfactory.

Environmental Aesthetics

A further ground for environmental preservation and for action to prevent environmental loss is to be found in people's appreciation of natural beauty, and the importance of opportunities for such appreciation remaining available for future people. Recognition of this has generated the subject of environmental aesthetics, and questions such as how natural beauty is to be recognized. Eugene C. Hargrove (1989) at one stage defended the views that everything in nature is beautiful, and that we have the same sort of duty to preserve natural beauty as to preserve artistic beauty. But these claims are difficult to defend.

Subsequently, Allen Carlson (2010) proposed five requirements for a satisfactory theory of natural beauty. One is to avoid anthropocentrism and a focus on human viewpoints, instead taking into account 'nature as a whole'. But this salutary aim may be too demanding. His second requirement is avoidance of being obsessed by scenery, and adopting the standpoint of mere spectators; here Carlson upholds Rolston's advocacy of 'embodied participation, immersion and struggle' (Rolston 1998). While these are salutary suggestions, 'scenic experiences often prove to be seminal ones' (Attfield 2014 [2003]: 117). Carlson next requires seriousness as opposed to superficiality, and appreciation which is true to its object. Yet, as Emily Brady (2003) has responded, appreciation of nature can instead be moulded by people's perceptual capacities and the imaginative responses they can trigger; think of 'Ode to Autumn' by John Keats.

Carlson now specifies that theories of environmental aesthetics should aspire to objectivity, implying the need for scientific understanding. Such understanding can sometimes assist. But, as Noël Carroll (2004) has commented, appreciation of nature can sometimes take the form not of scientific awareness but of our being emotionally aroused, for example by the grandeur of a waterfall, and such experiences can sometimes satisfy the requirement of objectivity. Hence, aesthetic theories can avoid both subjectivism and relativism without having to be science-oriented.

Carlson's final requirement is moral engagement; to support environmentalism, aesthetic appreciation cannot be completely separated from ethical awareness. But once again, this requirement needs refinement. Thus one person's purely aesthetic response (e.g., Coleridge's awareness of 'caverns measureless to man') can motivate a desire to preserve such caverns on the part of others, even if there was no such desire on the part of the poet. (For a discussion of aesthetic appreciation of nature through the medium of poetry, see Attfield 2014 [2003]: 118–20. For a poet inspired by Buddhism who has inspired both appreciation of nature and desire to preserve it, Gary Snyder (born 1930), see https://www.poetryfoundation.org/poets/gary-snyder.)

The themes discussed in this chapter are far from exhausting the full range of environmental philosophy, more of which is discussed in the coming chapter, 'Green Issues and Movements'. But this chapter discloses the origins of the community of environmental philosophers, how it has enormously broadened in scope as it has developed, and some of the thinking from adjacent fields, such as the Gaia theory, which has often served to inspire or influence it.

Recommended reading

Attfield, Robin (1981). 'The Good of Trees', *Journal of Value Inquiry*, 15: 35–54.
Attfield, Robin (1991 [1983]). *The Ethics of Environmental Concern*, 2nd edn. Athens: University of Georgia Press.
Attfield, Robin (2014 [2003]). *Environmental Ethics: An Overview for the Twenty-First Century*. 2nd edn. Cambridge: Polity.
Brady, Emily (2003). *Aesthetics of the Natural Environment*. Edinburgh: Edinburgh University Press.
Callicott, J. Baird (1980). 'Animal Liberation: A Triangular Affair', *Environmental Ethics*, 2: 311–428.
Goodpaster, Kenneth E. (1978). 'On Being Morally Considerable', *Journal of Philosophy*, 75: 308–325.
Jamieson, Dale (2007). 'When Utilitarians Should be Virtue Theorists', *Utilitas*, 19(2): 287–308.
Lovelock, James (1979). *Gaia: A New Look at Life on Earth*. Oxford: Oxford University Press.
McShane, Katie (2013). 'Environmental Ethics', in Hugh LaFollette (ed.), *International Encyclopedia of Ethics*. Oxford: Blackwell Publishing.
Mathews, Freya (2010). 'Planetary Collapse Disorder: The Honeybee as Portent of the Limits of the Ethical', *Environmental Ethics*, 32: 353–383.
Midgley, Mary (2001). *Gaia: The Next Big Idea*. London: Demos.
Naess, Arne (1973). 'The Shallow and the Deep, Long-Term Ecology Movement: A Summary', *Inquiry*, 16: 95–109; repr. in Robin Attfield (ed.), *The Ethics of the Environment*. Farnham: Ashgate, 2008, pp. 115–120.
Palmer, Clare, McShane, Katie and Sandler, Ronald (2014). 'Environmental Ethics', *Annual Review of Environment and Resources*, 39: 419–442.
Poetry Foundation (2020). https://www.poetryfoundation.org/poets/gary-snyder.
Regan, Tom (1983). *The Case for Animal Rights*. Berkeley: University of California Press.
Rolston, Holmes, III (1988). *Environmental Ethics: Duties to and Values in The Natural World*. Philadelphia, PA: Temple University Press.
Routley (later Sylvan) Richard (1973). 'Is There a Need for a New, an Environmental Ethic?' *Proceedings of the World Congress of Philosophy*. World Congress of Philosophy, Varna (Bulgaria), pp. 205–210; repr. in Robin Attfield (ed.), *The Ethics of the Environment*. Farnham: Ashgate, 2008, pp. 3–12.

Sandler, Ronald and Cafaro, Philip (eds), *Environmental Virtue Ethics*. Lanham, MD: Rowman & Littlefield.

Singer, Peter (1975). *Animal Liberation: A New Ethics for Our Treatment of Animals*. New York: Avon.

Singer, Peter (1979). *Practical Ethics*. Cambridge: Cambridge University Press.

Sterba, James (1995). 'From Biocentric Individualism to Biocentric Pluralism'. *Environmental Ethics*, 17: 101–207.

Taylor, Paul W. (1986). *Respect for Nature: A Theory of Environmental Ethics*. Princeton, NJ: Princeton University Press.

VanDeVeer, Donald (1979). 'Interspecific Justice', *Inquiry*, 22: 55–79.

Varner, Gary (1998). *In Nature's Interests*. New York: Oxford University Press.

Whitney, Elspeth (1993). 'Lynn White, Ecotheology and History', *Environmental Ethics* 15(2): 151–169.

9

Green Issues and Movements

Green issues yet to be discussed include ecofeminism, environmental justice, biodiversity preservation and rewilding, and advocacy of environmental stewardship and other forms of ecotheology; these issues are discussed in this chapter. (Issues of climate change and of pollution will be discussed in Chapter 10.) Some of these issues are perforce associated with particular movements, while further Green movements will also figure in the current chapter, including ones located as far apart as Germany, Kenya, India and Ecuador.

However, a long shadow has been cast over some of these movements, as a result of the ecological sympathies of the German philosopher Martin Heidegger (1889–1976). Heidegger wrote profoundly about the domination of technology over humanity and about the meaning of dwelling in the land; he wanted humanity to become nature's 'Shepherd' (Bramwell 1989: 11); but he also joined and supported the Nazi (National Socialist) Party. This shadow became all the more sinister because support for versions of ecological thought were propounded by a faction within the Nazi regime itself, led (until 1941) by Rudolf Hess (Bramwell 1989: 197).

Since the defeat of Nazism, some contemporary Western philosophers (such as David Cooper) have admired Heidegger's ecological insights, while others (such as Christopher Norris) have rejected everything he stood for because of his Nazism. Meanwhile post-war German ecologists, both theorists such as Rudolf Bahro (1935–97) and political leaders such as Petra Kelly (1947–92), have taken care to distance themselves from every vestige of Nazi ecology, and to present versions of Greenness opposed to state centralism, and at the same time opposed to nuclear weapons and nuclear energy. There is in any case no necessary connection between advocacy of environmentalism and authoritarian or fascistic tendencies, and no need for environmentalists concerned about other species to be any less concerned about our own.

Clarity about these matters has not been assisted by Anna Bramwell's presentation of ecologism, which is supposedly never anthropocentric (1989: 16), as if such anthropocentric philosophers as David Cooper, Bryan Norton and John O'Neill had never lived, and which is also somehow associated with the 'eco-socialism' of the post-war UK Labour government of 1945–51, all 'physical remnants' of which are (in 1989) being 'thankfully destroyed' (Bramwell 1989: 235). It is unclear whether these 'remnants' are supposed to include the much-praised Town and Country Planning Act of 1947, or even the much-treasured National Health Service (inaugurated in 1948). Bramwell's resulting conglomerate ('Ecologism') is an unhistorical caricature, informative as her text often is on details of Green and German history.

Ecofeminism

A whole range of distinctive Green platforms have in fact been presented, and not only in Germany. While 'Deep Ecology', which originated in Norway, has already been discussed in Chapter 7, a movement with which it has often been contrasted, that of ecofeminism, originated both in USA and in Australia, although the term 'ecofeminism' was introduced in France by Françoise D'Eaubonne in 1974. Early ecofeminists developed the insight of Simone de Beauvoir (1908–86) that patriarchal (male-dominated) systems and societies treat women and nature alike as 'other'. This insight was taken further by the American philosopher Karen Warren, who claimed that there are structural links connecting exploitative relations between men and women and exploitative relations between humanity and nature. These forms of oppression, she suggested, are so closely linked that neither can be overcome without due attention being paid to the other (Warren 1990). While ecofeminism has contributed other important insights, this has continued to be one of its central themes.

Others have drawn attention to there being many forms of oppression and domination, including racism, class division, exploitation of workers and the persecution of religious, cultural and sexual minorities, as well as sexism and the human domination of nature. This being so, equity would suggest that they should all be tackled as and when they arise, if necessary simultaneously. Ecofeminists would not need to disagree, but often assert close historical connections between the oppression of nature and that of women. For example, Carolyn Merchant (1990 [1980]) contrasted pre-modern (supposedly) respectful attitudes to 'mother Earth' (diverging here from the historical claims of Lynn White) and early modern and subsequent advocacy of exploring nature's secrets through mining and experimentation, not least through the practice of vivisection. Whether or not these changing historical attitudes bear out a necessary connection between attitudes to women and to nature, the suggested historical links have been held to require that the exploitation of women and of nature be considered and treated together.

However, these two forms of oppression seem not to be jointly present in every society that harbours one of them. The Ethiopian philosopher Workineh Kelbessa (2012) relates that within his own society (the Oromo) women are often oppressed, but that nature and wildlife are not. A possible inference is that the links between these forms of oppression are limited to particular societies and epochs, at most. Arguably, however, these links are far from universal even in Western societies, where women often play a leading part in oppressive practices such as fox-hunting and other blood sports, and are thus to be found among nature's oppressors rather than among the victims of oppression.

Besides, Western societies and attitudes to nature are not uniformly oppressive. Certainly, many (of both genders) consume the products of factory farms. Yet many others campaign against this practice, and still others take action to protect wildlife. Thus, claims about oppression should not be overgeneralized, as some ecofeminists recognize (Gaard 2017). All kinds of systematic oppression should be contested, oppression of women included. But there does not seem to be the systemic correlation between the exploitation of women and of nature that some ecofeminists assert.

Nevertheless, in the process of diagnosing these kinds of oppression, ecofeminists have come up with valuable correctives to much previous environmental thought. For example, they have criticized an excessive emphasis on dualisms, such as the representation of nature and culture as polar opposites, with no overlap and nothing in common. Ecofeminists such as Warren have challenged such dualistic thinking. Thus treating nature and culture as antithetical can foster such travesties as regarding only untouched wilderness and its creatures as valuable and worth preserving, opposing ecological restoration and its outcomes as deceptive simply because it depends on human (and therefore cultural) inputs (Elliot 1982; Katz 1992), or (differently) urban contempt for rural life (as lacking in culture). (Ecological restoration will be returned to later in this chapter.) Yet the human engagement with nature largely takes the forms of farming and gardening (both of them aspects of culture); and any refusal to recognize the dependence of both of them on nature indicates a truncated view of the spheres both of nature and of culture.

Ecofeminists have also valuably foregrounded the role of emotions such as compassion, and decried excessive emphasis on reason, particularly in ethics. The Australian philosopher Val Plumwood has rightly stressed the importance of emotional sensitivity, particularly in relations with animals, and how reliance on reason and on principles alone (as in Kantian ethics) can fail to motivate the performance of responsibilities that we intellectually endorse, and produce unnecessary self-division (Plumwood 1991). Plumwood's advocacy of 'critical ecofeminism' has recently been taken further by Greta Gaard in a book of that title (2017). In a similar vein, Mary Midgley has criticized the kind of atomistic individualism that ignores both our complete dependence on others in infancy and childhood, and our willingness in adulthood to care for others. This kind of individualism characteristically misrepresents society as a contract between rational but emotionally stunted individuals imprisoned in their own self-interest (Midgley 1983, 2010).

Such insights into contract theory and human motivation comprise valuable contributions both to ethics and to political theory. Ecofeminism has further reminded us of our embodied and socially embedded situation (Benhabib 1992). Yet caution is in place before each and every woman is regarded as a victim of oppression, as early ecofeminism seemed to imply. Nor, however, should we underestimate the agency of women, and their ability to influence and change the future of the planet. (Some brief passages within this section may also be found in Attfield 2018a.)

Social Ecology and Bioregionalism

Further ecological movements should here be introduced, albeit more briefly. Social ecology stresses the evil of social degradation, and the need for social transformation as a precondition of environmental restoration (the theme of the next section). Hierarchy and domination are seen as the fundamental problems, and the leading social ecologist, Murray Bookchin, regards cities and urban development as crucial to 'ecological society' (1974, 1989). There is less emphasis on the preservation of species or ecosystems. Effectively, social ecology has an anthropocentric approach.

Bioregionalism, by contrast, emphasizes living in place, and the restoration both of nature and society in each locality. In more extreme versions, it supports the autonomy of regions, as defined (for example) by their watersheds, and promotes self-sufficiency within them; cosmopolitan critics see this as liable to constrain people's access to the wider achievements of human culture. But its proposals for urban and community development, and its advocacy of giving priority to local produce, have won greater support (Sale 1985; Berg et al. 1990; Beavis 1991).

Ecological Restoration

Before further ecological issues and movements are considered, a brief consideration of ecological restoration is in place, already discussed passingly in an earlier section, is appropriate. This subject was also touched on in connection with the proposed damming of the Hetch Hetchy valley (in Chapter 4), when the dam's proponents undertook that the new reservoir above the dam would be encircled by scenic trails, and thus that no eventual loss of scenic enjoyment was to be feared from the dam's construction. Similar offers from would-be developers, for example of open-cast mines, to restore the scenic qualities of their site of operations after those operations have been completed, have figured among the reasons for suspicion and scepticism about ecological restoration as a whole.

Some philosophers have rejected ecological restoration in general. Robert Elliot (1982), for example, has argued that, while restorations are possible, they invariably have less value than what they seek to restore, because they are 'fakes', lacking the evolutionary origins of natural organisms and assemblages. It can be granted that a thing's aesthetic value might depend in part on its origins. Yet, intrinsically, the value of a flourishing tree in a botanical garden may be the same as that of such a tree in a forest.

Eric Katz (1992) went further, and claimed that restorations of nature are impossible, since they are artefacts, whereas natural entities are undesigned, autonomous and capable of self-realization. Yet restored woodlands, for example, largely come about through natural processes (after an original human intervention); so they are not properly artefacts, and are just as capable of developing in accordance with their evolved capacities as are wild creatures and scenes. They can even have greater value than what preceded them; as Sylvan replied in an unpublished essay, an ecosystem that has been impoverished by the 'creaming' of some of its species can attain greater biodiversity value if the 'creamed' species are reintroduced from elsewhere (Sylvan 1992: 23).

Restorations can in fact take several forms. A river such as the Thames, once severely polluted and (in its lower reaches) entirely lacking fish, can be restored through pollution control and the reintroduction of fish species. Differently, species that have become extinct in one country can be restored through reintroduction from another; examples include the return of red kites (*Milvus milvus*) to Wales and much of England, and of the beaver (*Castor fiber*) to several English rivers. No one would call the regimented plantations of pines and firs of the (British) Forestry Commission 'restoration'. But that term could be used of the large-scale reforestation of Cuba, of parts of Pakistan, and particularly of Ethiopia, a country large areas of which were deforested in recent civil wars.

Yet restoration has its limits. As Emma Marris (2011) has argued, it is simply not feasible to restore even the wilder stretches of Hawaii to their condition prior to white settlement, let alone to that prior to human settlement, for humanly introduced species have become indigenized and integral to what others have recently called 'novel ecosystems' (Hobbs et al. 2006). A novel ecosystem can be understood as 'a new species combination that arises spontaneously and irreversibly in response to anthropogenic land use changes, without correspondence to any historic ecosystem' (Murcia et al. 2014: 548). (The ongoing debate about novel ecosystems cannot be further discussed here.)

One form of ecological restoration is rewilding, or practices of conservation aimed at restoring and protecting natural processes and core wilderness areas, providing connectivity between such areas, and protecting or reintroducing apex predators and keystone species. An example is the reintroduction of wolves (*Canis lupus*) to Yellowstone National Park. Practices of rewilding can make a difference to protecting natural processes without even coming close to restoring territories to their uncultivated state. Thus the reinstatement of riverside corridors of forest in North Borneo (involving curtailment of palm-oil plantations) is allowing species such as orangutans to retain a sufficient habitat of connected forest for survival, at least in some places. Even in suburbia, practices of less frequent mowing of lawns and of planting verges with wild flowers can allow the return of insects and of birds, both undergoing serious current decline.

Future Generations and Future Ethics

Since the Enlightenment, there has been a growing realization that current generations can make a significant difference to what follows. The importance of this has been acknowledged through international agreement at the Rio Summit of 1992 about the need for sustainable development, in which provision for future generations to satisfy their own needs is recognized (WCED 1987; see also Chapter 7).

It has been argued by Derek Parfit (1984) that the obligations of the current generation to facilitate as good a quality of life as possible for future generations hold good, irrespective of the fact that most future people cannot currently be identified. Certainly, our ability to foresee their preferences imposes a limit on our duties in their regard. But there is no room for doubt that future generations will need a relatively pollution-free environment, access to clean water, and opportunities to feed themselves (Attfield 2018a: 35–7), and little doubt that they will benefit from access to the cultural heritage of humanity, and to as close as possible a range of species and ecosystems as the current generation has inherited. Practices such as discounting future interests turn out to have a more slender basis than is often assumed, and should be restricted to clear cases of uncertainty rather than applied across the board (Attfield 2018a: 32–5).

These considerations underlie the importance of the Montreal Convention, which restricted the use of and trade in chemical propellants that had been found to be undermining the ozone layer, and thus our natural protection (and that of other animal species) against skin cancer (Montreal Protocol 1987). China and India, which were on the point of producing such chemicals, were persuaded, through offers of technology transfer, to adopt substitutes. Later, when a hole in the ozone layer over the Arctic was discovered, as well as one already known to exist over the Antarctic, the convention was strengthened; currently, the ozone layer is said to be beginning to recover, a process that may be complete in another five or six decades if the convention continues to be observed. The adoption of the Montreal Convention itself was thus a clear example of an application of the precautionary principle (internationally adopted at Rio in 1992). This principle can be paraphrased as follows. When there is reason to believe that serious and/or irreversible harm is in prospect, lack of complete scientific consensus should not be regarded as a reason against taking preventive action (Parker 1998). There was much greater consensus once the Arctic ozone hole was discovered, but action was crucially needed (as this subsequent discovery bore out) no later than 1987. This key decision was a vital contribution to all future generations, and also demonstrates the possibility of successful action in face of global environmental issues.

In the concluding chapter we turn to the issue of climate change. This is an even harder issue to resolve, but what has been said, both about obligations to future generations and about the precautionary principle, will once again be found to be critically relevant.

The Ethics of Biodiversity

Biodiversity refers to the diversity on our planet of species, subspecies and habitats. There are estimated to be some nine million species on Earth, of which fewer than two million have been discovered. Sadly, they are being lost at an alarming and increasing rate, many disappearing prior to being discovered at all. A large proportion of species live either in tropical forests or on coral reefs, and both these kinds of habitat are currently endangered and subject to destruction.

Grounds to cherish and preserve this diversity include the principle of plenitude, deriving from ancient Greek philosophy – the principle that the more diverse the world is the better (Lovejoy 1936; see Chapter 1). This principle was almost universally accepted in the West until its rejection by the Romantic writer Schelling (see Chapter 2) in the early nineteenth century.

Other grounds have more recently been put forward for the preservation of biodiversity, as in Bryan Norton's book *The Preservation of Species* (1986), by way of multiple benefits to humanity. Elliot Sober (1986), however, doubts whether biodiversity has any value other than aesthetic value; assuredly, it has a great deal of such value, as the phenomenon of ecotourism bears out, not to mention the boost to the spirits of birdsong, rightly assumed when Rachel Carson (2000 [1962]) imagined the impact of a spring without it. Sober considers that the argument from possible future uses (e.g., medicinal uses of forest leaves) amounts to no more than an argument from ignorance, but I have replied (2011b) that it is rather an argument grounded in actual medical discoveries and thus from the probability of further such discoveries. There are in fact many such discoveries of potential human uses of wild nature, for food as well as medicine; for example, the Brundtland Report (as mentioned in Chapter 7) cites a perennial variety of wild maize, found in a Mexican forest under threat of destruction at the time, which could prove crucial to world food production (WCED 1987: 155). Wild species can also be considered resources because they supply timber, roofing materials, and fibres for clothing and biomass for kindling.

A further ground relating to human interests is the value of the scientific research which the continued existence of wild nature makes possible. We do not need to hold, with Karen Borza and Dale Jamieson (1990), that knowledge is intrinsically valuable in order to recognise that there is a strong cultural argument here in support of preservation, and that such research contributes to the education of future generations, and to our understanding of other global problems.

A different ground for preservation has been presented by Mark Sagoff (1974), which could be extended to apply to the preservation of much biodiversity. Sagoff suggests that free-flowing rivers and species such as eagles should be preserved because they symbolize American values such as freedom. While such arguments clearly have their limits, since other nations will cherish different symbols, this argument could also be applied within British culture to preserving the White Cliffs of Dover, Wordsworth's Lake District or the 'Banks of Green Willows' celebrated by George Butterfield. Yet too many species and habitats go uncelebrated for this argument to uphold preservation in general.

As it happens, many (but not all) of the species omitted from coverage by Sagoff's argument are covered by that of the Indian environmentalist Vandana Shiva (1997). Shiva points out that biodiversity has long served as a common resource (of food, medicines, fuel and housing materials) for rural people in the Third World, who have preserved it (not least for these reasons, but also because of its intrinsic worth). Multinational corporations are widely seeking to exploit it, but are not dependent on it in the same way as poor people are. Her case, then, is an appeal to environmental justice (discussed in the coming section); and certainly, while there could in some cases be developmental gains from uses of wild species, the interests of the poor should not be disregarded.

By way of a different argument, it is sometimes suggested that endangered species have rarity value as such; but it is implausible that value increases in inverse proportion to numbers (except for market value, which can sometimes fluctuate in this way). It is more cogent that the value of the last surviving members of a species is grounded in the value that future members of the species would have if the species is allowed to survive, value that depends on the survival of its current members. This basis can be appealed to by biocentrists, and in relevant cases by sentientists (see Chapters 2 and 8).

The case for preservation is in any case strengthened when the intrinsic value of present and future organisms or creatures is recognized. While this argument is not always conclusive for practical purposes, and can sometimes be outweighed, it is always relevant when (for example) the destruction of ancient woodlands or of coral reefs is in question. It only gains in importance when we consider that large numbers of bird, insect, fish and mammalian species are currently at risk of extinction (Greenfield 2020). Alongside climate change and pollution, biodiversity loss figures among the three major ecological problems, to which we will return in Chapter 10.

Environmental Justice and the Environmental Justice Movement

Environmental justice refers to fair distributions of environmental costs and benefits. While anthropocentrists limit its scope to discriminatory distributions among human beings, biocentrists can (and some do) include distributions affecting both human beings and other species as well (Attfield and Humphreys 2016, 2017). However, 'Environmental Justice' has also become the name of a movement that objects to unfair distributions of environmental harms such as pollution (among human beings), and to inadequate procedures for deciding such matters, as where the people of a locality lack a say in decisions affecting themselves and their locality, and generally lack recognition of minority peoples, even where decision-making procedures are in theory satisfactory.

This movement was inaugurated when the citizens of Warren County in North Carolina, most of whom were African Americans, protested without success at the siting of a toxic dump of polychlorinated biphenyl (PCB) in their community. This protest led to a study in 1987 by the United Church of Christ Commission for Racial Justice, which disclosed that hazardous waste sites tended to be situated in areas with large minority populations (Payne and Newman 2005). Further examples have included the contamination of Navajo lands in Arizona through uranium mining, and the exposure of Navajo miners to levels of radioactivity far above allowable limits. Examples have not been lacking within the USA in more recent decades.

Besides, practices of this kind are far from confined to the United States. Western companies have often dumped toxic wastes at sites in West Africa, and electronic wastes, full of heavy metals and other toxic substances, have been exported as far afield as India, Africa, Bangladesh and China. Weak regulation of such sites has often allowed children to use risky practices in attempting to recover saleable materials (Hourdequin 2015). Particular examples have included the dumping of dioxin-laden industrial ash from Philadelphia in Guinea and Haiti (1987) and of PCB-contaminated chemical waste from Italy in Nigeria (1988). Accordingly, this practice fully deserves James Sterba's (1998b) label of 'environmental racism'.

An even more flagrant example occurred when containers of toxic waste were dumped a short distance off-shore along more than 400 miles of the eastern coastline of Somalia in the 1990s, when that country had no government able to object. Subsequently, waves from the Sumatran tsunami of 2004 (from thousands of miles away) fortuitously and calamitously broke open many of these containers and spread the contents (radioactive materials included) along the adjacent coast, probably causing some of the local cancer clusters as well as scores of untimely deaths (Kelbessa 2012). This deadly pollution is likely to continue until the recently installed government of Somalia manages to curtail it. Thus the environmental justice movement turns out to carry worldwide implications.

This movement recognizes the need for intergenerational justice as well as justice between contemporaries. It also claims to be concerned about birds and wetlands (Payne and Newman 2005); but it seems so far to have given a low priority to rectifying injustices between species. However, by foregrounding the kinds of oppression that had previously gone unnoticed, it has shown that environmentalism cannot be confined to preserving the quality of life of the comfortable, in agreement with what Naess (1973) had argued long before.

Stewardship and Ecotheology

The ancient, biblical and patristic origins of the belief that the role of humanity is to be stewards of nature, answerable to God, have been presented in Chapter 1, as have replies to some of its modern critics such as White, Passmore and Coates. Passmore's criticism, however, concerned its supposed lack of influence in early and medieval Christianity rather than its message, since he regarded this tradition as one of the seeds of the kind of positive attitude to nature needed in the modern world (Passmore 1974). In Chapter 2 we encountered the explicit revival of the language of stewardship by Calvin, and its application to the natural world by Sir Matthew Hale, followed by thinkers such as John Ray and Alexander Pope.

Thus, when Lynn White (1967) effectively challenged the Christian world to rediscover the attitudes of St Francis, one central response was to reaffirm the teachings of advocates of stewardship, not least through the inauguration of the John Ray Initiative (founded 1997). Other responses included historical correctives, as when Susan Bratton (1988) disclosed that, far from being exceptional, Francis stood in a long line of saints and ascetics whose friendly relations with animals exercised a widespread influence in the medieval period. Calvin de Witt (2000), a Christian environmentalist and scientist, has advanced seven biblical arguments for the stewardship of creation. A further response was that of the current Pope, who chose to adopt the name of Francis and, in the encyclical *Laudato si'*, advocated a form of social justice that included justice towards animals and care for the natural world, regarding this as a development of the social teaching of the Catholic Church (Pope Francis 2015). There were yet further responses to White, as when Richard Bauckham (2010) presented an account of the Bible as teaching that the place of humanity is to be found in a 'community of creation': see later in this section. But let us focus for the present on stewardship.

While the modern advocacy of stewardship began as a Jewish (Helfand 1986) and Christian teaching, and presupposed answerability to God, and is also now widely recognized as a specifically Islamic doctrine, with answerability owed to Allah (e.g., Masri 1992), stewardship was soon taken up by secular think-tanks and campaigning groups, for whom answerability could instead be, for example, to humanity, or to the community of moral agents (Attfield 2015 [1999]: 57–61). For example, David Pearce and his fellow-authors of *Blueprint 2* (1989) wrote: 'Humanity should act as nature's stewards and conserve natural resources and the environment, for their own sake and to preserve the interests of other creatures.' Indeed, the language of secular stewardship can be traced back to Karl Marx (1967, vol. 3: 776: see Attfield 2015 [1999]: 58–9). Thus, stewardship has ceased to be confined to religious contexts.

Commitment to different versions of stewardship has been widely applied in practice. Wesley Granberg-Michaelson (2020) depicts the impact of one version, which stressed the 'Integrity of Creation', on the ecumenical movement, including the churches of India, Africa and Latin America. Back in 1989, the Ecumenical Patriarch of Constantinople, Dimitrios I, issued a 'Message on the Day of Prayer for the Protection of Creation', including among the threats to 'the life of our planet' the so-called 'phenomenon of the greenhouse' (Kerber 2020: 352). Fazlun Khalid (2013) recounts that when the Islamic version, for which humanity is God's *Khalifah* (caliph) of the Earth, accountable to God for its use and care, became available in Kiswahili to the fishermen of Zanzibar, they at once abandoned their longstanding practice of fishing by dynamiting coral reefs, because this involved disobedience to Allah. The secular version, which borrows from the Bible the belief that people now alive do not own the Earth, but hold it in trust for their successors, was expressed in the British Conservative government's White Paper 'This Common Inheritance' (1990), and led indirectly to the significant British contribution to the Kyoto agreement on climate change (under a Labour government) of 1997.

Stewardship has also been widely criticized, most forcefully by Clare Palmer. She rightly remarks (1992) that the idea that universal management is needed is a nonsense. But advocates of stewardship need not support this idea, and can favour letting alone large tracts of the Earth – for example, virtually the whole Antarctic continent.

Palmer goes on to conclude that 'stewardship is inappropriate for some of the planet some of the time, some of it for all of the time (the deep oceans), and all of it for some of the time – that is, before humanity evolved and after its extinction' (1992: 79). But, as was just noted, stewardship does not mean interventionism, and is compatible with letting-be (for example, the deep oceans). Besides, granted that there was no human responsibility before there were human beings, and that such responsibility will cease when humans become extinct, responsibility remains relevant for the intervening period for the entire sphere that humans can affect, which currently means not only the Earth but also much of the solar system and parts of outer space beyond it. If the extensive power of humanity is not deployed responsibly, global problems will be intensified. Thus the extent of modern technology actually makes attitudes and policies reflecting stewardship indispensable.

However, ecotheology extends beyond advocacy of stewardship. Richard Bauckham argues in *The Bible and Ecology* that although in the Bible nature is de-divinized (and thus not to be worshipped), 'it is not desacralized', and thus continues to reflect the nature of its creator (2010: 86). This, as Ailsa Hunt remarks, makes it a fit object for a 'respectful environmental ethic' (2019: 147). Bauckham cites Psalm 148, in which the whole of nature praises God, and implicitly (alongside humanity) forms a 'community of creation' (2010: 76–80).

A different ecotheological approach is provided by Jürgen Moltmann, who, in *God in Creation* (1985), accepts the distinctness of God and creation, but represents each as profoundly involved in the other. He thus advocates panentheism, which we have encountered as the stance of Luther (see Chapter 2), while at the same time remaining firmly trinitarian. A similar but less overtly trinitarian approach has been presented by Arthur Peacocke, writing from the stance of an Anglican scientist (2004, 2007). Panentheist beliefs readily foster respect for nature and concern to preserve it from degradation and pollution.

Yet another kind of ecotheology takes an ecofeminist form, supplementing the kinds of ecofeminism discussed earlier in this chapter. Grace Jantzen, for example, rejects panentheism for putting too great a distance between God and the world, and adopts instead the view that God is embodied, just as humans are. This stance is presented in *God's World: God's Body* (1984), an explicitly pantheistic work. However, the big problem for this kind of theology is that it precludes belief in creation. This problem is avoided by Sally McFague, who accepts talk of the world as God's body, but regards it as metaphorical: we are 'invited to see the creator in the creation, the source of all existence in and through what is bodied forth from that source' (1993: 133–4; see also Deane-Drummond 2008: 151). At the same time, McFague urges her readers to cease from regarding the world as a machine and to recognise its subjectivity (see Deane-Drummond 2008: 151), a claim that appears to come too close to pantheism after all. But this makes her version of panentheism problematic, since the metaphor of the world as God's body seems to be taken too far. Space prevents a review of further versions of ecotheology. (For a more detailed account, see Deane-Drummond 2008; for a defence of the common elements of the stances of Moltmann and Peacocke, see Attfield 2019.)

Ecotheology, whether or not in versions based on belief in the human stewardship of nature, has exercised a growing influence through the ecumenical movement, from the early days in which 'the greenhouse phenomenon' was first publicized by Dimitrios in 1989, to the movement's grass-roots influence in places such as Brazil, Cameroon, Fiji, Indonesia, USA and Uruguay, as related by Kerber (2020: 351, 356). While the movement has failed to galvanize transformative global action (Granberg-Michaelson 2020: 350), it has exercised a valuable influence in preparing governments and electorates to take ecological problems seriously.

Green Political and Social Movements

If we set aside the environmentalism of some Nazis, Green political movements in Europe originated with post-war protests against nuclear weapons and nuclear energy. The ecofeminist Petra Kelly (1947–92) joined such a campaign in West Germany on returning from the USA after her sister had died of radiation-induced cancer, and became leader of the German Greens (*die Grünen*) in 1979. Besides campaigning against nuclear energy, this group was vocal about acid rain and its capacity to defoliate forests, and against the stationing of cruise and Pershing medium-range missiles in Germany, which increased the chances of an outbreak of nuclear war. The Greens won representation in the *Bundestag* (federal parliament) in 1983, and increased it in 1987, but lost it in the post-unification election of 1990. Not long after that, Kelly died (Connelly 2018). Earlier, in 1988, the USA began removing medium-range missiles from Germany, under a treaty signed by President Reagan and Mikhail Gorbachev, which preceded the ending of the Cold War.

Green representation in parliament in Germany was soon restored through merging with Alliance 90 (a grouping of civil rights activists), and in 1998 the *Grüne Partei* (Green Party) entered government in coalition with the Social Democrats. Their main achievement was the decision of 2000 to phase out the use of nuclear energy; renewable energy was promoted at the same time. These achievements led to increased representation in 2002, and a second term in government, albeit in partnership with a weakened Social Democrat party. In 2003, the German Greens gained thirteen seats in the European Parliament elections, one of those elected being Daniel Cohn-Bendit, who had previously represented in that parliament the Greens of France. However, because of further Social Democrat losses in the 2005 election, the coalition fell from power, and the Greens returned to opposition.

In the following period, though, they came to power in different state elections through an alliance with the Christian Democrats in Hamburg (2008), with the Free Democrats in Saarland (2009) and with the Social Democrats in North Rhine-Westphalia (2010), and have subsequently held power in coalitions in several other states, becoming the senior partner in a coalition in Baden-Württemberg from 2011. These coalitions have perforce involved compromises, as well as advances – for example, in matters of public transport. In the 2019 European elections the Greens won twenty-one seats (coming second), and their national support has continued gradually to increase (Lehmann 2019). Earlier, following the disaster of 2011 affecting the Fukushima power station in Japan, eight nuclear power stations in Germany were permanently closed down (*Encyclopaedia Britannica* n.d.).

The earliest Green political parties were in New Zealand and Tasmania (Dann 2011), but their achievements, like those of the Green Party in Britain, have been less extensive than those of the Greens of Germany, partly because of different electoral systems. At the time of writing, the British Green Party has one Member of Parliament, two members of the House of Lords, and (up to 31 January 2020) seven members of the European Parliament. For a time, they also formed a minority administration in the city of Brighton, where their sole MP, Caroline Lucas, has her constituency. However, there is a strong environmentalist voice within the Labour Party, in the form of the Socialist Environmental and Resources Association (SERA), and also among the Liberal Democrats, the Scottish National Party and Plaid Cymru. The French Greens have fared slightly better, securing fourteen members of the European Parliament from 2009 to 2014, and seventeen members of the National Assembly from 2012 to 2017. But in each case, they fell back at subsequent elections.

There are Green parties and campaigns in many other countries. In Kenya, for example, Wangari Maathai (1940–2011) led the women in tree-planting and founded the Green Belt Movement, which began planting trees in the 1970s, and eventually planted fifty million, partly for the sake of poverty relief and partly to restore areas where trees had been cleared for farming and plantations. In 1989, Maathai resisted the building of a sky-scraper in Uhuru Park, Nairobi (a park that is effectively a national monument), and in 1998 successfully resisted office-building in Karua Forest. In 2002, she was elected to parliament, and in 2004 she was awarded the Nobel Peace Prize (Green Belt Movement 2019).

Meanwhile in India, Vandana Shiva (born 1952) founded the women's movement 'Navdanya', literally meaning 'nine seeds', symbolizing the protection of biological and cultural diversity (Navdanya 2019). (Shiva has already been mentioned above, in the section 'The Ethics of Biodiversity'.) She is an advocate of sustainability through the renewal of traditional cultures, and one of the leaders of the International Forum on Globalization (along with Ralph Nader and Jeremy Rifkin), and active in the anti-globalization movement (Chatterjee 2011). Other Asian countries too have Green movements; surprisingly, members of the Green Party of Kyrgyzstan assisted the author in navigating the Metro of Boston, Massachusetts in 1998.

While Green campaigning activity in the USA has not been as conspicuous as that of Western Europe, the Climate Emergency Declaration Resolution in Congress, at the time of writing, has no fewer than than seventy co-sponsors, including several Democratic Party presidential candidates (Climate Emergency Movement 2019: 2). As we have seen (Chapter 7), Barry Commoner stood for president on an ecological ticket as long ago as 1980. More recently former Vice-President Al Gore, after being narrowly defeated in the presidential election of 2000, produced a book about global warming, *An Inconvenient Truth* (2006; it was made into a film of the same name the same year). There is also a significant and longstanding environmentalist lobby, with the Sierra Club (see Chapter 4) prominent within it.

Nor is environmentalist campaigning absent from Latin America, where campaigners (including people from local and indigenous communities) are often pitted against logging interests. Conflicts of this kind have led to the untimely deaths of some environmentalists, both in Brazil and in Mexico, as BBC reports confirm. In terms of biodiversity, Latin America contains some of the greatest 'hot-spots', which local people as well as scientists are eager to preserve. The cloud-forests of Costa Rica are being preserved (among other means) through ecotourism; while places of even greater diversity, such as the Yasuni Nature Reserve in Ecuador, have been the focus of schemes by which Western national and regional governments have contributed funding for development on condition that ecosystems are left intact and the minerals beneath them are left in the ground. Sadly, in the case of the Yasuni Reserve, these efforts have proved unsuccessful (Attfield 2015 [1999]: 156–7).

One characteristic policy of many (though not all) environmentalists should be mentioned here: opposition to economic growth. Konrad Ott (2012) has distinguished four forms of such opposition. The first simply rejects treating Gross Domestic Product (GDP) as the criterion of national well-being, and replacing it with goals like quality of life and happiness. Most Green parties would support this approach, which reduces the importance of growth rates, without insisting they become negative. A second approach aims to reduce the impacts of growth on natural systems, and pursue strong sustainability, which sets firm limits on the substitution of natural substances and products with artificial ones, and seeks to preserve most (but not all) wild species (Daly 1995). Again, most Green parties would endorse this approach, despite some possible loss of growth.

A third approach seeks to restore communal practices and conviviality and related virtues; such societies would supposedly not miss the growth they might forgo. Since this approach might disadvantage the poor, not all Green parties would support it. Ott's fourth approach regards capitalist forms of production and distribution as incompatible with de-growth, and aims to replace them with cooperative or communal structures. Some Green parties aspire to this kind of transformation, holding that capitalist growth cannot continue for ever; Naomi Klein (2014) appears to share this view. But others prioritize the civil liberties that could be at risk.

Green parties have recently received added support as a result of the Extinction Rebellion movement. Intergovernmental Panel on Climate Change (IPCC) scientists revealed during 2018 that there were just twelve years in which to reduce carbon and other greenhouse gas emissions, before it would otherwise be too late to attain the targets of the Paris Agreement of 2015 (Watts 2018). More than one thousand governments (local or national), representing 265 million people, have declared climate emergencies (Climate Emergency Movement 2019). Speeches given by the Swedish schoolgirl Greta Thunberg have further strengthened this movement, generating strikes by schoolchildren, and a growth in support for parties such as the Greens of Germany. We return to these developments in Chapter 10.

The Earth Charter (2000)

Before this chapter closes, attention should be drawn to *The Earth Charter*, the product of the independent Earth Charter Commission (2000), set up as a result of the Earth Summit of 1992 to produce a statement of values and principles for a sustainable future. This charter emerged from an extensive process of international consultation, and was formally approved by thousands of organizations, including UNESCO and IUCN (International Union for the Conservation of Nature).

The Preamble expresses the need for 'a sustainable global society, founded on respect for nature, universal human rights, economic justice and a culture of peace', and goes on to outline ecological, social and international problems, the related challenges, and the responsibilities of all human beings as both national and global citizens. The text proceeds to present principles of 'respect and care for the community of life' and of 'ecological integrity', while also calling for 'social and economic justice' and for 'democracy, nonviolence and peace'. In its closing section, 'The Way Forward', the charter acknowledges that choices between values need to be made, but encourages finding ways to harmonize the values presented earlier through a new sense of global interdependence.

Significantly, this charter adopts a biocentric stance, recognizing 'that every form of life has value regardless of its worth to human beings' (Earth Charter Commission 2000: 2). Besides expressing concern for all current creatures, it also recognizes the needs of future generations. There is much else too that Greens and environmentalists in general can welcome. Thus environmental conservation and rehabilitation are to be integral to all development initiatives; viable nature reserves, both terrestrial and maritime, are to be established and safeguarded, and the recovery of endangered species and ecosystems is to be promoted. Renewable resources are to be managed sustainably (2000: 2). At the same time poverty is to be eradicated, and human development is to be pursued in an equitable and sustainable manner, involving gender equality and universal access to education and healthcare (2000: 3). Further, the knowledge, values and skills needed for a sustainable way of life are to be integrated into systems of education (2000: 4).

The Earth Charter, in fact, embodies almost everything that environmentalists could look for. Its implementation is a different matter. But as in the matter of the universal acclamation for sustainable development at the Rio Conference of 1992, the near-universal endorsements of this charter supply opportunities for campaigners to claim that many of their campaigns have already been accepted in principle (in theory, that is) by the authorities that they need to win over. Those, however, in need of a motivational boost in order to be spurred to further action should read Naomi Klein's *On Fire: The (Burning) Case for a Green New Deal* (2019).

This chapter has traced the progress of many environmentalist campaigns and movements, as well as surveying recent thought about obligations to our successors and about the relations of environmentalism and religion. The next chapter explains the global environmental crisis, and the Conclusion summarizes some of the main findings of this book.

Recommended reading

Attfield, Robin (2015 [1999]). *The Ethics of the Global Environment*, 2nd edn. Edinburgh: Edinburgh University Press.
Bauckham, Richard (2010). *The Bible and Ecology: Rediscovering the Community of Creation*. Waco, TX: Baylor University Press.
Bratton, Susan Power (1988). 'The Original Desert Solitaire: Early Christian Monasticism and Wilderness', *Environmental Ethics*, 10(1): 31–53.
Daly, Herman E. (1995). 'On Wilfred Beckerman's Critique of Sustainable Development', *Environmental Values*, 4(1): 49–55.
Earth Charter Commission (2000). *The Earth Charter*. https://earthcharter.org/invent/images/uploads/echarter_english.pdf.
Elliot, Robert (1982). 'Faking Nature', *Inquiry*, 25: 81–93.
Hourdequin, Marion (2015) *Environmental Ethics: From Theory to Practice*. London: Bloomsbury.
Katz, Eric (1992). 'The Big Lie: Human Restoration of Nature', *Research in Philosophy and Technology*, 12: 231–241.
Kelbessa, Workineh (2012). 'Environmental Injustice in Africa', *Contemporary Pragmatism*, 9(1): 99–132.
Klein, Naomi (2014). *This Changes Everything: Capitalism vs. the Climate*. New York: Simon & Schuster.
Klein, Naomi (2019). *On Fire: The (Burning) Case for a Green New Deal*. New York: Simon & Schuster.
Marris, Emma (2011). *Rambunctious Garden: Saving Nature in a Post-Wild World*. London: Bloomsbury.
Masri, Al-Hafiz B. A. (1992). 'Islam and Ecology', in Fazlun Khalid and Joanne O'Brien (eds), *Islam and Ecology*, 1st edn. London: Cassell.
Midgley, Mary (1983). *Animals and Why They Matter*. Harmondsworth: Penguin.
Naess, Arne (1973). 'The Shallow and the Deep, Long-Term Ecology Movement: A Summary', *Inquiry*, 16: 95–109; repr. in Robin Attfield

(ed.), *The Ethics of the Environment*. Farnham: Ashgate, 2008, pp. 115–120.
Norton, Bryan ed. (1986). *The Preservation of Species*. Princeton, NJ: Princeton University Press.
Ott, Konrad (2012). 'Variants of De-growth and Deliberative Democracy: A Habermasian Proposal', *Futures*, 44: 571–581.
Palmer, Clare (1992). 'Stewardship: A Case Study in Environmental Ethics', in J. Ball et al. (eds), *The Earth Beneath*, 1st edn. London: SPCK, pp. 67–86.
Parfit, Derek (1984). *Reasons and Persons*. Oxford: Clarendon Press.
Pope Francis (2015). *Laudato Si'*. https://laudatosi.com/.
Sagoff, Mark (1974). 'On Preserving the Natural Environment', *Yale Law Journal*, 84: 205–267.
Sale, Kirkpatrick (1985). *Dwellers in the Land: The Bioregional Vision*. San Francisco, CA: Sierra Club Books.
Shiva, Vandana (1997). *Biopiracy: The Plunder of Nature and Knowledge*. Boston, MA: South End Press.
Sterba, James (1998b). *Justice for Here and Now*. New York: Cambridge University Press.
Warren, Karen (1990). 'The Power and Promise of Ecological Feminism', *Environmental Ethics* 12: 121–146.
WCED (World Commission on Environment and Development) (1987). *Our Common Future* (the 'Brundtland Report'). Oxford: Oxford University Press.

10

The Environmental Crisis

This chapter depicts the environmental crisis of the twenty-first century. The Conclusion then summarizes some of the main strands of environmental thought portrayed in this book, many of which have contributed to contemporary environmentalism. These strands offer hope that citizens, corporations, countries and international bodies can address the environmental crisis, and avert environmental disaster.

In 2000, Paul J. Crutzen and Eugene F. Störmer proposed that a new geological epoch had begun, which they named the 'anthropocene', since this was the epoch when humanity had come to occupy a central geological and ecological role. They suggested regarding it as having started in the latter part of the eighteenth century, because the global effects of human activities had become much more noticeable in the two centuries from that time. Since their proposal, others have suggested either an earlier start date for the anthropocene (such as the invention of ships or of agriculture) or, alternatively, a later one (the world wars of the twentieth century). But this is, on all accounts, the period when human impacts are considered to have become predominant over the entire surface of the Earth.

This new epoch-designation rapidly became controversial, when Crutzen (2006) proposed a form of climate engineering to combat climate change, evincing a belief in technocratic solutions. But it is one thing to propose a new geological age, and another to propose that human technology should be employed to resolve all the problems. However, Crutzen also performed a valuable service when (in 1982) he introduced to the world the subject of the nuclear winter likely to follow a nuclear war, with dark skies likely to jeopardize harvests and most of Earth's species (Crutzen and Birks 1982: see also Chapter 7 for the related alert from Paul Ehrlich).

In any case, Crutzen's proposed epoch-designation can also be used to supply a dramatic way of demonstrating that the Earth is now beset by an environmental crisis, of which the triple manifestations are atmospheric and marine pollution, biodiversity loss and climate change. These are the issues to be discussed in the present chapter. In some ways they overlap (carbon emissions are, after all, a form of pollution), and climate change can contribute to biodiversity loss. There are of course other ecological problems (desertification, shortages of fresh water, loss of topsoil, shrinkage of inland seas), some of which also overlap with each other, or with the trio just mentioned (for example, climate change contributes to the shrinkage of seas such as the Aral Sea and the Dead Sea, and to the growth of deserts). But the global and pervasive nature of the three central problems, and the concern they have aroused, warrant their being selected for special attention.

Pollution

Passmore defines pollution as 'matter and physical processes in the wrong place' (since radiation and noise, as well as physical substances, can be forms of pollution). A place, he adds, can be the wrong place either aesthetically, or because human health is endangered, or because wildlife is placed at risk (1974: 45–6). A narrower but more informative definition is that of Erich Weber: 'the presence of substances in the ambient atmosphere, resulting from the activity of man or from natural processes, causing adverse effects to man and the environment' (1982: 241). But there can also, as we shall see, be pollution of the land, the oceans, the stratosphere and outer space, as well as of the atmosphere.

However, we can reasonably begin with air pollution. As Derek Elsom says, this used, up to the 1960s, to appear to consist in a series of localized problems around emission sources and urban areas, although that was bad enough to cause fatalities, as in the great smog of London (a blend of smoke and fog) of 1952. The rapid increase in petrol-powered vehicles supplemented emissions from domestic fires and factories to produce nitrogen oxides, carbon monoxide, hydrocarbons such as benzene, sulphur dioxide and particles of lead (Elsom 1992: 3–4). This problem was partially allayed in Britain by the Clean Air Act (1956) and its implementation, which included the designation of areas where only smokeless fuel could be burned. But the air quality of most urban areas and highways worldwide soon deteriorated further through the further increase of petrol-powered vehicles and the introduction of diesel-powered ones, with their distinctive contribution of nitrogen oxides and of particulates, minuscule particles of substances such as carbon and sulphuric acid, severely harmful to human respiratory tracts. At the same time, long-range transport of sulphur and nitrogen compounds has made air pollution global in extent (Elsom 1992: 4). To these toxic chemicals should be added the worldwide distribution of the radiation from the nuclear tests of the early part of the Cold War, which spread substances such as strontium 90, concealed, for example, in milk, until the Nuclear Test Ban Treaty ended such testing in 1963 (Freedman 2020).

The sulphurous and nitrous impacts of industry and power stations have also produced the widespread problem of acid rain, generated downwind from industrial areas. Acid rain has led to widespread defoliation of forests, for example in eastern Canada, affected by smoke from the eastern United States, in the Czech Republic, through fumes from Germany, and in Scandinavia, affected by emissions from Britain. As Elsom relates, this has put pressure on governments to reduce national emissions of sulphur dioxide and oxides of nitrogen by as much as 75–90 per cent (1992: 4).

Yet levels of air pollution, largely from petrol-powered and diesel-powered traffic, have continued to rise in urban areas, making the air of many towns and cities a toxic brew, particularly for children and elderly people. Most of Africa, northern Europe, Arabia, India and China are particularly badly affected (World Pollution Map 2019). Air pollution, indeed, is said to kill prematurely seven million people every year. Thus, quite apart from the pollution that greenhouse gases produce (see later in this chapter), air pollution has become a global problem, and is widely recognized as a significant component of the global environmental emergency.

With marine pollution, there is a similar story, of a more readily visual variety. For all the main shipping lanes of Earth's seas and oceans are currently affected by oil slicks from tankers. Yet most oceanic pollution comes from the land, such as the thousand-mile-wide belt of plastic trash in the northern Pacific Ocean. Much of this plastic eventually breaks down into microplastics, which pervade the entire water column, are virtually impossible to recover and are deleterious to the health of both marine creatures and human beings. These discoveries, widely publicized through the television programmes of David Attenborough, have led in many countries to campaigns against the kinds of plastic that cannot be recycled (single-use plastics) (Parker 2019).

Besides aerial and marine pollution, there are many other kinds. Chemical pollution, such as that released at Bhopal in India, has become notorious. A leak at a pesticide factory there led to 600,000 people being exposed to poisonous gases, with between 4,000 and 16,000 fatalities. Toxic material remains at the site, and numerous disabled children continue to be born (Taylor 2014). There are, sadly, many other examples of land pollution, such as the radioactive contamination at Fukushima, where, in 2011, a tsunami caused a nuclear power station to malfunction (*Encyclopaedia Britannica* 2019), and discharges of hormone-mimicking chemicals such as dioxins, which have the unintended side-effect of disrupting the functioning of hormones secreted by the human body (Hormone Health Network/Endocrine Society 2020).

Pollution of the stratosphere may become a comparable problem, with the detritus of space explorations floating above our heads. The pollution of outer space would be just as troubling, except that stratospheric detritus is prone to fall to Earth (and has sometimes done so), prompting international discussions about related insurance issues and where the responsibility for compensating victims lies. The suggested plan of adding sulphur aerosols to the stratosphere could, in due course, easily exacerbate atmospheric pollution.

Nevertheless, the main kinds of pollution are pollution of the atmosphere and the oceans. Both are global problems of increasing extent, and could well justify claims about a global environmental emergency even without the problems of biodiversity loss and of climate change.

Biodiversity Loss

A range of suggested grounds for preserving biodiversity have already been considered in Chapter 9. Here it remains to convey the extent and seriousness of the recent and ongoing losses to species, subspecies and habitats, and responses to them of the recent past and the present.

The World Wildlife Fund (WWF) *Living Planet Report* (2014) reports that, between 1970 and 2010, the planet lost 52 per cent of its biodiversity. According to John P. Rafferty (2019), the 'massive conversion of forests, wetlands, grasslands, and other terrestrial ecosystems has produced a 60 percent decline (on average) in the number of vertebrates worldwide since 1970, with the greatest losses in vertebrate populations occurring ... in South and Central America (89 percent)'. While the declines in some other orders have been smaller, the pattern is repeated across the species, with particularly heavy declines among species of birds and of insects. Deforestation and the acidification of oceans (Böhm and

Ott 2019) have been strong contributing factors. A 2019 international scientific report noted that up to one million plant and animal species are facing extinction as a result of human activities (IPBES 2019).

Elizabeth Maruma Mrema, the acting Executive Secretary of the UN Convention on Biological Diversity, warns that 'the destruction of life-supporting ecosystems such as coral reefs and rainforests means that humans risk living in an "empty world" with "catastrophic" consequences for society' (Greenfield 2020). Mrema, Greenfield adds, is 'responsible for spearheading a Paris-style agreement for nature' due to be 'negotiated this year'. Mrema speaks of the need for 'transformative action to make a difference' (Greenfield 2020).

Greenfield (2020) further relates that during May 2019, world-leading scientists warned that nature is disappearing at a rate ten to hundreds of times higher than the average for the past ten million years. He adds that experts had earlier warned that humans are driving the sixth mass extinction event in Earth's history.

One rapid and recent disappearance may serve as symbolic of this overall decline. The biocentrist philosopher Freya Mathews wrote in 2010 how honeybees were suffering from colony collapse disorder, in which hives in many parts of the world are left 'eerily empty, marie-celeste like'. For example, between 2007 and 2010 a third of all honeybees in the United States mysteriously disappeared (2010: 357). The cause is unclear, but pesticides are suspected. Yet one-third of our crops depend on honeybees for pollination, as do many wild plant species; honeybees are a keystone species in planetary ecosystems. For Mathews. this disorder is a symptom and portent of a wider '*Planetary* Collapse Disorder', and of 'the unravelling of the larger context of meaning itself', that is, of the biosphere (2010: 367). We have to hope against hope that this unravelling can be halted.

Another advocate of action to address biodiversity loss has been David Attenborough (born 1926). Through television programmes such as 'Blue Planet 2', this veteran maker of wildlife films has popularized the scale and urgency of this and related problems. Recently, he joined forces with the young Swedish climate change campaigner Greta Thunberg (born 2003) to revive the passions and galvanize the energies of people of intermediate ages, and of their governments.

It is thus of great importance that the upcoming UN Convention on Biological Diversity conference should agree effective measures to limit the ongoing losses to biodiversity, building on the agreement reached at Nagoya in 2010. Meanwhile, it remains indisputable that biodiversity loss is a significant and serious component in the current global environmental crisis, urgently needing to be addressed. Granted that we cannot preserve everything, an internationally coordinated effort is urgently needed to preserve as many species, subspecies, habitats and ecosystems as possible.

Climate Change: Scientific and Ethical Issues

Climate change in the form of emissions of carbon dioxide and of other greenhouse gases such as methane and nitrous oxide is itself a form of pollution, and also a prominent cause of biodiversity loss (EPA n.d.). Additionally, it is disrupting communities and global ecosystems through the melting of Arctic and Antarctic ice and the consequent rise of sea and ocean levels, through its generation of more frequent and more intense climate events such as storms, heat waves, droughts and wildfires, through its displacement of people whose land has ceased to be productive and through its driving of many species (including some of the vectors of disease) to higher altitudes and higher latitudes (NASA 2020). Meanwhile, the carbon dioxide in the atmosphere has risen from pre-industrial levels of 280 parts per million (ppm) to more than 400 ppm; and several recent years have been the hottest ever recorded (Attfield 2018a: 106)

Further, despite a few dissenting voices, the vast majority of scientists believe that human activity is the dominant cause of these changes. In 1995, the IPCC declared that human responsibility for global warming was 'more likely than not'. By 2001, they declared it 'likely', and by 2007 'very likely'. By 2013 they affirmed that it was 'extremely likely'. In 2018 (as we saw in the previous chapter), they insisted that 'rapid, far-reaching and unprecedented changes in all aspects of society' were needed within twelve years if the target of the Paris Agreement of 2015 of limiting average temperatures to 1.5 degrees above pre-industrial levels was to be attained (Watts 2018).

The current scientific consensus about global warming being anthropogenic (mainly caused by human activity) dates from around 1990. Long before, however, the Swedish scientist Svante Arrhenius (1859–1927) proposed that a halving of carbon dioxide levels could have caused the Ice Ages, and that a doubling of these levels, liable to be occasioned by the greenhouse effect, could generate a rise of 5–6 degrees (Celsius). After decades of debate (when some scientists were more concerned about global cooling than about global warming), and eventually the new evidence of an ice-bore of 1987 from central Antarctica that appeared to confirm Arrhenius's calculations, the IPCC was set up in 1988, and soon produced increasing levels of agreement in support of the anthropogenic theory (Sample 2005). This was also just before the Ecumenical Patriarch of Constantinople Dimitrios wrote of 'the phenomenon of the greenhouse' (1989; see Chapter 9).

Despite the crescendo of scientific agreement about anthropogenic climate change, a small minority of scientists and a vocal array of journalists and politicians persist in denying that climate change is anthropocentric. (Climate change denial is everywhere an outlier among scientists; but the fossil fuel industry has systematically purveyed disinformation, successfully promoting such denial; see Oreskes and Conway 2010.) However, such disagreement falls within the scope of the precautionary principle, unanimously accepted at the Rio Conference on Environment and Development of 1992. The weak form of this principle, as there agreed, declares that lack of scientific consensus is not to count as a reason against action where there is reason to believe that serious or irreversible harm is in prospect (see Chapter 7). But even the sceptics cannot deny that there is reason to believe precisely that this is the case with climate change, even if they deny that the reasons are conclusive. So everyone who accepts this principle, including the sceptics, should accept the ethical case for vigorous and concerted action.

The ethical case has other dimensions as well. Some of these are presented in the 2005 *White Paper on the Ethical Dimensions of Climate Change*. Thus it is reckless and wrong to inflict harms, such as the impacts of severe weather events, on people (for example, most Africans) who have contributed little or nothing to their genesis; and it is also wrong avoidably to lower the quality of life of future generations, who are liable to suffer from a greater intensity and frequency of extreme weather events, and from the inundation of coasts, deltas, flood-plains and small islands (Brown et al. 2005). Further, avoidably inflicting harms on people who have not contributed to them and cannot avoid them amounts to an infringement of their human rights, as Simon Caney (2010) has forcefully argued. There again, it is widely agreed to be wrong avoidably to eradicate species, except to prevent greater evils. And finally, it is wrong to neglect to compensate the relatively innocent victims of climate change (Attfield 2018a). Thus, the ethical case for strong and concerted action to mitigate climate change, and to foster adaptation where such change is irreversible, is itself irresistible.

The same conclusion is reached by the economists Gernot Wagner and Martin Weitzman (2015). They warn against assuming that, even if climate change will be costly, the losses can be compensated by increasing GDP. For example, if the global food supply were to reduce, starving people would not be assisted by the production of more iPhones. Wagner and Weitzman accept the case for across-the-board discounting (which is open to contestation), and also pay insufficient heed to risks to wildlife; but they still warn that, given 'business-as-usual', there is a 10 per cent chance of the rise of average temperatures catastrophically exceeding 6 degrees (Celsius). They were also concerned about emissions from hydrofluorocarbons (HFCs); but they may subsequently have taken comfort from the Kigali agreement of 2016, which, if implemented, will phase out these emissions. In any case, their conclusion remains clear: strong and concerted action to mitigate climate change is an imperative that cannot wait. Similarly, Bruno Latour (2018) has argued that contemporary politics needs to focus on the Earth and on the need for international political action to secure a common future for the whole of humanity.

Climate Change: Schemes and Policies

There are, however, different views about how entitlements to emit greenhouse gases should be allocated and how mitigation and adaptation should be paid for. One widely supported stance, called 'Contraction and Convergence', was put forward by Aubrey Meyer, and has long been supported by Dale Jamieson (among others). The underlying principle is that everyone has an equal right to emit greenhouse gases (whether directly or from domestic or farmed animals). Hence the permissible global total of emissions for a given year should be calculated and then apportioned between the various states of the world; and this should increasingly be done in proportion to their human population. Countries wishing to emit above their entitlement would have to purchase some of the quota of countries not using their full entitlement. The scheme would, therefore, be redistributive, supplying poor countries with additional resources, at least in the early stages. Increasingly, the criteria would diverge from current practice and converge globally (Convergence), and the permissible total would contract for the sake of global sustainability (Contraction), in accordance with the slogan 'Contraction and Convergence' (Mayer 2005; Jamieson 2001; Attfield 2018a).

Two dangers should at once be mentioned. Poor countries might, out of desperation, sell entitlements needed by themselves; but this danger could be overcome by agreeing a ceiling on emissions-trading (as a proportion of any nation's quota). There again, populations might be boosted to generate a larger national entitlement; but this dangerous incentive could be averted by agreeing an early cut-off date for population numbers, rather than a later one.

Another apparent criticism was that it was unfair to disregard the emissions of the past; initially the reply was that what matters is restricted to the present and the future. But a scientific discovery (or rather its implications) has resuscitated this criticism. In a 2009 paper in *Nature*, Malte Meinshausen and others showed that, if humanity is to have a 50 per cent chance of avoiding an average temperature rise of more than 2 degrees, its all-time total of carbon emissions has to be limited to a total of one trillion tonnes of carbon. There again, for either a 75 per cent chance of 2 degrees or for a 50 per cent chance of limiting average temperature rise to 1.5 degrees, the limit is around three-quarters of a trillion tonnes, or 750 billion tonnes. These figures have become known as 'humanity's carbon budget'.

Unfortunately, 55 per cent of the budget of one trillion tonnes had already been emitted by 2009, and the remainder of that budget was likely to be emitted by 2044; and a yet higher percentage had already been emitted if the lower carbon budget were to be adopted, together with a likely still earlier date for the emission of the rest to be complete (Meinhausen et al. 2009). An implication was that the countries responsible for the 55 per cent already emitted could not fairly claim that their populations should be treated equally in the present with those of countries with much lower historical emissions.

This problem does not of itself demolish Contraction and Convergence. For that system could be modified to involve equal per capita emissions since 1990, the date when the fact that human emissions were changing the climate became widely known, or perhaps from somewhat earlier, as suggested by Meyer. But in the absence of such a modification, some other scheme seems needed, both to reduce the entitlements of countries much of whose wealth derives from emissions of the past, and to permit the development of countries whose relative poverty corresponds to low historical emissions. Otherwise poorer countries could present a case for compensation for their suffering the effects of the emissions of others.

A different system, called 'Greenhouse Development Rights', was put forward in 2008 by Paul Baer, Tom Athanasiou, Shivan Kartha and Eric Kemp-Benedict. In order to fund the development of poorer countries, as well as climate mitigation and adaptation, they recommended a system that recognizes everyone's right to such development, to be funded by an international tax on everyone with a higher income than the average for Spain at that time (Baer et al. 2008; Attfield 2018a).

Following the death of Baer, this proposal was revised by Athanasiou and Kartha (together with Christian Holz), so as to take account of humanity's carbon budget, and the 1.5 degree (Celsius) target agreed at the Paris conference of 2015. These authors have attempted to apportion the remaining carbon budget (and the mitigation of carbon emissions) on the twin bases of countries' historical responsibility and their economic capacity. The overall aim remains to respect rights to development at the same time as distributing emissions quotas. The product, their Climate Equity Reference Project, seeks to show what equity would call for, whether responsibility is limited to the period since 1990, or is traced back to 1950 or even 1850. Once again, an intergovernmental body would be authorized to implement this scheme (Holz et al. 2015; Attfield 2018a).

Yet the negligible prospect of international agreement being reached in adopting such a comprehensive solution, and in entrusting such an intergovernmental body with powers on this scale, suggest that it is preferable for climate issues at global level to be tackled separately. If so, then an adjusted version of Contraction and Convergence, while less comprehensive in its aims and scope, appears preferable after all. Others, it should be acknowledged, have proposed a global auction of emission entitlements, on the basis that the operation of market forces would generate the most efficient distribution (Tickell 2008). But auctions are all too prone to favour countries and corporations with enough financial muscle to outbid the others, and thus are unlikely to generate outcomes that could be accepted as just.

At the actual Paris Conference, the organizers took the view that no centrally administered system or regimen for the distribution of entitlements and burdens would prove acceptable, and accordingly invited all participant countries to submit pre-conference voluntary commitments of their own. This probably induced countries that might have been reluctant to participate to do so, and thus to share in the decisions to adopt a ceiling of either 2 degrees (Celsius), or 1.5 degrees if possible (UNFCCC 2015). But unfortunately, despite the agreed ceiling, the aggregated voluntary commitments were far from sufficient to generate either of the limits just mentioned, and made much more likely a (catastrophic) rise in average temperatures of some 3 degrees (Celsius).

Fortunately, it was also agreed that there would be a series of review conferences, at which the levels of these commitments could be ratcheted up. But unfortunately, President Trump decided in 2017 to withdraw the USA from the agreement, and confirmed this decision in 2019 (Holden 2019). The only silver lining to this decision is that many American states and corporations are maintaining their commitment, to an extent that they may actually outdo what the Obama administration was proposing (EDF 2020).

Meanwhile, there has been increasing discussion of schemes to reduce the carbon dioxide present in the atmosphere (carbon dioxide removal, or CDR) or to reflect back incoming solar energy (solar radiation management, or SRM), schemes that fall under the broad heading of climate engineering. Some forms of CDR are relatively innocuous, such as growing more trees, which sequestrate considerable quantities of carbon dioxide, as also are some forms of SRM, such as painting roofs white, to reflect solar radiation and prevent its absorption. These are commendable schemes, but unfortunately have long lead times, and cannot make enough difference on the timescale needed (Ott 2011).

This drawback has led others to propose saturating the oceans with iron filings so as to foster the growth of algae, to absorb oceanic carbon dioxide (a more radical form of CDR). But this would threaten ocean ecosystems, and would risk changing the colour of the oceans to bright green (Ott 2011). A less obnoxious form of CDR would be carbon capture and storage, which would extract carbon dioxide, for example from power stations, and store it underground (Jelley 2020: 90–2). But the technology is as yet unproven, and in the absence of safe storage, the stored gas might leak out, cancelling the expected gain. It is to be hoped that the necessary technology will improve, but at present it cannot be relied on.

Hence the attractiveness of the kind of proposal made by Crutzen (2006), to release particles of sulphur into the upper atmosphere, so as to reflect sunlight and heat back into space. This was first proposed as a measure to supplement mitigation, but has subsequently been suggested as a solution to the problem of the continual increase of average temperatures. But this process could well acidify the atmosphere, and might also contribute to the growing problem of the acidification of the oceans. There is also the problem that, once initiated, suspending it would lead to such rapid increases of temperature that it might have to be continued indefinitely. There again, the sky could well cease to be blue (Ott 2011). Such a technological fix would best be avoided, because of its potential detrimentally to assault the planetary biosphere.

Another form of SRM has been suggested, that of 'marine cloud brightening'. Oceanic clouds would be treated with materials such as sea salt, and would then, being brighter, reflect back more sunlight than at present. But initiating this process could generate further climate change through increased rainfall (Ott 2011). Another reason for caution about this proposal is the risk that it could adversely affect the cycle of monsoons. Accordingly, all these more radical forms of climate engineering should best be avoided, at least unless all else fails; arguably, they should not even be researched, unlike such comparatively innocuous schemes as roof-painting and tree-planting (Gardiner 2011).

Together with pollution and biodiversity loss, climate change forms an unprecedented global problem, and, like them, it requires urgent attention. Nor should we forget the other issues, which these problems exacerbate, such as desertification, water shortages, soil erosion and the shrinkage of inland seas. Never before in human history have ecological problems been so vast or the need for solutions so pressing.

Recommended reading

Berry, Robert J. (ed.) (2006). *Environmental Stewardship: Critical Perspectives – Past and Present*. London: T&T Clark.

Brown, Donald et al. (2005). *White Paper on the Ethical Dimensions of Climate Change*. College Park, PA: Rock Ethics Institute, Penn State University.

Crutzen, Paul J. and Störmer, Eugene F. (2000). 'The "Anthropocene"', *IGBP Newsletter* (Newsletter of the International Geosphere-Biosphere Programme), 41: 17–18.

Holz, Christian, Kartha, Sivan and Athanasiou, Tom (2015). *Climate Equity Reference Project*. https://climateequityreference.org/.

Hormone Health Network/Endocrine Society (2020). https://www.hormone.org/your-health-and-hormones/endocrine-disrupting-chemicals-edcs.

IPCC (Intergovernmental Panel on Climate Change) (2020). https://www.un.org/en/sections/issues-depth/climate-change/.

Jelley, Nick (2020). *Renewable Energy: A Very Short Introduction*. Oxford: Oxford University Press.

Latour, Bruno (2018). *Down to Earth: Politics in the New Climatic Regime*, trans. Catherine Porter. Cambridge: Polity.

Meinshausen, M. et al. (2009). 'Greenhouse Gas Emission Targets for Limiting Global Warming to 2°C', *Nature*, 458 (30 April): 1158–1163.

Meyer, Aubrey (2005). *Contraction & Convergence: The Global Solution to Climate Change*. Schumacher Briefing No. 5. Totnes: Green Books.

Oreskes, Naomi and Conway, Erik M. (2010). *Merchants of Doubt: How a Handful of Scientists Obscured the Truth on Issues from Tobacco Smoke to Global Warming*. London: Bloomsbury

Sample, Ian (2005). 'The Father of Climate Change'. https://www.theguardian.com/environment/2005/jun/30/climatechange.climatechangeenvironment2.

Taylor, Alan (2014). 'Bhopal: The World's Worst Industrial Disaster, 30 Years Later'. https://www.theatlantic.com/photo/2014/12/bhopal-the-worlds-worst-industrial-disaster-30-years-later/100864/.

UNFCCC (2015). 'The Paris Agreement'. https://unfccc.int/process-and-meetings/the-paris-agreement/the-paris-agreement.

Wagner, Gernot and Weitzman, Martin L. (2015). *Climate Shock: The Economic Consequences of a Hotter Planet*. Princeton, NJ: Princeton University Press.

Watts, Jonathan (2018). 'We Have 12 Years to Limit Climate Change Catastrophe, Warns UN', *Guardian*. https://www.theguardian.com/environment/2018/oct/08/global-warming-must-not-exceed-15c-warns-landmark-un-report.

WWF (World Wildlife Fund) (2014). 'Living Planet Report'. https://www.worldwildlife.org/pages/living-planet-report-2014.

Conclusion

This book has traversed many centuries and many cultures. Its main theme has been the environmental thought of the West, broadly construed, with occasional comparisons with the thought and traditions of other civilizations (such as that of India), and a few references to their distinctive environmentalism.

The Christian, Jewish and Islamic tradition of humanity being stewards or trustees of the natural world has its critics (for example, Palmer 1992; Smith 2010: 386), yet it motivates many to environmental activism, some because of their religious commitments, and some whose perspective is entirely secular (Berry 2006). Passmore (1974) must have had in mind a secular version of the stewardship tradition in commending it as a promising approach with ancient origins.

The other tradition selected by Passmore as offering the seeds of an environmentally enlightened approach, that of cooperation with nature, also continues to animate those who understand humanity as enhancing or helping to complete God's work of creation (Southgate 2006). Some secular versions of this approach have their dangers. Yet the idea of enhancing the natural world in ways that respect and blend with its processes can be reconciled with the project of preserving its species and habitats, and is expressed in numerous gardens and botanical gardens, and also in many forms of farming, permaculture included (Suh 2014).

A quite distinct strand of environmental thought emerged with the evolutionary discoveries of Darwin and of Wallace. Evolutionary theory also has its dangers, as in the form of its offshoot, social Darwinism;

yet Darwinism has fostered such environmentally crucial fields of study as the sciences of ecology and ethology. It has also continued to supply inspiration for thinkers opposed to individualist models of society, and stressing the importance of social cooperation, both as a desirable policy and as a component of Darwinism, thinkers such as Kropotkin, and more recently Midgley (2010).

Appreciation of wild places and wilderness can be ascribed to a distinctively American aesthetic tradition, apparent in Thoreau, Muir and the Sierra Club (though it was also present in the European Romantic Movement, and in earlier figures like Basil the Great). The American tradition of establishing national parks has spread round the world, first to Canada and then to the national parks of the United Kingdom and of its former empire. National parks in Africa have sometimes involved the eviction of the previous human inhabitants, or the confiscation of their lands. One such area in South Africa was appropriated during the Apartheid period for inclusion in the Kruger Park, but returned to its previous owners shortly after Apartheid was overthrown, and was wisely retained by them as forest so that they could receive an income from ecotourism (Robins and van der Waal 2008; Maluleke 2018). The model of terrestrial national parks has led to the establishment of maritime reserves; arguably, both kinds of reserve need to be expanded if the planet's remaining biodiversity is not to be lost.

Many have been attracted to ecocentrism and to loyalty to the biosphere or to the planet by the (diverse) works of Clements, Leopold and Lovelock. Yet the more empirical and pragmatic approach of Tansley and of Gleason has inspired different forms of environmental ethic such as biocentrism, particularly when combined with modern humanitarianism.

The humanitarian tradition has contributed to two twentieth-century movements, the animal welfare movement of Singer and others, and the animal rights movement led by Regan. The ethics of these movements has contributed to environmentalism by reinforcing biocentrism. So too has ethology, the science of animal behaviour, of which the main representative discussed in this book has been E. O. Wilson. Midgley has criticized the excesses of sociobiology, but used the findings of ethology to fortify an ethic that takes individual animals seriously, as well as their contributions to ecosystems (Midgley 1979a, 1979b, 1983).

Another strand contributing to environmentalism has been resistance to deforestation, as expressed in many places and periods, and not least by George Perkins Marsh. Reforestation is now widely understood as vital in the struggle for climate change mitigation, while the preservation of forests is equally crucial for the preservation of biodiversity.

Resistance to pollution has been another motif in the growth of environmentalism. Longstanding concerns about nuclear pollution, not least from nuclear testing, were recently renewed by the Fukushima disaster (2011), while air pollution is now recognized to be a major source of urban mortality worldwide. Some of the remedies turn out to overlap with those for climate change, by way of the decarbonization of transport. Maritime pollution, involving both hydrocarbons and plastic, has also generated international concern, and led to campaigns against the avoidable use of plastic as well as oil. Change is going to require reconfiguring both national and global economies, as well as changes of lifestyles, and thus to be systemic as well as domestic.

Yet environmental concern and activism owe much to poets, whose influence often long outlives them, from Virgil to Wordsworth, and from Gerard Manley Hopkins to Gary Snyder. Poets, while often ignored in their day, are often, as Shelley remarked, 'the unacknowledged legislators of the world' (1840 [1821]). The teaching of religions (particularly theistic religions) must also be recognized as relevant. While Lynn White's presentation of Judaeo-Christian beliefs and attitudes was largely inaccurate, his estimate of the influence of religion was arguably more insightful. Even if ideas are not the ultimate drivers of history, the cosmic assumptions and intuitions of multiple agents (and electorates) have often been crucial, and may yet prove to be no less so.

White rightly held that many Christians (and others) had interpreted (perhaps 'misinterpreted' would be a better term) their religion in ways that justified a domineering attitude to nature and a despotic role for humanity (White 1967). Not only have anthropocentric approaches become widely acceptable (not least in economics), but egoistic forms of individualism have been combined with them to the detriment of both society and the natural world. Bacon's aspiration to 'effect all things possible' (Chapter 2) has had far-ranging impacts, but it was the later apostles of science-based and technology-based exploitation whose responsibility for climate change, biodiversity loss and pollution has been greater and more direct.

Awareness of all this has led many to attribute environmental problems to capitalism. This theory is defensible with regard to unregulated capitalism, which widely proves to be a sufficient condition of the problems that comprise the current environmental crisis. Yet it should also be remembered that it was a communist regime that, through economic expansionism and exploitative agricultural planning, caused the shrinking of the Aral Sea (UCL Home 2007) (an ongoing problem for Kazakhstan and Uzbekistan), and another communist regime that has been responsible for questionable constructions such as the Three Gorges Dam (Wines 2011) and expansion of coal-fired power stations (Ambrose 2019), as well as of electricity generation from renewable energy. Ecologically informed regulation is needed within systems such as that of China as well as those of Europe and the Americas.

In any case, we cannot wait for the overthrow of any given economic or political system, because action to address the environmental crisis is urgently needed in the present. Concerted global plans and early action are needed, not least at the 2020 conferences on biodiversity and on climate change (postponed, at the time of writing, to 2021, because of the Covid-19 pandemic). Maritime and air pollution too require prompt and globally pervasive action to preserve both humanity and other species.

What is needed, then, as Marx once said in his eleventh thesis on Feuerbach, is to change the world (1924 [1845]). But not only does this not preclude interpreting it; a requirement for changing it beneficially, justly and defensibly is understanding it. The role of the historian, as of the philosopher, is to understand it; and to that role, my hope is that this book has made a small contribution.

Recommended reading

Suh, Jungho (2014). 'Towards Sustainable Agricultural Stewardship: Evolution and Future Directions of the Permaculture Concept', *Environmental Values*, 23(1): 75–98.

Watts, Jonathan (2018). 'We Have 12 Years to Limit Climate Change Catastrophe, Warns UN', *Guardian*. https://www.theguardian.com/environment/2018/oct/08/global-warming-must-not-exceed-15c-warns-landmark-un-report.

WWF (World Wildlife Fund) (2014). 'Living Planet Report'. https://www.worldwildlife.org/pages/living-planet-report-2014.

References

Aiken, W. (1996 [1977]). 'The "Carrying Capacity" Equivocation', in W. Aiken and H. LaFollette (eds), *World Hunger and Morality*, 2nd edn. Upper Saddle River, NJ: Prentice-Hall, pp. 16–25.

Allaby, M. (1996). *Basics of Environmental Science*, 2nd edn. London: Routledge.

Allee, W., Emerson, A., Park, O., Park, T. and Schmidt, K. (1949). *Principles of Animal Ecology*. Philadelphia, PA: W. B. Saunders Co.

Ambrose, J. (2019). 'China's Appetite for Coal Power Returns Despite Climate Pledge', *Guardian*, 20 November. https://www.theguardian.com/world/2019/nov/20/china–appetite–for–coal–power–stations–returns–despite–climate–pledge–capacity.

Attfield, R. (1981). 'The Good of Trees', *Journal of Value Inquiry*, 15: 35–54.

Attfield, R. (1991 [1983]). *The Ethics of Environmental Concern*, 2nd edn. Athens: University of Georgia Press.

Attfield, R. (1987). *A Theory of Value and Obligation*. Beckenham, UK: Croom Helm. Republished 2020, London: Routledge.

Attfield, R. (1994). *Environmental Philosophy: Principles and Prospects*. Aldershot: Ashgate.

Attfield, R. (1995). *Value, Obligation and Meta-Ethics*, Amsterdam: Rodopi. Republished 2019, Leiden: Brill.

Attfield, R. (1998a). 'Environmental Ethics (Overview)', in R. Chadwick ed., *Encyclopedia of Applied Ethics*, vol. 2. San Diego: Academic Press, pp. 73–81.

Attfield, R. (1998b). 'Responsibility for the Global Environment', *International Journal of Applied Philosophy*, 12: 181–186.

Attfield, R. (2006). *Creation, Evolution and Meaning*. Aldershot: Ashgate.

Attfield, R. (ed.) (2008). *The Ethics of the Environment*, Farnham: Ashgate.

Attfield, R. (2009a). 'Mediated Responsibilities, Global Warming and the Scope of Ethics', *Journal of Social Philosophy*, 40(2), 225–236.

Attfield, R. (2009b). 'Social History, Religion and Technology: An Interdisciplinary Investigation into White's "Roots"', *Environmental Ethics*, 31(1): 31–50

Attfield, R. (2011a). 'Cultural Evolution, Sperber, Memes and Religion', *Philosophical Inquiry*, 35(3–4): 36–55.

Attfield, R. (2011b). 'Sober, Environmentalists, Species and Ignorance', *Environmental Ethics*, 33(3): 307–316.

Attfield, R. (2012a). 'Environmental Ethics: An Overview', in *Encyclopedia of the Life Sciences*. Chichester: John Wiley & Sons. http://www.els.net.

Attfield, R. (2012b). *Ethics: An Overview*. London: Bloomsbury.

Attfield, R. (2014 [2003]). *Environmental Ethics: An Overview for the Twenty-First Century*, 2nd edn. Cambridge: Polity.

Attfield, R. (2015 [1999]). *The Ethics of the Global Environment*, 2nd edn. Edinburgh: Edinburgh University Press.

Attfield, R. (2016). *Wonder, Value and God*. London: Routledge.

Attfield, R. (2018a). *Environmental Ethics: A Very Short Introduction*. Oxford: Oxford University Press.

Attfield, R. (2018b). 'Environmental Philosophy and Environmental Ethics for Sustainability', in T. Marsden (ed.), *The SAGE Handbook of Nature*, vol. 1. Los Angeles, CA: Sage, pp. 38–58.

Attfield, R. (2019). 'Panentheism, Creation and Evil', *Open Theology*, 5: 166–171.

Attfield, R. and Attfield, K. (2016). 'The Concept of "Gaia"', in *Encyclopedia of the Life Sciences*. Chichester: John Wiley & Sons. http://www.els.net.

Attfield, R. and Humphreys, R. (2016). 'Justice and Non-human Animals, Part I', *Bangladesh Journal of Bioethics*, 7(3): 1–11.

Attfield, R. and Humphreys, R. (2017). 'Justice and Non-human Animals, Part II', *Bangladesh Journal of Bioethics*, 8(1): 44–57.

Baer, P., Athanasiou, T., Kartha, S. and Kemp-Benedict, E. (2008). *The Greenhouse Development Rights Framework: The Right to Development in a Climate Constrained World*, 2nd edn. Berlin: Heinrich Böll Stiftung. https://www.sei.org/publications/right-development-climate-constrained-world-greenhouse-development-rights-framework/.

Bartram, W. (1958). *The Travels of William Bartram: Naturalist's Edition*, ed. Francis Harper. New Haven, CT: Yale University Press.

Bauckham, R. (2010). *The Bible and Ecology: Rediscovering the Community of Creation*. Waco, TX: Baylor University Press.

Beavis, M. (1991). 'Stewardship, Planning and Public Policy', *Plan Canada*, 31(6): 75–81.
Benhabib, S. (1992). *Situating the Self: Gender, Community and Post-Modernism in Contemporary Ethics*. New York: Routledge.
Berg, P., Magilavy, D. and Zuckerman, S. (1990). *A Green City Program for the San Francisco Bay Area and Beyond*. San Francisco, CA: Wingbow Press.
Berry, R. J. (ed.) (2006). *Environmental Stewardship: Critical Perspectives – Past and Present*. London: T&T Clark.
Blackstone, W. (1974). *Philosophy & Environmental Crisis*. Athens: University of Georgia Press.
Böhm, F. and Ott, K. (2019). *Impacts of Ocean Acidification: An Analysis from an Environmental Ethics Perspective*. London: Metropolis.
Bookchin, M. (1974). *The Limits of the City*. New York: Harper & Row.
Bookchin, M. (1989). *Remaking Society*. Montreal: Black Rose.
Borza, K. L. and Jamieson, D. (1990). *Global Change and Biodiversity Loss: Some Impediments to Response*. Boulder, CO: Center for Space and Geosciences Policy, University of Colorado.
Brady, E. (2003). *Aesthetics of the Natural Environment*. Edinburgh: Edinburgh University Press.
Bramwell, A. (1989). *Ecology in the 20th Century: A History*. New Haven, CT: Yale University Press.
Bratton, S. P. (1988). 'The Original Desert Solitaire: Early Christian Monasticism and Wilderness', *Environmental Ethics*, 10(1): 31–53.
Brown, D. et al. (2005). *White Paper on the Ethical Dimensions of Climate Change*. College Park, PA: Rock Ethics Institute, Penn State University.
Bugbee, H. (1999 [1958]). *The Inward Morning*. Athens: University of Georgia Press.
Bugbee, H. (2017 [1974]). 'Wilderness in America', in D. Rodick, (ed.), *Wilderness in America: Philosophical Writings of Henry G. Bugbee*. New York: Fordham University Press, pp. 84–93.
Burrow, J. (ed.) (1985). *The Origin of Species*. London: Penguin Classics.
Cahen, H. (1988). 'Against the Moral Considerability of Ecosystems', *Environmental Ethics*, 10(3): 195–216.
Callenbach, E. (1978). *Ecotopia*. London: Pluto Press.
Callicott, J. B. (1980). 'Animal Liberation: A Triangular Affair', *Environmental Ethics*, 2(1): 311–428.
Callicott, J. B. (1984). 'Non-Anthropocentric Value Theory and Environmental Ethics', *American Philosophical Quarterly*, 21: 299–309.
Callicott, J. B. (1989a). 'American Indian Land Wisdom? Sorting Out the Issues', in J. B. Callicott, *In Defense of the Land Ethic: Essays in Environmental Philosophy*. Albany: State University of New York Press, pp. 203–219.

Callicott, J. B. (1989b). 'Traditional American Indian and Western European Attitudes to Nature: An Overview', J. B. Callicott, *In Defense of the Land Ethic: Essays in Environmental Philosophy*. Albany: State University of New York Press, pp. 177–201.

Callicott, J. B. (2016). 'The Historical Roots of Environmental Philosophy', in T. LeVasseur and A. Peterson (eds), *Religion and Ecological Crisis: The 'Lynn White Thesis' at Fifty*. New York: Routledge, pp. 33–46.

Cameron, L. (2017). *Sir Arthur Tansley* (Oxford Bibliographies series). http://www.oxfordbibliographies.com.view/document/obo-9780199830060-0094.

Caney, S. (2010). 'Climate Change, Human Rights and Moral Thresholds', in S. Gardiner, S. Caney, D. Jamieson and H. Shue (eds), *Climate Ethics: Essential Readings*. Oxford: Oxford University Press, pp. 163–177.

Carey, J. (2005). *The Faber Book of Science*. London: Faber & Faber.

Carlson, A. (2010). 'Contemporary Environmental Aesthetics and the Requirements of Environmentalism', *Environmental Values*, 19(3): 289–314.

Carroll, N. (2004). 'On Being Moved by Nature: Between Religious and Natural History', in A. Carlson and A. Berleant (eds), *The Aesthetics of Natural Environments*. Peterborough, Canada: Broadview Press, pp. 89–107.

Carson, R. (1941). *Under the Sea Wind*. New York: Simon & Schuster.

Carson, R. (1951). *The Sea Around Us*. Oxford: Oxford University Press.

Carson, R. (1955). *The Edge of the Sea*, New York: Mariner Books.

Carson, R. (2000 [1962]). *Silent Spring*. London: Penguin Classics.

Carson, R. (2017 [1965]). *The Sense of Wonder: A Celebration of Nature for Parents and Children*, New York: Open Road Media.

Carus-Wilson, E. M. (1954), 'An Industrial Revolution in the Thirteenth Century', in E. M. Carus-Wilson, *Essays in Economic History*, vol. I. London: Edward Arnold, pp. 41–60.

Cassidy, V. (2007). *Henry Chandler Cowles: Pioneer Ecologist*, Poland: Kedzie Productions.

Cérézuelle, D. (2018). 'Introduction', *The Green Light: A Self-Critique of the Ecological Movement*, trans. Christian Roy. London: Bloomsbury Academic, pp. xxi–xxx.

Chadwick, O. (1973). 'Evolution and the Churches', in C.A. Russell (ed.), *Science and Religious Belief: A Selection of Recent Historical Studies*. Maidenhead: Open University Press, pp. 282–293.

Charbonneau, B. (2018 [1980]). *The Green Light: A Self–Critique of the Ecological Movement*, trans. Christian Roy. London: Bloomsbury Academic.

Chatterjee, D. K. (2011). 'Vandana Shiva', in *Encyclopedia of Global Justice*, vol. I. New York: Springer, pp. 999–1001.

Clark, S. (1977). *The Moral Status of Animals*. Oxford: Clarendon Press.
Clark, S. (1983). 'Gaia and the Forms of Life', in R. Elliot and A. Gare (eds), *Environmental Philosophy: A Collection of Readings*. St Lucia: University of Queensland Press.
Clements, F. (1904). *The Development and Structure of Vegetation*. Lincoln, NE: Botanical Seminar.
Clements, F. (1905). *Research Methods in Ecology*. Lincoln, NE: University Publishing Company.
Clements, F. (1916). *Plant Succession: An Analysis of the Development of Vegetation*. Washington, DC: Carnegie Institute of Washington.
Clements, F. and Chaney, R. (1949 [1935]). 'Ecology in the Public Service', in B. Allred and E. Clements (eds), *Dynamics of Vegetation: Selections from the Writings of F. E. Clements*. New York: H. W. Wilson, pp. 249–254.
Clements, F. and Pound, R. (1898). *The Phytogeography of Nebraska*. Lincoln: University of Nebraska.
Clements, F. and Shelford, V. (1939). *Bio-Ecology*. London: Chapman & Hall.
Climate Emergency Movement (2019). *10 Years to Zero: A Newsletter of the Climate Emergency Movement*. New York: The Climate Mobilization.
Coates, P. (1998). *Nature: Western Attitudes since Ancient Times*. Berkeley: University of California Press.
Collin, N. (1793). 'An Essay on Those Inquiries in Natural Philosophy, Which Are at Present Most Beneficial', *Transactions of the American Philosophical Society*, vol. 3.
Commoner, B. (1966). *Science and Survival*. London: Gollancz.
Commoner, B. (1971). *The Closing Circle: Confronting the Environmental Crisis*. New York: Alfred A. Knopf.
Commoner, B. (1976). *The Poverty of Power*. New York: Random House.
Commoner, B. (1990). *Making Peace with the Planet*. New York: Pantheon Books.
Connelly, C. (2018). *Great European Lives: Petra Kelly*. https://www.theneweuropean.co.uk/top–stories/great–european–lives–petra–kelly–1–5713431.
Cottingham, J. (1978). '"A Brute to the Brutes?": Descartes' Treatment of Animals', *Philosophy*, 53: 551–559.
Craige, B. (2002). 'Eugene Odum (1913–2002)', in *New Georgia Encyclopedia*. https://www.georgiaencyclopedia.org/articles/geography-environment/eugene-odum-1913-2002.
Crutzen, P. (2006). 'Albedo Enhancement by Stratospheric Sulfur Injections: A Contribution to Resolve a Policy Dilemma?', *Climatic Change*, 77(3–4): 211–219.
Crutzen, P. and Birks, J. (1982). 'The Atmosphere After a Nuclear War: Twilight at Noon', *Ambio*, 11(2/3): 73.

Crutzen, P. and Störmer E. (2000). 'The "Anthropocene"', *IGBP Newsletter*, 41: 17–18.
Daly, H. (1977). 'The Steady-State Economy: What, Why and How?', in D. Pirages (ed.), *The Sustainable Society: Implications for Limited Growth*. New York: Praeger, pp. 107–130.
Daly, H. (1995). 'On Wilfred Beckerman's Critique of Sustainable Development', *Environmental Values*, 4(1): 49–55.
Dann, C. (2011). 'The Development of the First Two Green Parties: New Zealand and Tasmania', in *From Earth's Last Islands: The Global Origins of Green Politics*. https://web.archive.org/web/20110515170932/http://www/globalgreens.org/literature/dann/chapterfive.html.
Darwin, C. (1859). *On the Origin of Species*. London: John Murray.
Darwin, C. (1871). *The Descent of Man, and Selection in Relation to Sex*. London: John Murray.
Darwin, C. (1985). 'An Historical Sketch', in J. Burrow (ed.), *The Origin of Species*. London: Penguin Classics.
Darwin, C. (2009 [1872]). *The Expression of the Emotions in Man and Animals*, ed. Sharon Messenger. London: Penguin Classics.
Darwin, F. (ed.), (1887/8). *The Life and Letters of Charles Darwin*, 2. vols. London: J. Unray.
Dawkins, R. (1989). *The Selfish Gene*, 2nd edn. Oxford: Oxford University Press.
de Waal, F. (1996). *Good Natured: The Origins of Right and Wrong in Humans and Other Animals*. Cambridge, MA: Harvard University Press.
de Witt, C. B. (2000). 'Creation's Environmental Challenge to Evangelical Christianity', in R. J. Berry (ed.), *The Care of Creation: Fostering Concern and Action*. Leicester: Inter-Varsity Press, pp. 65–67.
Deane-Drummond, C. 2008, *Eco-Theology*. London: Darton, Longman & Todd.
Denis, L. (2000). 'Kant's Conception of Duties Regarding Animals: Reconstruction and Reconsideration', *History of Philosophy Quarterly*, 17: 405–423.
Derr, T. (1973). *Ecology and Human Liberation*. Geneva: WSCF Books.
Dicks, H. (2019). 'Being Like Gaia: Biomimicry and Ecological Ethics', *Environmental Values* 28(5): 601–620.
Dobzhansky, T. (1937). *Genetics and the Origin of Species*. New York: Columbia University Press
Dryden, J. (1958). *The Poems of John Dryden*. ed. James Kinsley. Oxford: Oxford University Press
Dubos, R. (1970). 'Can Man Adapt to Megalopolis?', *The Ecologist*, October.
Dubos, R. (1972). *The God Within*. New York: Scribner.
Dubos, R. (1974). 'Franciscan Conservation and Benedictine Stewardship',

in D. and E. Spring (eds), *Ecology and Religion in History*. New York: Harper & Row, pp. 114–136.

Earth Charter Commission (2000). *The Earth Charter*. https://earthcharter.org/invent/images/uploads/echarter_english.pdf.

Ecologist (1972). *A Blueprint for Survival*. Harmondsworth: Penguin.

EDF (Environmental Defense Fund) (2020). 'California Leads Fight to Curb Climate Change'. https://www.edf.org/climate/california-leads-fight-curb-climate-change.

Egerton, F. (2012). *Roots of Ecology: Antiquity to Haeckel*. Berkeley: University of California Press.

Ehrlich, P. (1970). *The Population Bomb*. New York: Ballantine Books.

Ehrlich, P. and Ehrlich, A. (1972). *Population, Resources, Environment*. San Francisco, CA: Freeman.

Ehrlich, P. and 19 others (1983). 'Long-term Biological Consequences of Nuclear War', *Science* 222(4630), 23 December: 1293–1300.

Ehrlich, P., Sagan, C. et al. (1985). *The Cold and the Dark: The World After Nuclear War*. New York: W. W. Norton.

Elliot, R. (1982). 'Faking Nature', *Inquiry*, 25: 81–93.

Elsom, D. M. (1992). *Atmospheric Pollution: A Global Problem*, 2nd edn. Oxford: Blackwell Publishers.

Elton, C. (1927). *Animal Ecology*. London: Sidgwick and Jackson. Repr. 2001, Chicago: University of Chicago Press.

Elton, C. (1930). *Animal Ecology and Evolution*. Oxford: Clarendon Press.

Elton, C. (1958). *The Ecology of Invasions by Animals and Plants*. London: Methuen. Repr. 2000, Chicago: University of Chicago Press.

Elton, C. (1966). *The Pattern of Animal Communities*. New York: Methuen.

Emerson, R. (1883 [1836]) 'Nature', in R. Emerson, *Nature, Addresses and Lectures: The Works of Ralph Waldo Emerson*, 14 vols. Boston, MA: Standard Library.

Emerson, R. (1990 [1836]). *Nature*, in Richard Poirier (ed.), *Ralph Waldo Emerson* (The Oxford Authors). Oxford: Oxford University Press.

Encyclopaedia Britannica (1998a). 'Dust Bowl: Historic Region, United States', *Encyclopaedia Britannica*. http://www.britannica.com/placeDust-Bowl.

Encyclopaedia Britannica (1998b). 'Johannes Eugenius Bülow Warming', https://www.britannica.com/biography/Johannes-Eugenius-Bulow-Warming.

Encyclopaedia Britannica (2019) 'Fukushima Accident'. https://www.britannica.com/event/Fukushima-accident.

Encyclopaedia Britannia [n.d.]. 'German Daily Life and Social Customs'. *https://www.britannica.com/place/Germany/Daily-life-and-social-customs*.

EPA (Environmental Protection Agency, US) (n.d.). 'Greenhouse Gas Emissions'. https://www.epa.gov/ghgemissions.

Fiering, N. (1976). 'Irresistible Compassion: An Aspect of Eighteenth-Century Humanitarianism', *Journal of the History of Ideas*, 37: 195–218.

Fisher, R. (1930). *The Genetical Theory of Natural Selection*. Oxford: Oxford University Press.

Forbes, S. (1991 [1887]). 'The Lake as a Microcosm', in L. Real and J. Brown, *Foundations of Ecology: Classical Papers with Commentaries*. Chicago, IL: University of Chicago Press, pp. 14–27.

Ford, E. B. (1964). *Ecological Genetics*. London: Methuen.

Freedman, L. (2020). 'Nuclear Test–Ban Treaty', *Encyclopaedia Britannica*. https://www.britannica.com/event/Nuclear-Test-Ban-Treaty.

Gaard, G. (2017). *Critical Ecofeminism: Ecocritical Theory and Practice*. Lanham, MD: Lexington Books.

Gardiner, S. (2011). 'Some Early Ethics of Geoengineering the Climate: A Commentary on the Values of the Royal Society Report', *Environmental Values*, 20(2): 163–188.

Gardner, W. H. (1953). *Poems and Prose of Gerard Manley Hopkins*. Harmondsworth: Penguin Books.

Gillispie, C. (1969). *Genesis and Geology*, 2nd edn. Cambridge, MA: Harvard University Press.

Glacken, C. J. (1967). *Traces on the Rhodian Shore: Nature and Culture in Western Thought from Ancient Times to the End of the Eighteenth Century*. Berkeley: University of California Press.

Gleason, H. (1991 [1926]). 'The Individualistic Concept of the Plant Association', in L. Real and J. Brown (eds), *Foundations of Ecology: Classical Papers with Commentaries*. Chicago: University of Chicago Press, pp. 98–117.

Goldin, O. (1997). 'The Ecology of the *Critias* and Platonic Metaphysics', in L. Westra and T. Robinson (eds), *The Greeks and the Environment*. Lanham, MD: Rowman & Littlefield, pp. 73–80.

Goodman, L. E. (2019). 'Darwin's Heresy', *Philosophy* 94 (367): 43–86.

Goodman, R. (2018). 'Transcendentalism', in E. Zalta (ed.), *The Stanford Encyclopedia of Philosophy* (Fall edn). https://plato.stanford.edu/archives/fall2018/entries/transcendentalism/.

Goodpaster, K. (1978). 'On Being Morally Considerable', *Journal of Philosophy*, 75: 308–325.

Gore, A. (2006). *An Inconvenient Truth: The Planetary Emergency of Global Warming and What We Can Do About It*. Emmaus, PA: Rodale Press.

Gould, S. (1997). *Life's Grandeur: The Spread of Excellence from Plato to Darwin*. Harmondsworth: Penguin.

Gould, S. and Lewontin, R. (1994). 'The Spandrels of San Marco and the Panglossian Paradigm: A Critique of the Adaptationist Programme', in E. Sober (ed.), *Conceptual Issues in Evolutionary Biology*, 2nd edn. Cambridge, MA: MIT Press, pp. 73–90.

Gould, S. and Vrba, E. (1998). 'Exaptation: A Missing Term in the Philosophy of Form', in D. Hull and M. Ruse (eds), *The Philosophy of Biology*. Oxford: Oxford University Press, pp. 52–71.

Granberg-Michaelson, W. (2020). 'Climate Change and the Ecumenical Movement', in E. Conradie and H. Koster (eds), *Christian Theology and Climate Change*. London: T&T Clark, pp. 340–351.

Gray, A. (1860). 'Natural Selection not Inconsistent with Natural Theology', *Atlantic Monthly*, 6: 109–116, 229–239, 406–425.

Green Belt Movement (2019), *Wangari Maathai*. https://www.greenbeltmovement.org/wangari-maathai.

Greenfield, P. (2020). 'Humans risk living in an empty world, warns UN official', *Guardian*, 20 January, p. 3.

Grime, J. P. (2002 [1979]). *Plant Strategies, Vegetation Processes and Ecosystem Properties*. Chichester: John Wiley.

Grober, U. (2007). *Deep Roots: A Conceptual History Of 'Sustainable Development' (Nachhaltigkeit)*. Berlin: Wissenschaftszentrum Berlin für Sozialforschung.

Guite, M. (2017). *Mariner: A Voyage with Samuel Taylor Coleridge*. London: Hodder & Stoughton.

Haeckel, E. (1876 [1868]). *The History of Creation*. New York: D. Appleton and Co.

Hagen, J. (2018). 'Frederic Edward Clements', *Encyclopaedia Britannica*. https://www.britannica.com/biography/Frederic-Edward-Clements.

Hagen, J. (2019). 'Henry Chandler Cowles', *Encyclopaedia Britannica*. https://britannica.com/biography/Henry-Chandler-Cowles.

Haldane, J. B. S. (1932). *The Causes of Evolution*. London: Longmans, Green.

Hardin, G. (1968). 'Tragedy of the Commons', *Science*, 162: 1243–1248.

Hardin, G. (1974). 'Living on a Lifeboat', *Bioscience*, 24.

Hargrove, E. C. (1989). *Foundations of Environmental Ethics*. Englewood Cliffs, NJ: Prentice-Hall.

Hawken, P. (2017). *Drawdown: The Most Comprehensive Plan Ever Proposed to Reverse Global Warming*. New York: Penguin.

Helfand, J. (1986). 'The Earth Is the Lord's: Judaism and Environmental Ethics', in E. Hargrove (ed.). *Religion and Environmental Ethics*. Athens: University of Georgia Press, pp. 38–52.

Hilton, R. and Sawyer, P. (1963), 'Technical Determinism: The Stirrup and the Plough', *Past and Present*, 24: 90–100.

Hippocrates (1923). 'Airs, Waters, Places', in *Hippocrates with an English*

Translation by W. H. S. Jones, vol. I. Cambridge, MA: Harvard University Press, pp. 70–137.

HM Government (1990). *This Common Inheritance: Britain's Environmental Strategy*. Cm 1200. London: HMSO.

Hobbs, R. et al. (2006). 'Novel Ecosystems: Theoretical and Management Aspects of the New Ecological World Order', *Global Ecology and Biogeography*, 15: 1–7.

Holdcroft, D. and Lewis, H. (2001). 'Consciousness, Design and Social Practice', *Journal of Consciousness Studies*, 8(8): 43–58.

Holden, E. (2019). 'Trump Begins Year-long Process to Formally Exit Paris Climate Agreement', *Guardian*, 5 November. https://www.theguardian.com/us-news/2019/nov/04/donald-trump-climate-crisis-exit-paris-agreement#img-3.

Holz, C., Kartha, S. and Athanasiou, T. (2015). *Climate Equity Reference Project*. https://climateequityreference.org/.

Hormone Health Network/Endocrine Society (2020). https://www.hormone.org/your-health-and-hormones/endocrine-disrupting-chemicals-edcs.

Hourdequin, M. (2015). *Environmental Ethics: From Theory to Practice*. London: Bloomsbury.

Hughes, J. D. (1983). *American Indian Environments*. El Paso: Texas Western Press.

Hughes, J. D. (1994). *Pan's Travail: Environmental Problems of the Ancient Greeks and Romans*. Baltimore, MD: Johns Hopkins University Press.

Hume, C. W. (1957). *The Status of Animals in the Christian Religion*. London: Universities' Federation for Animal Welfare.

Hunt, A. (2019). 'Pagan Animism: A Modern Myth for a Green Age', in A. Hunt and H. Marlow (eds), *Ecology and Theology in the Ancient World: Cross-Disciplinary Perspectives*. London: Bloomsbury, pp. 137–152.

Hunter, C. (2018). 'Clinton Hart Merriam: From Teenage Taxidermist to National Geographic Founder', *National Geographic*. https://blog-nationalgeographic.org/2018/01/25/clinton-hart-merriam-from-teenage-taxidermist-to-national-geographic-founder/.

Hursthouse, R. (1999). *On Virtue Ethics*. Oxford: Oxford University Press.

Hutchinson, G. (1974). 'Attitudes towards Nature in Medieval England: The Alphonso and Bird Psalters', *Isis*, 65: 5–37.

Huxley, J. (1942). *Evolution: The Modern Synthesis*. London: Allen & Unwin.

Huxley, T. H. (1863). *Evidence as to Man's Place in Nature*. New York: D. Appleton.

Huxley, T. H. (1894 [1888]). 'The Struggle for Existence in Human Society', in T. Huxley, *Evolution and Ethics, and Other Essays*, vol. 9. New York: D. Appleton, pp. 195–236.

IGBP (International Geographers – Biosphere Programme) (2001). *Amsterdam Declaration on Earth System Science.* http://www.igbp.net/about/history/2001amsterdamdeclarationonearthsystemscience.4.1b8ae20512db692f2a680001312.html.

International Union for the Conservation of Nature (1980). *World Conservation Strategy.* Gland, Switzerland: IUCN/UNEP/WWF.

IPBES (Intergovernmental Science-Policy Platform on Biodiversity and Ecosystem Services) (2019). 'Extinction Due to Human Activity'. https://www.britannica.com/topic/Intergovernmental-Science-Policy-Platform-on-Biodiversity–and–Ecosystem–Services.

IPCC (Intergovernmental Panel on Climate Change) (2020). https://www.un.org/en/sections/issues-depth/climate-change/.

Jamieson, D. (1995). 'Ecosystem Health: Some Preventive Medicine', *Environmental Values,* 4: 333–344.

Jamieson, D. (2001). 'Climate Change and Global Environmental Justice', in C. Miller and P. Edwards (eds), *Changing the Atmosphere: Expert Knowledge and Environmental Governance.* Cambridge, MA: MIT Press.

Jamieson, D. (2007). 'When Utilitarians Should be Virtue Theorists', *Utilitas,* 19(2): 287–308.

Jantzen, G. (1984). *God's World: God's Body.* London: Darton, Longman & Todd.

Jelley, N. (2020). *Renewable Energy: A Very Short Introduction.* Oxford: Oxford University Press.

John Ray Initiative (2020). https://www.jri.org.uk.

Jones, H. (2019). Personal communication (29 July).

Kant, I. (2005 [1785]). *Groundwork of the Metaphysic of Morals,* trans. Thomas K. Abbott, ed. Lara Denis. Peterborough, ONT: Broadview. https://www.earlymoderntexts.com/assets/pdfs/kant1785.pdf.

Katz, E. (1992). 'The Big Lie: Human Restoration of Nature', *Research in Philosophy and Technology,* 12: 231–241.

Kelbessa, W. (2012). 'Environmental Injustice in Africa', *Contemporary Pragmatism,* 9(1): 99–132.

Kerber, G. (2020). 'A Response to Wesley Granberg-Michaelson', in E. Conradie and H. Koster (eds), *Christian Theology and Climate Change.* London: T&T Clark, pp. 351–356.

Kingsley, C. (1930 [1863]). *The Water Babies.* London: Hodder and Stoughton.

Kirchner, J. W. (1992). 'The Gaia Hypotheses: Are They Testable? Are They Useful?' in S. Schneider and P. Boston (eds), *Scientists on Gaia.* Cambridge, MA: MIT Press. Repr. in L. Pojman (ed.), *Environmental Ethics: Readings in Theory and Application.* Boston, MA: Jones and Baldwin, 1994, pp. 146–154.

Khalid, F. (2013). 'Muslims, the Environment and the Challenge of the Emerging Order'. Unpublished address delivered at Cardiff University, February.

Klein, Naomi (2014). *This Changes Everything: Capitalism vs. the Climate.* New York: Simon & Schuster.

Klein, Naomi (2019). *On Fire: The (Burning) Case for a Green New Deal.* New York: Simon & Schuster.

Kropotkin, P. (1899), *Fields, Factories and Workshops.* Reissued as *Fields, Factories and Workshops (Tomorrow)*, ed. C. Ward. London: Unwin, 1974.

Kropotkin, P. (1902). *Mutual Aid: A Factor of Evolution.* London: William Heinemann.

Las Casas, B. de (1992 [1552]). *A Short Account of the Destruction of the Indies*, trans. N. Griffin. London: Penguin Books.

Latour, Bruno (2018) *Down to Earth: Politics in the New Climatic Regime*, trans. Catherine Porter. Cambridge: Polity.

Lear, L. (1997). *Rachel Carson: Witness for Nature.* New York: Henry Holt. Repr. 1998, London: Allen Lane.

Lecky, W. E. H. (1913 [1869]), *History of European Morals from Augustus to Charlemagne*, 2 vols. London: Longmans, Green.

Lehmann, A. (2019). 'Greens Are on the Rise. But the Nation is Divided', *Guardian*, 24 June. https://www.theguardian.com/commentisfree/2019/jun/24/german-greens-rise-nation-divided.

Lenton, T. (1998). 'Gaia and Natural Selection', *Nature*, 30 July, 394: 439–447.

Leopold, A. (1925). 'Wilderness as a Form of Land Use', *Journal of Land and Public Utility Economics*, I.

Leopold, A. (1926). Contribution to *National Conference on Outdoor Recreation Proceedings 1926*, 69th Cong., 1st Sess., Senate Doc. 117, 14 April. Washington, DC.

Leopold, A. (1966 [1949]). *A Sand County Almanac with Other Essays on Conservation from Round River.* New York: Oxford University Press

Leopold, A. (1953). *Round River: From the Journals of Aldo Leopold*, ed. L. B. Leopold. New York: Oxford University Press.

Leopold, A. (1979 [1923]). 'Some Fundamentals of Conservation in the Southwest', *Environmental Ethics*, 1(2): 131–141.

Leopold, A. and Brooks, A. (1933). *Game Management.* New York: C. Scribner's Sons.

Lewontin, R. (1970). 'The Units of Evolution', *Annual Review of Ecology and Systematics*, 1: 1–23.

Lindberg, D. (1992). *The Beginnings of Western Science: The European Scientific Tradition in Philosophical, Religious and Institutional Context, 500 BC to AD 1450.* Chicago, IL: University of Chicago Press.

Lindeman, R. L. (1942). 'The Trophic-Dynamic Aspect of Ecology', *Ecology*, 23(4): 399–417.

Lindstrøm, T. (2010). 'The Animals of the Arena: How and Why Could Their Destruction and Death Be Endured and Enjoyed?', *World Archaeology*, 42(2): 310–323.

Linzey, A. (1976). *Animal Rights: A Christian Assessment of Man's Treatment of Animals*. London: SCM Press.

Lloyd, G. (2018). *Reclaiming Wonder: After the Sublime*. Edinburgh: University of Edinburgh Press.

Lovejoy, A. O. (1936). *The Great Chain of Being: A Study of the History of an Idea*. Cambridge, MA: Harvard University Press.

Lovelock, J. (1979). *Gaia: A New Look at Life on Earth*. Oxford: Oxford University Press.

Lovelock, J. (1990). 'Hands Up for the Gaia Hypothesis', *Nature*, 344: 100–102.

Lovelock, J. (2006). *The Revenge of Gaia: Why the Earth is Fighting Back – and How We Can Still Save Humanity*. London: Penguin.

Lowenthal, D. (2000 [1958]). *George Perkins Marsh*. Seattle: University of Washington Press.

McCrea, R. (1910). *The Humane Movement: A Descriptive Survey*. New York: Columbia University Press.

McFague, S. (1993). *The Body of God: An Ecological Theology*. London: SCM Press.

McRobie, G. (1982). *Small Is Possible*. London: Abacus Books.

McShane, K. (2004). 'Ecosystem Health', *Environmental Ethics*, 26(3): 227–245.

McShane, K. (2013). 'Environmental Ethics', in H. LaFollette (ed.), *International Encyclopedia of Ethics*. Oxford: Blackwell Publishing.

Maluleke, G. (2018). 'Rethinking Protected Area Co-Management in the Makuleke Region, South Africa'. PhD dissertation. Stellenbosch University, South Africa.

Malin, J. (1956). *The Grassland of North America: Prolegomena to Its History with Addenda*. Chicago, IL: University of Chicago Press.

Margulis, L. (1998). *The Symbiotic Planet*. London: Phoenix Press.

Marris, E. (2011). *Rambunctious Garden: Saving Nature in a Post-Wild World*. London: Bloomsbury.

Marsh, G. P. (1965 [1864]). *Man and Nature: Physical Geography as Modified by Human Action*, ed. David Lowenthal. Cambridge, MA: Harvard University Press.

Marsh, G. P. (2003 [1864]). *Man and Nature: Or, Physical Geography as Modified by Human Action*, ed. David Lowenthal. Seattle: University of Washington Press.

Marsh, G. P. (1970 [1874]). *The Earth as Modified by Human Action*,

A New Edition of Man and Nature. St. Clair Shores, MI: Scholarly Press.
Martin, R. (2015). *Shakespeare and Ecology*. Oxford: Oxford University Press.
Marx, K. (1924 [1845]), 'Theses on Feuerbach'. https://www.marxists.org/archive/marx/works/1845/theses/index.htm.
Marx, K. (1967). *Capital*, 3 vols. New York: International.
Masri, A. (1992). 'Islam and Ecology', in F. Khalid and J. O'Brien (eds), *Islam and Ecology*. London: Cassell.
Mathews, F. (2010). 'Planetary Collapse Disorder: The Honeybee as Portent of the Limits of the Ethical', *Environmental Ethics*, 32: 353–367.
Mayr, E, (1982). *The Growth of Biological Thought*. Cambridge, MA: Belknap Press of Harvard University Press.
Meadows, D. H. et al. (1974 [1972]). *The Limits to Growth*. London: Pan Books.
Meinshausen, M. et al. (2009). 'Greenhouse Gas Emission Targets for Limiting Global Warming to 2°C', *Nature*, 458 (30 April): 1158–1163.
Merchant, C. (1990 [1980]). *The Death of Nature: Women, Ecology and the Scientific Revolution*. San Francisco, CA: HarperCollins.
Meyer, A. (2005). *Contraction & Convergence: The Global Solution to Climate Change*. Schumacher Briefing No. 5. Totnes: Green Books.
Midgley, M. (1979a). *Beast and Man: The Roots of Human Nature*. Brighton: Harvester Press.
Midgley, M. (1979b). 'Gene-Juggling', *Philosophy*, 54: 438–458.
Midgley, M. (1983). *Animals and Why They Matter*. Harmondsworth: Penguin.
Midgley, M. (2000). 'Why Memes', in H. Rose and S. Rose (eds), *Alas, Poor Darwin*. London: Jonathan Cape, pp. 67–84.
Midgley, M. (2001). *Gaia: The Next Big Idea*. London: Demos.
Midgley, M. (2010). *The Solitary Self: Darwin and the Selfish Gene*. Slough: Acumen.
Midgley, M. (2014 [2010]). *The Solitary Self: Darwin and the Selfish Gene*. London: Routledge.
Migne, J. (ed.) (1844–63). *Patrologiae Cursus Completus . . . Series Latina*. Paris: J. P. Migne.
Mill, J. (1920 [1848]). *Principles of Political Economy*, ed. W. J. Ashley. London: Longmans, Green.
Miller, G. (1993). *Environmental Science: Sustaining the Earth*. Boston, MA: Wadsworth.
Mishan, E. (1971). 'The Economics of Hope', *The Ecologist*, January.
Moltmann, J. (1985). *God in Creation: An Ecological Doctrine of Creation*, trans. M. Kohl. London: SCM Press.

Montreal Protocol on Substances that Deplete the Ozone Layer (1987). www.ciesin.org/TG/PI/POLICY/montpro.html.
Moore, G. E. (2003). *Principia Ethica*. Cambridge: Cambridge University Press.
Moore, K. D. (2005). 'The Truth of the Barnacles: Rachel Carson and the Moral Significance of Wonder', *Environmental Ethics*, 27(3): 263–277.
Muir, J. (1912). *The Yosemite*. New York: The Century Company.
Muir, J. (1992 [1916]). *The Eight Wilderness Discovery Books*. London: Diadem Books.
Murcia, C. et al. (2014). 'A Critique of the "Novel Ecosystem" Concept', *Trends in Ecology and Evolution*, 29(10): 548–553.
Myerson, J. (2000). *Transcendentalism: A Reader*. New York: Oxford University Press.
Naess, A. (1973). 'The Shallow and the Deep, Long-Term Ecology Movement: A Summary', *Inquiry*, 16: 95–109. Repr. in R. Attfield (ed.), *The Ethics of the Environment*. Farnham: Ashgate, 2008, pp. 115–120.
NASA (2020), 'The Effects of Climate Change'. https://climate.nasa.gov/effects/.
Nash, R. F. (2014 [1967]). *Wilderness and the American Mind*, 5th edn. New Haven, CT: Yale University Press.
Nash, R. F. (1989). *The Rights of Nature: A History of Environmental Ethics*. Madison, WI: University of Wisconsin Press.
National Academy of Sciences (1994). https://www.ncbi.nlm.nih.gov/books/NBK236347/.
Navdanya (2019). *Navdanya: The Earth Family*. http://www.navdanya.org/site/.
Nomanul Haq, S. (2001,). 'Islam', in D. Jamieson (ed.), *A Companion to Environmental Philosophy*. Malden, MA: Blackwell, pp. 111–129.
Norton, B. (ed.) (1986). *The Preservation of Species*. Princeton, NJ: Princeton University Press.
Nussbaum, M. (2006). *Frontiers of Justice: Disability, Nationality, Species Membership*. Cambridge, MA: Belknap Press of Harvard University Press.
Odum, E. (1953). *Fundamentals of Ecology*. Philadelphia, PA: Saunders.
Oreskes, N. and Conway, E. M. (2010). *Merchants of Doubt: How a Handful of Scientists Obscured the Truth on Issues from Tobacco Smoke to Global Warming*. London: Bloomsbury.
Ott, K. (2011). 'Domains of Climate Ethics', *Jahrbuch für Wissenschaft und Ethik*, 16: 95–112.
Ott, K. (2012). 'Variants of De-growth and Deliberative Democracy: A Habermasian Proposal', *Futures*, 44: 571–581.
Paley, W. (1810 [1802]). *Natural Theology; or Evidences of the Existence*

and Attributes of the Deity collected from the Appearances of Nature, in W. Paley (ed.) *The Works of William Paley*, vol. I. Boston, MA: Joshua Belcher, 1810.

Palmer, C. 1992, 'Stewardship: A Case Study in Environmental Ethics', in J. Ball et al. (eds), *The Earth Beneath*. London: SPCK, pp. 67–86.

Palmer, C. (2003). 'An Overview of Environmental Ethics', in A. Light and H. Rolston III (eds), *Environmental Ethics: An Anthology*. Oxford: Blackwell, pp. 15–37.

Palmer, C., McShane, K. and Sandler, R. (2014). 'Environmental Ethics', *Annual Review of Environment and Resources*, 39: 419–442.

Parfit, D. (1984). *Reasons and Persons*. Oxford: Clarendon Press.

Parker, J. (1998). 'Precautionary Principle', in R. Chadwick (ed.), *Encyclopedia of Applied Ethics*, vol. 3. San Diego, CA: Academic Press, pp. 633–641.

Parker, L. (2019). 'The World's Plastic Pollution Crisis Explained'. https://www.nationalgeographic.com/environment/habitats/plastic-pollution/.

Parsons, H. (1978). *Marx and Engels on Ecology*. Westport, CT: Greenwood Press.

Passmore, J. (1970). *The Perfectibility of Man*. London: Duckworth.

Passmore, J. (1974). *Man's Responsibility for Nature*. London: Duckworth.

Passmore, J. (1980), *Man's Responsibility for Nature*, 2nd edn. London: Duckworth (includes some additional essays).

Payne, D. and Newman, R. (2005). 'United Church of Christ Commission for Racial Justice', in D. Payne and R. Newman (eds), *The Palgrave Environmental Reader*. New York: Palgrave Macmillan, pp. 259–264.

Peacocke, A. (2004). 'Articulating God's Presence in and to the World Unveiled by the Sciences', in P. Clayton and A. Peacocke (eds), *In Whom We Live and Move and Have Our Being*. Grand Rapids, MI: Eerdmans, pp. 137–154.

Peacocke, A. (2007). *All That Is: A Naturalistic Faith for the Twenty-First Century*, ed. P. Clayton. Minneapolis, MN: Fortress Press.

Pearce et al. (1989). *Blueprint 2: Greening the World Economy*. London: Earthscan.

Pepper, D. (1984). *The Roots of Modern Environmentalism*. London: Routledge.

Plumwood (formerly Routley), V. (1991). 'Nature, Self and Gender: Feminism, Environmental Philosophy and the Critique of Rationalism', *Hypatia*, 6: 3–27.

Ponting, C. (1991). *A Green History of the World*. London: Sinclair Stevenson.

Pope Francis (2015). *Laudato Si'*. https://laudatosi.com/.

Popper, K. (1960). *The Poverty of Historicism*, 2nd edn. London: Routledge & Kegan Paul.

Rajan, S. (ed.) (2017). *Genealogies of Environmentalism: The Lost Works of Clarence Glacken.* Charlottesville: University of Virginia Press.

Ray, J. (1691). *The Wisdom of God Manifested in the Works of Creation.* London: John Rivington, John Ward, Joseph Richardson.

Rafferty, J. (2019). 'Biodiversity Loss'. https://www.britannica.com/science/biodiversity-loss.

Regan, T. (1981). 'The Nature and Possibility of an Environmental Ethic', *Environmental Ethics*, 3: 19–34.

Regan, T. (1983). *The Case for Animal Rights.* Berkeley: University of California Press.

Richardson, L. (2015). 'Thinking Like a Mountain', *The Paris Review*, 30 July.

Ridler, A. (ed.) (1966). *Thomas Traherne: Poems, Centuries and Three Thanksgivings.* Oxford: Oxford University Press.

Robins, S. and van der Waal, K. (2008). '"Model Tribes" and Iconic Conservationists? The Makuleke Restitution Case in Kruger National Park', *Development and Change*, 39(1): 51–72.

Rodick, D. (ed.) (2017). *Wilderness in America: Philosophical Writings of Henry G. Bugbee.* New York: Fordham University Press.

Rolston, H. (1975). 'Is There an Ecological Ethic?', *Ethics*, 85: 93–100. Repr. in R. Attfield (ed.), *The Ethics of the Environment.* Farnham: Ashgate, 2008, pp. 13–29.

Rolston, H. (1988). *Environmental Ethics: Duties to and Values in The Natural World.* Philadelphia, PA: Temple University Press.

Rolston, H. (1998). 'Aesthetic Experience in Forests', *Journal of Aesthetics and Art Criticism*, 56: 157–166.

Rolston, H. (2005). 'Environmental Virtue Ethics: Half the Truth, but Dangerous as a Whole', in R. Sandler and P. Cafaro (eds), *Environmental Virtue Ethics.* Lanham, MD: Rowman & Littlefield, pp. 61–78.

Rosling, H. and Rosling, O. (2018). *Factfulness: Ten Reasons We're Wrong About the World – and Why Things are Better Than You Think.* London: Hodder & Stoughton.

Routley (later Sylvan) R. (1973). 'Is There a Need for a New, an Environmental Ethic?', *Proceedings of the World Congress of Philosophy.* Varna (Bulgaria), pp. 205–210. Repr. in R. Attfield (ed.), *The Ethics of the Environment.* Farnham: Ashgate, 2008, pp. 3–12.

Rowlands M. (1998). *Animal Rights: A Philosophical Defence.* London: Macmillan.

Ruse, M. (1996). *Monad to Man: The Concept of Progress in Evolutionary Biology.* Cambridge, MA: Harvard University Press.

Ruse, M. (2001). *Can a Darwinian Be a Christian?* Cambridge: Cambridge University Press.

Ruse, M. (2006). 'Evolution', in A. Grayling, A. Pyle and N. Goulder (eds), *Continuum Encyclopedia of British Philosophy*, vol. 2. London: Bloomsbury, pp. 1034–1043.
Ryberg, J. (1997). 'Population and Third World Assistance', *Journal of Applied Philosophy*, 14: 207–219.
Sagoff, M. (1974). 'On Preserving the Natural Environment', *Yale Law Journal*, 84: 205–267.
Sagoff, M. (2013). 'What Does Environmental Protection Protect?', *Ethics, Policy and Environment*, 16(3): 239–257.
Sale, K. (1985). *Dwellers in the Land: The Bioregional Vision*. San Francisco, CA: Sierra Club Books.
Sale, K. (1990). *Conquest of Paradise*. New York: Knopf Publishing Group.
Salt, H. (1890). *The Life of Henry David Thoreau*. London: R. Bentley.
Salt, H. (1894 [1892]). *Animals' Rights: Considered in Relation to Social Progress*. New York: Macmillan & Co.
Salt, H. (ed.) (1897). *Cruelties of Civilization: A Program of Humane Reform*. London: William Reeves.
Salt, H. (ed.) (1906). *The Writings of Henry David Thoreau in Twenty Volumes*. Boston, MA: Houghton Mifflin & Co.
Salt, H. (1928). Letter to the Editor of *The Spectator*, 21 January, p. 15.
Sample, I. (2005). 'The Father of Climate Change'. https://www.theguardian.com/environment/2005/jun/30/climatechange.climatechangeenvironment2.
Sandler, R. (2005). 'Introduction: Environmental Virtue Ethics', in R. Sandler, and P. Cafaro (eds), *Environmental Virtue Ethics*. Lanham, MD: Rowman & Littlefield, pp. 1–12.
Sandler, R. (2013). *The Ethics of Species*. Cambridge: Cambridge University Press.
Sandler, R. and Cafaro, P. (eds) (2005). *Environmental Virtue Ethics*. Lanham, MD: Rowman & Littlefield.
Santmire, P. (1985). *The Travail of Nature: The Ambiguous Ecological Promise of Christian Theology*. Philadelphia, PA: Fortress Press.
Sauer, C. (1925). *The Morphology of Landscape*, Berkeley, CA: University Press.
Schliephake, C. (2016). *Ecocriticism, Ecology, and the Cultures of Antiquity*. Lanham, MD: Lexington Books.
Schopenhauer, A. (2010 [1818–19]). *The World as Will and Representation*, vol. I, trans. and ed., J. Norman, A. Welchman and C. Janaway. Cambridge: Cambridge University Press.
Schumacher, E. F. (1973). *Small Is Beautiful: A Study of Economics As If People Mattered*. London: Blond & Briggs.
Schweitzer, A. (1923). *Civilization and Ethics: The Philosophy of Civilization Part II*, trans, John Naish. London: A. & C. Black.

Schweitzer, A. (1933). *Out of My Life and Thought: An Autobiography*, trans. C. T. Campion. New York: George Allen & Unwin.

Sears, P. (1935). *Deserts on the March*. Norman: University of Oklahoma Press.

Shapshay, S. (2017). 'Schopenhauer on the Moral Considerability of Animals', in S. Shapshay (ed.), *The Palgrave Schopenhauer Handbook*. Cham, Switzerland: Palgrave Macmillan, pp. 283–298.

Shelford, V. (1913). *Animal Communities in Temperate America as Illustrated in the Chicago Region: A Study in Animal Ecology*. Chicago, IL: Geographical Society of Chicago.

Shelley, P. (1840 [1821]). 'A Defence of Poetry', in M. Shelley (ed.), *Essays, Letters from Abroad, Translations and Fragments by Percy Bysshe Shelley*. London: Edward Moxon.

Shiva, V. (1997). *Biopiracy: The Plunder of Nature and Knowledge*. Boston, MA: South End Press.

Sierra Club (n.d.) *John Muir: A Brief Biography*. https://vault.sierraclub.org/john_muir_exhibit/life/muir_biography.aspx.

Simberloff, D. (2013). *Charles Elton* (Oxford Bibliographies series). https//www.oxfordbibliographies.com/view/document/obo-9780199830060/obo-9780199830060–0090.xml.

Singer, P. (1975). *Animal Liberation: A New Ethics for Our Treatment of Animals*. New York: Avon.

Singer, P. (1979). *Practical Ethics*. Cambridge: Cambridge University Press

Smith, M. (2010). 'Epharmosis: Jean-Luc Nancy and the Political Oecology of Creation'. *Environmental Ethics*, 32(4): 385–404.

Sober, E. (1986). 'Philosophical Problems for Environmentalism', in B. Norton (ed.), *The Preservation of Species*. Princeton, NJ: Princeton University Press, pp. 173–194.

Sober, E. (1998). 'Six Sayings about Adaptationism', in D. Hull and M. Ruse (eds), *The Philosophy of Biology*. Oxford: Oxford University Press, pp. 72–86.

Southgate, C. (2006). 'Stewardship and Its Competitors: A Spectrum of Relationships between Humans and the Nonhuman Creation', in R. G. Berry (ed.), *Environmental Stewardship: Critical Perspectives – Past and Present*. London, T&T Clark.

Southwood, T. R. E. (1971). *Ecological Methods: With Particular Reference to the Study of Insect Populations*. London: Chapman & Hall.

Spencer, H. (1862). *First Principles*. London: Williams and Norgate.

Steinbeck, J. (1939). *The Grapes of Wrath*. New York: Viking Books.

Sterba, J. (1995). 'From Biocentric Individualism to Biocentric Pluralism', *Environmental Ethics*, 17: 101–207.

Sterba, J. (1998a). 'A Biocentrist Strikes Back'. *Environmental Ethics*, 20: 361–376.

Sterba, J. (1998b). *Justice for Here and Now*. New York: Cambridge University Press.
Stoll, Mark (2015). *Inherit the Holy Mountain: Religion and the Rise of American Environmentalism*. Oxford: Oxford University Press.
Suh, J. (2014). 'Towards Sustainable Agricultural Stewardship: Evolution and Future Directions of the Permaculture Concept', *Environmental Values*, 23(1): 75–98.
Sylvan (formerly Routley), R. (1992). 'Mucking with Nature' (unpublished paper).
Tansley, A. G. (1935). 'The Use and Abuse of Vegetational Concepts and Terms', *Ecology* 16(3): 284–307.
Tansley, A. G. (1965 [1939]). *The British Islands and Their Vegetation*, 4th edn. Cambridge: Cambridge University Press.
Tansley, A. G. and Chipp, T. (1926). *Aims and Methods in the Study of Vegetation*. London: British Empire Vegetation Committee.
Taylor, A. (2014). 'Bhopal: The World's Worst Industrial Disaster, 30 Years Later'. https://www.theatlantic.com/photo/2014/12/bhopal-the-worlds-worst-industrial-disaster-30-years-later/100864/.
Taylor, P. W. (1986). *Respect for Nature: A Theory of Environmental Ethics*. Princeton, NJ: Princeton University Press.
Thomas, K. (1983). *Man and the Natural World: A History of the Modern Sensibility*. New York: Pantheon Books.
Thompson, I. (2014). *Landscape Architecture: A Very Short Introduction*. Oxford: Oxford University Press.
Thomson, J. A. (1910). *Darwinism and Human Life*. New York: Henry Holt.
Thoreau, H. (1968 [1854]). *Walden*. London: Dent.
Thoreau, H. (1989 [1854]). *Walden*. Princeton, NJ: Princeton University Press.
Thoreau, H. (1988 [1865]). *Cape Cod*, ed. J. J. Moldenhauer. Princeton, NJ: Princeton University Press.
Thoreau, H. (1906), *The Writings of Henry Thoreau*, ed. B. Torrey. Boston, MA: Houghton Mifflin Company.
Thoreau, H. (1973). *Reform Papers*, ed. W. Glick. Princeton, NJ: Princeton University Press.
Tickell, O. (2008). *Kyoto2: How to Manage the Global Greenhouse*. London: Zed Books.
Turner, E. (1964). *All Heaven in a Rage*. London: Michael Joseph.
UCL Home (2007). 'Aral Sea Shrinkage Caused by Humans'. https://www.ucl.ac.uk/news/2007/apr/aral–sea–shrinkage–caused–humans.
Udall, S. (1963). *The Quiet Crisis*. New York: Holt, Rinehart & Winston.
United Nations (1986). *Declaration on the Right to Development*. New York: United Nations.

United Nations Conference on Environment and Development (1992). 'Rio Declaration on Environment and Development', in W. Granberg-Michaelson (ed.), *Redeeming the Creation: The Rio Earth Summit: Challenges for the Churches*. Geneva: WCC Publications, pp. 86–90.

UNFCCC (2015). 'The Paris Agreement'. https://unfccc.int/process-and-meetings/the-paris-agreement/the-paris-agreement.

VanDeVeer, D. (1979). 'Interspecific Justice', *Inquiry*, 22: 55–79.

Varner, G. (1998). *In Nature's Interests*. New York: Oxford University Press.

Vaughan, H. (1976). *Henry Vaughan: The Complete Poems*, ed. A. Rudrum. Harmondsworth: Penguin.

Vivès, L. (ed.) (1872–8). *Oeuvres Complètes de Saint Augustin*, 34 vols. Paris: Librairie de Louis Vivès.

Waddell, H. (1995). *Beasts and Saints*. London: Darton, Longman & Todd.

Wagner, G. and Weitzman, M. L. (2015). *Climate Shock: The Economic Consequences of a Hotter Planet*. Princeton, NJ: Princeton University Press.

Wallace, A. (1869). 'Sir Charles Lyell on Geological Climates and the Origin of Species', *Quarterly Review*, 126: 359–394.

Wallace, A. (1872). *The Malay Archipelago: The Land of the Orangutan and the Bird of Paradise: A Narrative of Travel, with Studies of Man and Nature*. London: Macmillan.

Ward, B. (1966). *Spaceship Earth*. New York: Columbia University Press.

Ward, B. and Dubos, R. (1972). *Only One Earth: The Care and Maintenance of a Small Planet*. Harmondsworth: Penguin.

Warming, E. (1909 [1895]). *Oecology of Plants: An Introduction to the Study of Plant Communities*. Oxford: Clarendon Press.

Warren, K. (1990). 'The Power and Promise of Ecological Feminism', *Environmental Ethics*, 12: 121–146.

Watts, J. (2018). 'We Have 12 Years to Limit Climate Change Catastrophe, Warns UN', *Guardian*, 8 October. https://www.theguardian.com/environment/2018/oct/08/global-warming-must-not-exceed-15c-warns-landmark-un-report.

WCED (World Commission on Environment and Development) (1987). *Our Common Future* ('The Brundtland Report'). Oxford: Oxford University Press.

Weaver, J. and Flory, E. (1934). 'Stability of Climax Prairie and Some Environmental Changes Resulting from Breaking', *Ecology*, 15: 333–347.

Webb, W. (1931). *The Great Plains*. Boston, MA: Ginn and Co.

Weber, E. (1982). *Air Pollution: Assessment Methodology and Modeling*, vol. 2. New York: Plenum.

Weber, M. (2002 [1905]). *The Protestant Ethic and the Spirit of Capitalism*, trans. P. Baehr and G. C. Wells. London: Penguin Books.

Welbourn, F. (1975). 'Man's Dominion', *Theology*, 78: 561–568.
Whewell, W. (1837). *The History of the Inductive Sciences*. London: Parker.
Whewell, W. (1840). *The Philosophy of the Inductive Sciences*. London: Parker.
White, L. (1962). *Medieval Technology and Social Change*. Oxford: Clarendon Press.
White, L. (1967). 'The Historical Roots of Our Ecologic Crisis', *Science*, 155(37): 1203–1207.
White, L. (1973). 'Continuing the Conversation', in I. Barbour (ed.), *Western Man and Environmental Ethics*. London: Addison-Wesley, pp. 55–64.
Whitehead, A. N. (1979 [1929]). *Process and Reality*. New York: Free Press.
Whitney, E. (1993). 'Lynn White, Ecotheology and History', *Environmental Ethics* 15(2): 151–169.
Whitney, E. (2004). *Medieval Science and Technology*. Westport, CT: Greenwood Press.
Whitney, E. (2006). 'Changing Metaphors and Concepts of Nature', in D. Lodge and C. Hamlin (eds), *Religion and the New Ecology: Environmental Responsibility in a World in Flux*. Notre Dame, IN: University of Notre Dame Press, pp. 26–52.
Whittaker, R. (1975 [1970]). *Communities and Ecosystems*, 2nd edn. New York: Macmillan.
Wilcher, R. (ed.) (1986). *Andrew Marvell: Selected Poetry and Prose*. London: Methuen.
Wilkie, J. (1973). 'Buffon, Lamarck and Darwin: The Originality of Darwin's Theory of Evolution', in C. A. Russell (ed.), *Science and Religious Belief: A Selection of Recent Historical Studies*. London: University of London Press.
Wilkins, T. (1995). *John Muir: Apostle of Nature*. Norman: University of Oklahoma Press.
Williams, M. B. (1978). 'Discounting Versus Maximum Sustainable Yield', in R. Sikora and B. Barry (eds), *Obligations to Future Generations*. Philadelphia, PA: Temple University Press, pp. 169–185.
Wilson, E. O. (1975). *Sociobiology: The New Synthesis*. Cambridge, MA: Harvard University Press.
Wilson, E. O. (1984). *Biophilia*. Cambridge, MA: Harvard University Press.
Wilson, E. O. (1999). *Consilience*. London: Abacus.
Wines, M. (2011) 'China Admits Problems with Three Gorges Dam', *New York Times*. https://www.nytimes.com/2011/05/20/world/asia/20gorges.html.
Wordsworth, W. and Coleridge, S. (1800) *Lyrical Ballads*. London.
World Pollution Map (2019). https://www.google.com/search?client=firefox-b-d&q=global+air+pollution+map&tbm=isch&chips=q:global+air+pollution+map,g_1:air+quality&usg=AI4_-kRd9C4VMX2RjPz_FoLXf0

UGv9-k8Q&sa=X&ved=2ahUKEwjhlvzEsuDnAhXLQhUIHaU_Dz0Qg IoDKAB6BAgKEAQ&biw=1142&bih=791.
Worster, D. (1985 [1977]). *Nature's Economy: A History of Ecological Ideas*. Cambridge: Cambridge University Press.
Wright, S. (1931). 'Evolution in Mendelian Populations', *Genetics*, 16: 97–159.
Wright, S. (1932). 'The Roles of Mutation, Inbreeding, Crossbreeding and Selection in Evolution', *Proceedings of the Sixth International Conference of Genetics*, 1: 356–366.
WWF (World Wildlife Fund) (2014). *Living Planet Report*. https://www.worldwildlife.org/pages/living-planet-report-2014.

Index

acid rain 196, 205
acidification of oceans 206–7, 213
Acts of the Apostles 19, 20, 21, 35
adaptationism 79, 80
aesthetics, environmental 49, 93, 95, 125, 141, 175, 179–81, 187, 190, 197, 204
Africa 17, 27, 44, 105, 88, 104, 110, 127, 133, 144, 146, 147, 157, 192–3, 194, 201, 205, 209, 217
    see also Ethiopia; Kenya; South Africa, Republic of; Zanzibar
agent orange 143
Aiken, William 144, 162
Albert the Great 29–30, 86
Allee, Walter 128
American Society for the Prevention of Cruelty to Animals (ASPCA) 99–100
Amsterdam Declaration on Earth System Science (2001) 176
animal contests 17–18
Animal Ecology (Elton) 110–11, 121
Animal Liberation: A New Ethics for Our Treatment of Animals (Singer) 167, 182
animals, study of 15, 30, 40, 41, 64–6, 69, 72, 78, 89–90, 100, 104–6, 109, 110, 112, 117–18, 121, 129–32, 167–8, 171, 176, 186, 217
Animals and Why They Matter (Midgley) 140, 142, 169, 201
Antarctic 1, 137, 141, 189, 195, 208
'anthropocene' 203, 214
anthropocentrism 22, 28, 34, 39, 45, 86–7, 95, 112, 137, 156–7, 164, 172, 180
Antony, St 24–5, 28
Aquinas, Thomas 24/5, 29, 31, 35
Aral Sea 147, 204, 218,
Arctic 135, 189, 208
arguments for design 21, 31, 60–1, 75, 91
Aristotle 1, 12, 15–16, 23, 28, 45, 30–31, 40, 128, 155–6, 178
Arouet, François-Marie (Voltaire) 45, 46
Arrhenius, Svante 208–9
artefacts 187
Athanasiou, Tom 211, 214
atomism 12, 16–17, 34, 39–40, 41
Attenborough, David 205, 207
Attfield, Robin 3, 4, 6, 150, 164, 170, 178, 198
    articles and chapters 26, 34, 58, 79, 150, 155, 164, 166, 175–6, 181, 192, 196

Attfield, Robin (*cont.*)
  books 21, 29, 32, 43–4, 47, 51, 58, 73–4, 78–9, 80, 108, 137, 150, 160, 164, 170, 172, 178, 180, 181, 186, 189, 194, 199, 208, 209, 210, 211, 212
Augustine of Hippo, St. 18, 21, 23–4, 25, 125
Averroes 28, 31

Bacon, Francis 24, 39–41, 56, 91, 128
Baer, Paul 211
Baghdad 16, 28
Bahro, Rudolf 183
Bailey, Liberty Hyde 127, 128
Bangladesh 147, 192
Bartram, William 44, 51
Basil the Great, St. 6, 23, 25, 27, 31, 42, 87, 217
Bauckham, Richard 194, 195, 201
Beagle, The 61, 62
Beast and Man: The Roots of Human Nature (Midgley) 140, 142
Beatitudes (Gospel of Matthew) 155
beauty
  natural 6, 10–11, 13, 17, 23, 29, 37, 38–9, 40, 42, 51, 67, 94, 98, 123–5, 134, 154, 179–80
  sense of 11, 13, 17, 23, 42, 97, 140–1
Beecher, Henry Ward 100
Beethoven, Ludwig van 54
Bellamy, David 141–2
Benedict, St 25, 27, 31
  Rule of Benedict 25, 26
Benedictines 25, 29–30, 31, 36, 149, 156
Benhabib, Seyla 186
Bentham, Jeremy 33, 45, 96, 167
benzene 204
Beowulf 27
Bergh, Henry 92, 99–100
Bergson, Henri 74
Berry, Robert J. 214, 216
Bible, the 18, 19, 20, 22, 24, 35, 75, 84, 91, 155, 194
  intertestamental book / Apocrypha
    Wisdom of Solomon 20
  New Testament 18–20, 20–2, 26, 31
    Acts 19, 20–1, 35
    Mark 21

Matthew 21
Revelation 22
Romans 21–2, 29, 31, 91
Old Testament (the Hebrew Bible), 18–20, 22
  Deuteronomy 20
  Genesis 19–20, 42, 62, 75, 80
  Job 19, 22, 130
  Proverbs 20, 22
  Psalms 19–20, 22, 29, 31, 38–9, 52, 125, 195
'Binsey Poplars' (Hopkins) 123
biocentrism 21, 34, 92, 127, 157, 169–71, 178, 217
bioclimatology 13
'biocoenoses' 108, 120
biodiversity 17, 31, 69, 112, 125, 135, 137, 149, 161, 175, 183, 187, 190–1, 198, 206
  loss of 17, 140, 150, 191, 204, 206–7, 208, 213
biogeography 50, 63–4, 72, 104
Biophilia (Wilson) 140, 142
Black Elk 43–4
Blake, William 53
Blueprint for Survival (1972) 105, 148–51
Boehme, Jakob 36
Bonaventure, St 29
book of nature 24, 53, 91–2
Bookchin, Murray 186
Boyle, Robert 34, 41
Brady, Emily 180, 181
Bratton, Susan Power 24, 28, 32, 193, 201
Bridges, Robert 123
British Ecological Society 109
Brouwer, David 143, 168
Brown, Donald 209, 214
Brundtland, Gro Harlem 153, 158–61, 163, 190
  see also *Our Common Future*
Buddhism 155, 180
Burns, Robert 53

Cafaro, Philip 178, 182
Callenbach, Ernest 151
Callicott, J. Baird 14, 43, 92, 169, 172–3, 181
Calvin, Jean 3, 33–4, 35, 36, 37, 41, 56, 57, 58, 87, 193
Cambridge Platonists 34, 40

Canada 111, 205, 217
capital, natural 155
capitalism 47, 73, 101, 147, 199
Capon, Anthony 13
carbon capture and storage 213
Carson, Rachel 1, 4, 6, 7, 104, 120, 122, 135–9, 140, 141, 142, 145, 146, 147, 151, 190
   Silent Spring 4, 137–9, 143
Chadwick, Owen 75–6
Chambers, Robert 62
Charbonneau, Bernard 165
Chicago School (of ecologists) 128, 136
China 3, 8, 11, 61, 135, 189, 192, 205, 219
chlorofluorocarbons (CFCs) 161
Christianity 3, 5, 6, 8, 18, 19, 22–4, 26, 27, 29, 31, 52, 83, 91, 92
Chrysostom, St 22, 24, 31
Cicero, Marcus Tullius 17
Cistercians 31
Clare, John 4, 53–4, 57
Clark, Stephen R. L. 21, 177, 178
Clean Air Act (1956) 156, 204
Clements, Frederic 106–9, 110, 112–19, 120, 121, 127–8, 132, 135, 173, 217
   climax theory 107–9, 114–16, 120
climate change 46, 50, 133, 152, 156, 161, 183, 189, 191, 194, 199, 203–4, 206, 207, 208–14
Climate Emergency Movement 198, 199
climate engineering 203, 213
Climate Equity Reference Project 211–12, 214
Club of Rome 151–3
Coates, Peter 4, 7, 10, 11, 16, 17–18, 20, 24, 25, 26, 27, 28, 30, 32, 40–1, 43, 49, 52–5, 56, 58, 66, 68–9, 80, 193
Cohn-Bendit, Daniel 197
Coleridge, Samuel Taylor 50, 52–3, 59, 83, 84, 180
Collin, Reverend Nicholas 51
Commoner, Barry 2, 145, 146–8, 150, 162, 198
Comte de Buffon 48, 61
Conway, Erik M. 209, 214
Cooper, Anthony Ashley (Earl of Shaftesbury) 45

Córdoba 16, 28
Cosmas Indicopleustes 23
creation 2, 17, 19–25, 29, 36, 38, 39, 41, 42–3, 45, 52, 65, 78, 92, 130, 193–5, 196
   special 62, 65
crisis, environmental 5, 139, 162, 201, 203–14
Crutzen, Paul J. 203–4, 213, 214
Cuthbert, St 24–5, 31

Daly, Herman 158, 199, 201
Daoism 3, 11
Darwin, Charles 4, 8, 12, 33, 48, 57, 58, 60–80, 86, 89–91, 101, 104–5, 216
   Darwinism 4, 6, 47, 62, 65–6, 70–1, 74–80, 91, 101, 107, 122, 128, 177, 216–17
   Origin of Species 33, 60, 63–4, 66, 68, 82, 85, 86
   social Darwinism 72–4, 216
Darwin, Erasmus 48, 58, 61
Dawkins, Richard 78–80
DDT 1, 137, 139, 147
de Waal, Frans 71, 80
demand, ecological 150
Democritus of Abdera 12, 16
demographic transition 145–6, 150, 153
Derr, Thomas Sieger 36
Descartes, René 34, 38, 39–43
determinism 2, 5, 74, 79, 114, 140
   religious 5–6
   technological 5
Deuteronomy 20
development
   biological 62–4, 106
   sustainable 50, 144, 153, 157, 158–61, 163, 188–9, 200, 201, 209, 211
Die Grünen (German Greens) 196–7, 199
dimethyl sulphide 176–7
Dimitrios, Patriarch 194, 196, 209
Dobzhansky, Theodosius 77–8
domestication 5, 10, 89
domination of nature, human 31, 183, 184, 186
dominion 19, 31, 36, 37, 38, 57, 86, 127
Dryden, John 42

246 Index

Dubos, René 25, 31, 32, 139, 156–8
Only One Earth 157–8, 159
'dust bowl', the 109, 112–16

Earth Charter (2000) 200–1
Eckhart, Meister 35, 165
ecofeminism 183, 184–6, 195–6
ecologism 183–4
Ecology (journal) 106
Ecology
  science of 4, 65–8, 80, 103–20, 127–30, 139, 148
  as perspective 2, 31, 106, 120, 144, 147–8, 156, 164–6, 186
  economics 46, 56, 57, 61, 100, 102, 154, 218
'ecosystem', Paraguayan 66–7
ecosystems 2, 33, 67, 100, 109, 112, 115, 117–20, 130, 136, 137–8, 150–1, 156, 158, 160, 166, 167, 169, 171–3, 177, 186, 187, 189, 199, 200, 206–8, 213, 217
  'novel' 188
ecotheology 165, 183, 193–6
Ecuador 183, 198
Egerton, Frank N. 3, 4, 7, 14, 15, 16, 25, 32, 35, 43, 68, 85, 127, 136
Ehrlich, Paul 145–6, 156, 157, 160, 162, 204
Elliot, Robert 185, 187, 201
Ellul, Jacques 165
Elton, Charles 103, 109–12, 116, 117–18, 120, 121, 127, 132, 137
Animal Ecology 110–11
Emerson, Ralph Waldo 55–6, 57, 82–5, 91, 93, 101, 102
Empedocles 8, 9, 11–12, 14, 16, 30, 42, 48, 58, 64
endangered species *see* species, endangered
energy
  nuclear 70, 154–5, 156, 157–8, 160, 184, 196–7, 206
  renewable 132, 152, 160, 197, 200, 214, 219, 230
Engels, Friedrich 46–7, 86
environmental aesthetics *see* aesthetics, environmental

environmental crisis *see* crisis, environmental
environmental virtue ethics *see* virtue ethics, environmental
Environmental Justice Movement 183, 191–3
Environmental Protection Agency (EPA) 208
environmentalists 4, 15, 22, 33, 39, 104, 123, 148, 161, 184, 198, 199, 200–1
Epicureanism 16, 48, 64
Epicurus 12, 58
ethics, holistic 14, 169, 170, 172–5, 175–7
Ethiopia 185, 188
ethology 71, 80, 139–40, 217
Evelyn, John 1, 33, 41–2, 86, 88,
evolution, theories of 1, 8, 12, 48, 54, 56–8, 63–6, 68, 69–70, 71, 72, 77–80, 89, 105, 107, 111, 121, 132, 219
exaptation 67, 78–9, 81

Factfulness (Rosling) 145, 162
feedback loops 176
Fichte, Johann Gottlieb 55
Fisher, Ronald 77–8
food chains 66, 110, 117, 132, 137, 145
Forbes, Edward 103
Foreman, Dave 135
Fuller, Margaret 84
Francis I, Pope 29, 193–4, 215
Francis of Assisi, St 5, 20, 24, 28–29, 31, 38
Fukushima, Japan 197, 206, 218
Fundamentals of Ecology (Odum) 118, 121

Gaard, Greta 185, 186
Gaia (goddess) 14
Gaia theory 2, 8, 14, 175–7, 181
  see also Lovelock, James
Galapagos Islands 62, 104
Gassendi, Pierre 34, 39, 41
generations, future 28, 46, 77, 123, 131, 134, 154, 159–60, 174, 188–90, 209
genes 79–80, 139
Genesis 19–20, 42, 62, 75, 80
genetics 70, 75, 77, 78, 109

George, Henry 94, 100–1
Germany 29, 30, 33, 49, 54, 55, 57, 76, 83, 88, 183–4, 205
  Greens 196–7, 199
Gillispie, Charles Coulston 60, 62–3, 80
Glacken, Clarence J. 1, 19–20, 21, 22, 23–4, 26, 28, 29, 30–1, 32, 41, 42–3, 58, 61, 67, 69, 71–2, 81, 166
Gleason, Herbert 114, 116, 121, 173, 217
Godwin, William 50, 61
Goethe, Johann Wolfgang von 54, 61
Goodman, Lenn E. 69–70
Goodpaster, Kenneth 169–70, 172, 181
Gould, Stephen Jay 78–9, 80, 81
Gorbachev, Mikhail 196
Gore, Al 198
Granberg-Michaelson, Wesley 194, 196
Grant, Ulysses 3, 93
Gray, Asa 65, 76, 91
Gray, Thomas 17
Great Chain of Being 15, 16, 23, 31, 32, 45, 55, 57, 116
Green Belt Movement 198
Green movements 5, 30, 156, 183–4, 186–7, 196–7, 198–9
Green Party (Britain) 197
Green Revolution 145
'greenhouse' effect 158, 160, 177, 194, 196, 199, 205, 208–9, 210–11
Grime, J. P 104, 119, 121
Grisebach, August 104, 106
Guinea 192

Haeckel, Ernst 76, 88, 103, 148
Haiti 192
Haldane, J. B. S. 77
Hale, Sir Matthew 35, 36–7, 57, 87
Hardin, Garrett 144–5, 156, 157, 160, 162
  'Tragedy of the Commons' 144–5
  see also 'lifeboat' ethics
Hardy, Thomas 74
Hargrove, Eugene C. 167, 180
Hawaii 188
Hedge, Frederic Henry 83
Heidegger, Martin 183

Herbert, George 38,
Herder, Johann Gottfried 46, 73, 84
Hesiod 3, 9–11, 16, 26
Hetch Hetchy Valley 96–8
Hexaemeron 23
Hildegard of Bingen 24, 29–30
Hippocrates of Cos 12–13, 15, 16
Hobbes, Thomas 40, 140
Hobbs, Richard J. 188
homologies 61, 64
Hopkins, Gerard Manley 3, 4, 54, 120, 122–5, 138, 142, 218
  'Binsey Poplars' 123
  'Inversnaid' 123
  'Pied Beauty' 124–5
Hormone Health Network 206, 214
Hughes, J. Donald 9–10, 12, 17, 43, 105
humanitarianism 44, 45, 50, 57, 70, 74, 92, 99–101, 126, 169, 217
Hume, David 45
Humphreys, Rebekah 192
Hunt, Ailsa 195
Hutton, James 62, 175
Huxley, Julian 77, 110, 138
Huxley, Thomas Henry 60, 70–2, 74, 75–6, 77, 110, 138
hydrofluorocarbons (HFCs) 21

ideas, influence of 2–3, 5, 16, 27, 29, 30, 41–2, 56, 61, 65, 78, 79, 93, 125, 139, 156, 157, 218
immanence, divine 20, 23, 35–6, 195
  see also panentheism
India 8, 11, 61, 88, 135, 157, 183, 189, 192, 194, 198, 205, 206, 216
'Inversnaid' (Hopkins) 123
Irenaeus 22
Isaiah 19, 20, 22, 130
Islam 3, 15, 24, 27–8, 31, 194, 216

Jainism 11
Jamieson, Dale 173, 179, 181, 190, 210
Jantzen, Grace 195
Japan 79, 88, 133, 158, 161, 197
  see also Fukushima
Jesus 18, 21, 83
Job, Book of 19, 22, 130
Jonas, Hans 169
Judaism 18, 19

Kant, Immanuel 48–50, 51, 55, 57, 83, 84, 168
Kartha, Shivan 211–12, 214
Katz, Eric 185, 187, 210
Kazakhstan 218
Keats, John 53, 138, 180
Kelbessa, Workineh 185, 193
Kelly, Petra 183, 196
Kemp-Benedict, Eric 211
Kennedy, John F. 139
Kenya 183, 197–8
Kerber, Guillermo 194, 196
khalifa 27–8, 194
Khalid, Fazlun 194
Kigali agreement (2016) 210
Kimura, Motoo 79
Kingsley, Charles 65
Kirchner, James W. 176
kites, red 188
Klein, Naomi 199, 201
Kropotkin, Petr 70–1, 81, 105–6, 121, 151, 162, 217
Kruger Park 217
Kyoto agreement (1997) 161, 194
Kyrgyzstan 198

Lamarck, Jean-Baptiste 48, 58, 61, 62, 64, 68
  Lamarckism 48, 70, 73, 76
land ethic 14, 131–2, 134–5, 172
Las Casas, Bartolomé 45
Latour, Bruno 210, 214
Laudato Si' 29, 193, 202
Law of the Sea Convention 158
laws of history 47, 73
lead 204
Leibniz, Gottfried Wilhelm 34, 40, 45
Leopold, Aldo 4, 14, 87, 104, 108, 116, 117, 120, 121, 122, 125–35, 136, 142, 154, 165, 167, 169, 172, 173, 178, 217
  Sand County Almanac 129–35
  see also land ethic
Lewontin, Richard 78, 79, 80
Liddon, Henry 75
'lifeboat' ethics 144–5
Limits to Growth (Meadows et al.) 46, 151–4, 157, 158, 162
Lindberg, David 30
Lindeman, Raymond 30
Linnaeus 44, 51, 57, 101, 103, 110

Linzey, Andrew 22
Living Planet Report (2014) 206, 215, 219
Locke, John 17, 34, 41, 45, 83, 99–100
Longinus, *On the Sublime* 49
Lorenz, Konrad 71, 140
love of nature 6, 17, 67, 136, 140
Lovejoy, Arthur 15, 32, 190
Lovelock, James 2, 8, 14, 108, 175–81, 217
  see also Gaia theory
Lucretius 8, 16–17, 58
Lyell, Charles 62, 71, 88

Maathai, Wangari 197–8
maize 44, 161, 190
Man and Nature (Marsh) 1, 7, 82, 86–9, 102
Mark, Gospel of 21
Marsh, George Perkins 1, 3, 4, 7, 42, 82, 84, 85–91, 93, 94, 98, 101, 102 112, 126, 132, 144, 217
  Man and Nature 1, 7, 82, 86–9, 102
Marsh, James 84
Martin, Randall 37
Marvell, Andrew 38–9, 40
Marx, Karl 46–7, 73, 194, 219
Matthew, Gospel of 21
Meadows, Donella 36, 151–4, 158
  see also Club of Rome
meat-eating 19, 42, 133
Meinshausen, Malte 211
memes 79–80
Mendel, Gregor 75, 77
Merchant, Carolyn 14, 39–40, 58, 185
Merriam, C. Hart 104, 105, 106
Mexico 43, 129, 161, 198
Meyer, Aubrey 210–11
Midgley, Mary 71, 79, 81, 140, 142, 169, 177, 181, 186, 201, 207, 217
  Animals and Why They Matter 140, 169
  Beast and Man: The Roots of Human Nature 140
Mill, John Stuart 65–6, 96 , 99, 132, 149, 153
Miller, Hugh 63
Mishan, Edward 150

Moltmann, Jürgen 36, 195, 196
Montreal Convention/Protocol (1987) 161, 189
Moore, Barrington 106
Moore, G. E. 73–4
Moore, Kathleen Dean 137, 142
moral standing 131, 166, 168, 169, 170
Morris, William 155
Muir, John 4, 24, 82, 85, 91–99, 100, 101, 102, 132, 139, 159, 217
Mumford, Lewis 88, 149

Nader, Ralph 137, 198
Naess, Arne 14, 87, 164–7, 169, 173, 181, 193
Nagoya Conference (2010) 158, 161, 207
Nash, Roderick Frazier 4, 7, 42, 43, 45, 51, 58, 69, 74, 83–4, 84–5, 86–8, 91–101, 102, 107–9, 126–30, 135–8, 142, 156–7
national parks 3, 4, 89, 93–8, 135, 188, 217
   see also Yellowstone National Park; Yosemite National Park
nature 1–2, 5, 6, 8–12, 14, 17–18, 18–32, 34–42, 46–58, 60–4, 66–72, 82–9, 91–2, 99–101, 103, 105, 110–11, 113–18, 122–5, 127–8, 136–41, 144, 148, 154–5, 157, 165–6, 179–80, 183–7, 190, 193–6, 200, 204, 207, 216, 218
Navdanya women's movement 198
Nazi Party 183, 196
New Guinea 63, 72
New Testament *see* Bible, the
New Zealand 88, 197
Newman, John Henry 75, 122
Newton, Isaac 34, 40–1
Nigeria 192
North Borneo 188
Norton, Bryan 184, 202
Nuclear Test Ban Treaty (1963) 139
nuclear war 146, 196, 204
nuclear winter 146, 204
Nussbaum, Martha 15

oceans 52, 65, 87, 136, 138, 147, 176, 177, 195, 204, 205–6, 208, 213

Odum, Eugene 104, 116, 118–20, 121, 138
   Fundamentals of Ecology 118
oil slicks 141, 147, 205
Old Testament *see* Bible, the
Olmsted, Frederick Law 85.
Only One Earth: The Care and Maintenance of a Small Planet (Ward and Dubos) 157–8, 159, 162
oppression, systemic 101, 184–6, 193
orangutans 188
Oreskes, Naomi 209
Origen 22
Origin of Species, The (Darwin) 33, 60, 63–4, 66, 68, 80, 82, 85, 86
Ott, Konrad 199, 202, 213
Our Common Future 4, 158–61, 163, 202
   see also Brundtland, Gro Harlem
Ouspensky, Peter D. 128, 130
Ovid 11, 42
ozone layer 161, 169

palaeontology 48, 63, 64,
Paley, William 60–61
Palmer, Clare 164, 167, 170–1, 173–5, 181, 194–5, 202, 216
panentheism 34–6, 39, 43–4, 57, 58, 74, 99, 124, 195–6
Paraguay 66–7
Parfit, Derek 189, 202
Paris Conference (2015) 199, 207, 208, 211–2, 214
Passmore, John 2–3, 6, 13–14, 21, 22–3, 25, 29, 31, 32, 37–8, 47, 71, 73, 81, 86, 108, 166–7, 193, 204, 216
Pasteur, Louis 67–8
Paul, St 19–22, 31, 91
Peacocke, Arthur 23, 195, 196
Pearce, David 194
peoples, primitive 69–72
Pepper, David 4, 7, 66–7, 81, 105, 145, 151, 156, 162
'Pied Beauty' (Hopkins) 124–5
Pinchot, Gifford 4, 88, 95–8, 101, 125–6, 128, 129, 131, 158
'planetary collapse disorder' 207
plant communities *see* 'biocoenoses'
plantations 42, 47, 188, 198

plastic 146, 205, 218
Plato 3, 13–17, 37, 169
  see also Cambridge Platonists
plenitude, principle of 15, 190
Pliny the Elder 4, 10, 16, 41, 116
ploughing, heavy 5, 26
Plumwood, Val 186
Plutarch 17, 42
pollution 41, 46, 141, 144, 146, 151–7, 161, 166, 183, 188–9, 191, 192–3, 195, 204–6, 208, 213, 217–19
polychlorinated biphenyl (PCB) 192
Ponting, Clive 44–6, 59
Pope, Alexander 34, 41, 45, 57, 193
Porphyry 42
power stations, nuclear 197
  see also energy, nuclear
precautionary principle 161, 189, 209
preservation 4, 37, 43–4, 69, 82, 91–8, 101, 104, 127, 129–31, 135, 142, 154, 159–61, 165, 175, 179, 183, 186, 190–1, 217
progress, belief in 16, 46–7, 56–7, 61, 66, 71, 72–3, 76, 116, 129, 149
Proverbs 20, 22
Pusey, Edward 75
Pythagoreanism 11– 12

Rafferty, John P. 206
Rajan, S. Ravi 13, 50, 59, 61, 65, 67–72, 81, 90
Ray, John 23, 33, 37, 42–4, 57, 87, 132, 193
Reagan, Ronald 196, 217
Regan, Tom 168–9, 178, 181
Renaissance, the 4, 11, 14, 17, 28, 35
resource depletion 46, 145, 151, 161, 166
restoration, ecological 39, 88, 133, 185–8
Revelation, Book of 22
Ricardo, David 46
Rifkin, Jeremy 198
Right to Development, UN Declaration of the 159, 162
Rigi, Mount 54–5
Rio Conference (1992) 50, 144, 156, 160–2, 188–9, 200, 209
Rio Declaration (1992) 161–2

Rodick, David W. 165
Rolston, Holmes, III 131, 164, 165–7, 172, 174, 179, 180, 181
Romans, Book of 21–2, 29, 31, 91
Rosling, Hans 153, 162
  Factfulness 145
Round River, Wisconsin 120 121, 142
Rousseau, Jean-Jacques 49, 50–2, 72
Routley (later Sylvan), Richard 165–6, 167, 181, 187
Royal Society, the 34, 39–42
Royal Society for the Prevention of Cruelty to Animals (RSPCA) 99
Ruse, Michael 61, 63, 64, 66, 73, 74–5, 77–9, 81
Ruskin, John 155
Ryberg, Jesper 145, 162

Sagoff, Mark 173, 191, 202
Sale, Kirkpatrick 43, 187 202
Sand County Almanac, A (Leopold) 129–35, 142
Sandler, Ronald 170, 173, 174, 178, 181–2
Santmire, Paul 22–3, 29, 32, 35–6, 40, 59
Saxons 26
Scandinavia 44, 167, 205
Schelling, Friedrich 15, 34, 55, 56, 57, 190
Schiller, Friedrich 54
Schopenhauer, Arthur 49, 168
Schumacher, E. F. 154–6, 162
  Small Is Beautiful 154–6
Schweitzer, Albert 87, 127–8, 130, 134, 136, 142, 169
Scott, Peter Markham 141–2
Sears, Paul 113–14
selection, natural 1, 8–9, 12, 16, 48, 61–2, 63–80, 89–90
  see also Darwin, Charles
self-realization 187
Shelford, Victor 107–10, 121
Shelley, Percy Bysshe 53, 218
Shiva, Vandana 191, 198, 202
Sierra Club 95, 98, 102, 198, 217
Silent Spring (Carson) 4, 7, 137–9, 142, 143
Simberloff, Daniel 111–12

Singer, Peter 18, 167–71, 178, 182, 217
  Animal Liberation: A New Ethics for Our Treatment of Animals 167–8
Small is Beautiful (Schumacher) 154–6, 162
Smith, Adam 26, 46
Smith, Mick 216
Snyder, Gary 180, 218
Sober, Elliot 79, 81, 190
social Darwinism 72–4, 216
social ecology 186
Socialist Environmental and Resources Association 197
Society for the Prevention of Cruelty to Animals 46, 99, 100
sociobiology 139–40, 142, 217
solar radiation management (SRM) 212–13
Somalia 192–3
South Africa, Republic of 88, 217
Southwood, T. R. E. 119
special creation *see* creation, special
species
  endangered 141, 161, 190, 191, 200
  loss of 46, 133, 140, 160, 166, 191, 204, 206–8, 213, 218
  value of 92, 112, 160, 173–4
Spencer, Herbert 46, 47, 60, 71, 72–4, 76, 107–8
Spinoza, Baruch 34, 55, 57
Steinbeck, John 133, 121
Sterba, James 170, 173, 182, 192, 202
stewardship of nature, human 6, 8, 14, 19–20, 32, 36–7, 41, 57, 86–7, 132, 149, 157, 166, 177, 183, 193–6, 214, 216, 210
Stoics/Stoicism 15, 16, 148
Stoll, Mark 36, 91, 102
Stowe, Harriet Beecher 100
strontium 90 radioactive by-product, 137, 147, 205
Sturm und Drang 54
sublime, the 49, 51–2
Suh, J. 216, 219
sulphur dioxide 176, 204
Sumatra 192
survival of the fittest 69, 73–4
  see also Darwin, Charles

sustainability 12, 41, 95–6, 125, 148, 158–9, 198, 199, 210

Tansley, Sir Arthur 108–11, 114–17, 118–19, 120, 121, 135, 173, 217
Taylor, Paul W. 127, 170, 178, 182
technology 24, 47, 125, 128, 146, 148, 152, 155, 156, 164, 178, 183, 189, 195, 203, 213, 218
  high 140, 146–7, 150, 154, 155, 178, 195, 218
  intermediate 154–5, 156
  medieval 5, 26–7, 164
  'technological determinism' 5
Tennyson, Alfred Lord 122
Thames, River 133, 187
theocentrism 33–4, 36, 39, 57
Theodoret 23, 37
Theophrastus 1, 7, 13, 15–16, 23, 30, 31, 41, 86, 144
Thomas, Keith 42, 44–5, 59
Thomson, J. Arthur 67
Thoreau, Henry David 3, 56, 57, 59, 82, 84–7, 91, 93, 99, 100–1, 102, 127, 128, 132, 137, 139, 143, 217
  Walden 56, 59, 135
Three Gorges Dam 218
Thunberg, Greta 199, 207
Tickell, Oliver 212
Tinbergen, Nikolaas 140
tomatoes 44
'Tragedy of the Commons' (Hardin) 144–5, 162
Traherne, Thomas 3, 6, 38–9
Transcendentalists, the 4, 55–6, 82–84, 85, 89, 139
Transeau, Edgard 117–18
transmutation of species 60–3
Trump, Donald 212
Tryon, Thomas 41–2
Turner, J. M. W. 3, 54–5

Udall, Stuart 139
UNESCO 200
uniformitarianism 62
United Church of Christ 192
United Nations Framework Convention on Climate Change (UNFCCC) 50, 161
Uzbekistan 218

value
  aesthetic 93, 95, 97, 141, 175, 180, 187, 190, 217
  intrinsic 40, 114, 150, 155, 169, 172–5, 179, 187, 190, 191
  symbolic 174–5
  systemic 172–4
van Leeuwenhoek, Antoni 43
VanDeVeer, Donald 170, 178, 182
Varner, Gary 170, 182
Vaughan, Henry 39
vegetarianism 11, 19, 41–2, 168
Vestiges of the Natural History of Creation 62–3
Vietnam 143, 145
Vietnam War 143
Virgil 3, 6, 9–11, 16, 26, 41
virtue ethics, environmental 178–9, 182
Voltaire *see* Arouet, François-Marie
von Carlowitz, Hans Carl 42
von Humboldt, Alexander 13, 16, 23, 49–50, 58, 61, 63–4, 101, 103–4
Vrba, Elisabeth S. 78–9, 81

Wagner, Moritz 68, 79, 84, 102
Walden (Thoreau) 56, 59, 135
Wallace, Alfred Russel 60, 63, 69, 71–3, 90, 103, 216
Wallace Line, the 72
Ward, Barbara 157–8
  Only One Earth 157–8, 159
Webb, Walter 116
Weber, Max 36
Weismann, August 76
Weitzman, Martin L. 209, 214
Welbourn, Fred 36
Whewell, William 63
White, Gilbert 11, 47, 57
White, Lynn Jr. 5–6, 22, 25, 26–9, 31, 164, 173, 185, 193, 218
White Paper on the Ethical Dimensions of Climate Change (2005) 209, 214
Whitehead, Alfred North 14, 74
Whitney, Elspeth 14, 28, 30, 32, 165, 182
Whittaker, Robert H. 120, 121
wilderness 21, 25, 42, 43, 44, 51, 92, 93–8, 114, 123–4, 126, 128–9, 133, 134–5, 165, 166, 185, 188, 217
Williams, Mary B. 95, 158
Wilson, Edward O. 120, 139–40, 142, 217
  Biophilia 140
Wisdom of Solomon 20
wolves 10, 26, 29, 126, 135, 188
Wordsworth, William 3, 28, 48, 50–52, 55, 57, 59, 91, 122, 191, 218
World Commission on Environment and Development (WCED) 153, 158–9, 163, 202
World Conservation Strategy 159, 162
World Wildlife Fund (WWF) 206, 215, 219
Worster, Donald 4, 7, 11, 104–7, 110, 113–19, 121, 125–8, 136, 142
Wright, Sewell 77
Wytham Woods, Oxfordshire 111, 123

Yasuni Nature Reserve, Ecuador 198–9
Yellowstone National Park 3, 93–5, 97, 188
  see also national parks
Yosemite National Park 85, 91, 94–9
  see also national parks

Zanzibar 194
Zen Buddhism 5
Zhuangzi 11